Common Sense

—— *and* ——

REASONABLE ANSWERS

Published by Seacoast Press, an imprint of MindStir Media, LLC
1931 Woodbury Ave. #182 | Portsmouth, New Hampshire 03801 | USA
1.800.767.0531 | www.seacoastpress.com

Printed in the United States of America
ISBN-13: 978-1-7326291-8-9

Common Sense

— *and* —

REASONABLE ANSWERS

Warren William Luce

SEACOAST
PRESS

TABLE OF CONTENTS

INTRODUCTION

Perhaps you have read how the astronauts describe earth as stunningly beautiful, and the feelings they experience of awe, wonder and joy when they view it from space. Even we earthbound mortals stand in awe when we behold its majestic mountains, the tremendous expanse and power of its oceans and the magnificent towering forests, green pastures and waving fields of grain which give us sustenance and life.

Unfortunately, its remarkable inhabitants have gone astray, making it something less than the paradise that was intended for us. So what is our destiny? Is mankind to descend completely into uncivilized behavior and depravity and the world be destroyed in some Armageddon-like cataclysm as the theologians have convinced many to believe? Or do we have a choice? Can human behavior be changed? Can our world be changed for the better? Could mankind possibly achieve world peace?

I absolutely believe we can. God says so. In fact, he has told us the time is coming when "nation will not lift up sword against nation, nor will they learn war anymore." Given the state of our world it is hard to accept, isn't it? Yet, we should believe God and start thinking what must be done to achieve those goals. Obviously, we need to change our ways and do something different. But first we must change our perceptions. Perception is everything! Behavior modification, more often than not, is unsuccessful, but once perceptions have been altered, a change in behavior automatically follows.

We sorely need to change the perception of our own being. We have been conditioned, both by religion and in a secular sense, to believe that we are flawed, poor sinful beings, that it is human to err and it is our nature to cause all the hell that goes on in the world. That is all false. It has become the greatest, most harmful self-fulfilling prophecy in the history of mankind. We need to perceive ourselves as magnificent sentient beings, who have the power to choose right or wrong, who are masters of our own destiny, and who can control circumstances along the road that leads to it. We must to listen to God, who has told us we are "made in his image, wonderfully and respectfully made, the light of the world and salt of the earth and to let our light shine forth so as to make the world good."

Most of us are aware of the adverse effect that politics can have; a prime example being what the politicians are doing to the United States. We have a dysfunctional Congress, with the political parties, out of greed, vying for power and wealth, causing our country great harm, as well as having an undesirable effect on the rest of the world. While religion has done some good, we would be hard pressed to find any redeeming qualities in politics. They lend to corruption. They are polarizing. They are the prime cause of the U.S. financial problems. They are the direct cause of our dysfunctional Congress. They are a major factor in the Middle East conundrum. We need to get rid of political parties.

Religion is generally considered as something good to have. However, if we honestly analyze the effects that religion has had on humanity, we would have to conclude that it has caused mankind a great deal of grief. It has divided the human race like no other issue, causing discord, enmity and violence when it should be uniting people in harmony with one another and with God. It is at the root of much of the world's problems. It is a major cause of violence in the world, from the feeding of early Christians to the lions for entertainment, to the Crusades, the Inquisition, the Holocaust and many wars. Hitler thought he was doing God's will. The Japanese Shinto Authority believed it was their spiritual destiny to control the Far East and the Pacific, thus their attack on Pearl Harbor. Look at what Protestants and Catholics (so-called Christians) did to one another in Ireland. How about the Sunnis and Shiites blowing each other to bits because of their contradictory beliefs about Muhammad's successor? Much of the world's religious dogma needs to be questioned.

We are told that global terrorism is a serious threat to all of us. It is not. Our fear of terrorism is not justified. We have been brainwashed by both government and media hype to believe world terrorism poses a grave danger to U.S. national security and our individual safety. The facts dictate otherwise. Deaths from terrorism since 9/11 in the U.S. have been primarily at the hands of American terrorists. There is a better way to deal with terrorism.

We have been conditioned to believe that God is in charge of our world and wonder why He lets all the bad things happen to humanity. The truth is that God does not interfere in our lives. He has given us free choice and told us that we are to have dominion. Obviously, we have made some terrible choices. We are in charge and that is why bad things happen to good people; they are of our own doing. When we understand that and accept responsibility for our actions and things that happen in the world, then the world will change for the better.

Our perceptions of heaven, hell and death, are badly flawed, conditioned by false religious dogma. For example, we need to question the existence of hell. It is absurd to claim that God, whom we believe is perfect in love and justice, created such a terrible place where He sends people, including little children, to suffer eternally because they aren't perfect or do not believe in a certain religious dogma. A better understanding of these issues will greatly improve the human condition.

We need to open our minds to what we have tragically and unnecessarily done to our world and one another. We must awaken to the truth that through clear perception, the right choice and true application of thought, we have the power to right ourselves and thusly, our world. We all hope for a better and peaceful world. Hope springs eternal in the human heart but we need to understand it is love that will bring it to fruition. There is a universal human want to know that everything will turn out all right in the long run. This work provides that hope.

Chapter One

POLITICAL TREASON

The truth is that the United States Congress is committing treason, causing our country great harm. Treason is defined as betrayal of a trust, impairing the well-being of a state to which one owes allegiance or the crime of aiding and abetting an enemy of the state.

Surely, members of Congress have betrayed the trust given to them by us, the people, to govern responsibly. Without doubt, they have harmed the well-being of our country by their dysfunctional behavior; their refusal to work together to solve our country's problems. One of our worst enemies, even more so than terrorism, is our unsustainable annual deficit and rapidly mounting national debt. They are clearly aiding and abetting that enemy by deliberately refusing to compromise on curbing spending and increasing revenue so as to balance the budget. Unquestionably, by definition, they are guilty of treason.

Now, being a compassionate people, we are not in favor of hanging them, but other steps must be taken to bring them under control. We might get the President to have the Attorney General bring treason charges against a number of their leaders. However, that's not likely to go anywhere as the President is their accomplice and they would weasel their way out of it somehow or the Supremes would let them off. But they surely need to be tried for treason, in the court of public opinion, and appropriate punishment rendered, like throwing their asses out in the street at election time.

The words politics, political and politician have a negative connotation, implying scheming, sleaziness and even dishonesty. Webster defines politician as a word often used derogatorily with implications of seeking personal gain, of a schemer as distinguished from statesman. That surely describes what's going on in our government.

You've heard of the "sleaze factor." It is a phrase coined by a major news magazine referring to the political payoffs and influence peddling in Washington, D.C. Surely, you have seen the polls that rate respect and trust by profession, with politician at or near the bottom of the list? Will Rogers said we have the best congress money can buy. Even one of their own referred to himself and his colleagues as "gutless" for failure to do the right things. Richard North Patterson, in his marvelous novel, *Balance of Power*, speaks of the "sheer cowardice of politics," and rightly so.

The two political parties are polarized and generally unwilling to compromise in solving the serious problems that confront our nation. There is frequently a state of quarrelsome disagreement between the Administration and Congress, vying for power and political advantage. They don't seem to care about the tremendous damage they are inflicting on the country and the people.

They are serving special interest groups and playing partisan politics for the purpose of gaining re-election support, power and material possessions. Their priorities in governing are self, special interests, their party and lastly the good of the country. The bottom line is political expediency and a greater interest in their own well-being than that of the country. Their differences on issues are not because they are true ideologues but because they are scheming politicians vying for power.

Their job performance has been poor and that's being generous. For example, they and their predecessors have exhibited gross mismanagement of our nation's financial affairs, shackling us to that gargantuan national debt of $20 trillion. The interest alone of $432 billion every year is a huge burden on the taxpayers and a drag on the economy. If a private business was to handle its finances as Congress does the nation's, it would be bankrupt and those responsible fired or in prison.

Their devotion to their self and party interests rather than those of the country, and their subsequent failure to work together to solve our nation's problems are grossly irresponsible. Their dysfunctional behavior is outrageous and disgraceful. Good God Almighty, don't they see the serious, even disastrous, harm they are doing to the country, the people, and even themselves. We have a government of the politicians, by the politicians and for the special interests of which they are one, rather than a government of the people, by the people and for the people. Right now, their respect among the people is lower than a snake's belly (apologies to the snake).

I am getting a little carried away here out of frustration with politics and what the politicians are doing to our country. Therefore, in accordance with my philosophy of being kind and showing love to others, I have to say that it isn't entirely the fault of the individual politicians. They are good, decent people most of the time, just like the rest of us. Of course, they love their country. But, it seems that when they get into their political mode, their integrity suffers, their self-interest comes to the fore and they are willing to stray from doing the right thing so as to stay in power.

We, the people, must share the fault. By our votes, we pressure them to be everything to everyone; we want our share, and usually more, of the "pork." Hence, to keep our vote, they employ their spend, spend, spend authority. Groups of us pressure them through the lobby process to get our way. The corporations and wealthy exert heavy pressure to have it their way. They are caught up in the inefficient, divisive even corrupt political party system. Often their personal tendency to do the "right thing" is thwarted by having to be loyal to the party dictates. Still, if they exercised the integrity that they should, those practices would stop and they would always put the good of the nation and the people first.

We, the people, must give them better guidance by both our vote and correspondence when they get in office. As well, doing the "right thing" ourselves. Let's get one thing straight right up front. They seem to think they are in charge. They are not; we the people are! They need to write that down! They suffer the delusion of importance, power and indispensability when they are but servants; the hired help. They are dispensable and can be replaced. However, about ninety percent of the incumbents are reelected, and in that we are sending them the wrong message

We need to let them know that we want them to forget the damn politics and live up to their title of Honorable. Be statesmen and patriots, not politicians. Do what is right for their country, always! And guess what? When they do those things, they won't have to go through all that crap of "rubber chicken" dinners, shaking hands, "begging" for funds for their reelection. We'll keep them in their job because we're happy with their performance.

To reiterate, everything that they do must be in the interest of the country and the people. And that brings up the subject of special interests, on both sides of the political spectrum. They have been taking money from them in the way of political donations and in return influencing legislation that benefits their interests and harms the overall interests of the nation. That's acceptance of bribes, a criminal offense.

One of the most blatant, irresponsible and yes, tragic examples of Congress serving special interests is their subservience to the gun lobby; their failure to enact adequate gun control laws so as to protect the lives of American citizens. The spate of killing of our school children by use of automatic weapons is a direct result of that failure.

A 2013 UN study showed that, "While the specific relationship between firearm availability and homicide is complex, it appears that a vicious circle connects firearm availability and higher homicide levels." Lax gun laws in the United States result in 10,000 people killed every year by gun homicide. In Japan, with the strictest laws, fewer than 20 gun deaths occur annually.

Sensible gun laws, that will save lives, can be put in place without infringing on gun owners' Second Amendment rights. But Congress refuses to do so. It appears that support and donations from the gun lobby are more important to them than the lives of our school children. Despicable!

There are two principles that they need to write down and put where they can see them every day. They are, "the majority rules" and "compromise." Yes, we know they got their job through the "majority rules" principle when they got the most votes from their constituents. However, when they get on the team in Washington, the rules change.

They do need to look out for the interests of their constituents; however, their major responsibility is to the country as a whole. When they are sworn in they take an oath of allegiance to their country, not their state or district. And, as we well know, our country is very diverse, with a wide variety of interests. Obviously, all the interests of every group cannot be met and so "compromise" must be the by-word.

We understand that can be very difficult at times. That's when that other principle comes into play, "the majority rules." They need to understand that the great majority in our country is the middle of the roaders, the moderates, not those on the left or right. They are entitled to be heard, but because they are often antagonistic and uncooperative, their goals of having it only their way cannot be considered; the majority rules.

We moderates believe in the work ethic, something that Congress needs to pay more attention to. We've given them some leeway in their work days. However, they take entirely too much time off; they need to get back to work. They should get only thirty days paid vacation per year as do most government employees. They need to stop those "fact finding" junkets that we all know are pleasure trips at taxpayer expense. That's called embezzlement. If they want to know the facts, pick up the phone. That's why we have Foreign Service officers. Frequent recesses when they have so much work to do for the country is dereliction of duty.

We strongly believe in living within our means. We, the majority, have conservative values but are also compassionate and see the need for entitlements. We believe every American, indeed, every human being, is entitled to the basic needs of life--food, shelter and health care. But we also believe Americans are not entitled to be freeloaders in those respects or behave irresponsibly at taxpayers' expense, of which there is a great deal in our society. They need to address that problem.

Our Founding Fathers were dead set against political factions, warning that they breed corruption and deceit. How right they were. Yet, we accept politics as a normal and essential function of governing. We need to change that perception. Political parties aren't necessary or desired for a well-functioning government.

Surely, we can come up with a better system. Why not have all candidates running for a government office be required to run as an independent? Or we could keep our current system for the election process, then when sworn in, party affiliation is dropped and all members take an oath as an Independent. Do away with the "aisle;" congressional member seating would be alphabetical and by seniority. This would do away with voting along party lines; voting would be by the whole body Congress, with each member voting their conscience. There would be no more majority or minority.

America, you overwhelmingly disapprove of the poisoning, partisan politics that go on in our government. Then do something about it. Stop sending your "politician" back to Washington again and again. Drop your party affiliation and register as an Independent. Refuse to support a political party in any manner. This will encourage independents to run for office. You can then vote for the one whose platform agrees most closely with your beliefs. It only takes the will to do this.

We are fed up with the party politics that are so harmful to our country. We would do well to get rid of the party system. In analyzing its existence, we would have to conclude that it has brought very little benefit, but rather has caused us a great deal of woe. It is the foundation of dysfunction and corruption in government. It is the source that has polarized our nation. History records that a political party system began with deception and lying politicians and it certainly continues today.

"The United States Constitution has never formally addressed the issue of political parties. The Founding Fathers did not originally intend for American politics to be partisan. Alexander Hamilton and

James Madison, respectively, wrote specifically about the dangers of domestic political factions. George Washington was not a member of any political party at the time of his election or throughout his tenure as president. He warned against political parties; that they breed corruption and deceit."

How right they were! All politicians would be wise to take heed. The ranks of the independent voters are increasing rapidly. At this time the number of registered Independents in Arizona outnumber each of the Democrats and Republicans. The "handwriting is on the wall." So listen up, Congress people. You would do well to renounce your party affiliation and become independent. Not a member of an independent party but fully independent of obligation to any party or special interest. Your dysfunctional behavior is hurting our country and us. You're better than that. We know you do love the country, so be a true patriot, one who loves, supports and defends his country and its interests with devotion. It would be good to get rid of the word politician and call you patrioticians. We need an "American Spring," a revolution in how things are done there in Washington. Show that you love your country and do what's right for the people. Make history as the Congress that rose above politics, that really cared and did what was right for America. And when you do what's right for America, it will be good for the world.

Chapter Two
TERRORISM, WAR
AND VIOLENCE

The entire truth is not being told about terrorism. It has its roots in both religion and politics. The very first thing that must be done is for America to understand and acknowledge that we are a major part of the problem. Our unwise, politically rife foreign policy in the Middle East is a major cause of terrorism. Our lack of even-handedness in the issues there has been cited as a major reason for 9/11. Many countries there as well as others around the world see us as a hypocritical bully trying to force democracy and our values upon others, which they find offensive. The fact is that the major aggressor and promoter of terrorism in the Middle East is the United States. We will examine these issues later in this chapter and in detail in Chapter 10, The Middle East Solution.

But first, let's take a closer look at the America, whose government and values, we say the rest of the world would do well to emulate. We have some wonderful attributes but some serious faults, as well, of which we are in denial. Authors Oliver Stone, producer of historical films, and historian Peter Kuznick, in their work, *The Untold History of the United States*, document both the strengths and flaws we have exhibited throughout our history. Americans would do well to read it.

We claim to be a democracy, self-governance by and for the people. We are not! In reality, ours is a representative government. We elect officials and send them to Washington to represent our interests. Unfortunately, they often follow their own agenda and serve special interests to the detriment of the people. It is a government mired in dysfunction, corruption and enormous debt.

America is a real dichotomy. We have great wealth, yet immense debt. We have 530 billionaires and over 5,000,000 millionaires, yet 45 million people live in poverty. America is the land of freedom, opportunity and hope. Yet, it is also the land of despair and imprisonment in more ways than one--for the millions locked into the ghetto, into poverty, into the welfare system and in the prisons. The latter perhaps deservedly so, yet something is drastically wrong with a society that finds it necessary to incarcerate so many of its people. There seems to be a tug of war between the 'good guys' and the 'bad guys,' and between the 'haves' and 'have nots'. There are extraordinary acts of love and goodness, as well as heinous acts of violence. There are 94 million volunteers in America, helping others without thought of remuneration. Yet, there are many others who are greedy, dishonest, corrupt and indifferent to the needs of others. Still, the vast majority of Americans are full of decency and goodness, who are quick to come to the aid of others in times of disaster.

We have immense potential for greatness, for being that "shining light upon the hill," that others look to and wish to imitate. However, we have a long way to go, needing to understand that peace and well-being are not achieved by military force and materialism, but by love, caring and forgiveness, and then setting the example accordingly.

We are a violent nation, hardly a model for our children and the rest of the world to look up to. Our television shows, movies and video games that our children watch are rampant with violence. Other nations refer to us as "Violent America" and Washington D.C. as the "murder capitol" of the world. We seem to have a love affair with the "gun," there being 90 guns for every 100 people, more than any other country. We tend to use it to solve our disagreements with others, often on an individual basis and at other times on a grand scale by war. We are one of the biggest arms merchants in the world. We have assassinated four of our presidents; two have been shot but survived and a third shot at. There have been seventy-six massacres in our history beginning with such as the Boston massacre and the Indian massacres leading up to the recent ones at Oklahoma City, Columbine, Virginia Tech, Fort Hood, Tucson, Arizona, Newtown,

Connecticut and Parkland, Florida. We have been involved in forty-five wars since our inception, and tragically, most of them were unjust and unnecessary.

A *Just War Theory* put forth by theologians St. Augustine and Thomas Aquinas outlines the conditions and rules that must be adhered to in order to qualify as a just war.

They generally coincide with international law as pertains to war and are confirmed by the teaching of the Catholic Church. They are as follows:

1. Just Cause: A war must rise from a proper cause. The objective of a just war is to protect innocent life, defend human rights, punish injustice and restore peace.

2. Just Motive: A just war must be waged with right intentions, not vindictive motives.

3. Last Resort: Force is justified only as a last resort, when peaceful alternatives have been exhausted and no other viable options are perceived.

4. Probability of Success: A just war demands that there be a reasonable likelihood that war will achieve its aims.

5. Comparative Justice: Beyond the odds for victory, there must also be a realistic expectation that this victory in war will end more evil than the war itself causes.

6. Proportionality: Unnecessary violence is forbidden. Excessive fear mongering and inflating danger are illegitimate.

7. Discrimination: Non-combatants must never be targeted. Indiscriminate killing of the innocent is prohibited.

8. Reconciliation: A realistic hope and a plan of reconciliation should remain on the table throughout the effort and victory.

Considering those conditions and rules for just war, it is likely that there never has been a just war and likely never could be. We think of the Revolutionary War as just. It did not meet the requirements of Rules 1, 3, 4, 5 and probably 8. Basically, the goal of self-governance does not justify humans killing and maiming one another in an attempt to achieve that goal. We would have eventually attained our independence without the necessity of war. The Indian wars are a shameful black mark on our history; they met almost none of the rules. The Civil War was another unjust and unnecessary war. We think it was all about slavery, however, the over-riding reason to go to war was to prevent secession. Slavery was an ancillary issue. We are champions of self-determination; the South had a perfect right to secede. It is almost certain that reunion would have occurred. The slavery issue clearly would have been settled without the necessity of that bloody and brutal war—brother killing brother with bullets, bayonets and cannon balls.

Professional author Mel Barger brings the horror of that war into focus. "From 1861 to 1865, some of the worst savagery ever staged on Earth took place in North America. When it ended more than 620 thousand men were dead and many thousands more were blinded, crippled, disfigured, and otherwise maimed and injured. Towns and homes had been burned, railroads had been torn up, crops had been destroyed, and forests had been ravaged. Had a visitor from Outer Space witnessed this tragedy, he could only have assumed that millions of people in the United States had somehow gone temporarily insane."

Author Pat Buchanan makes a pretty good case against WWII in his book *The Unnecessary War.* It did solve the Hitler problem but at what terrible cost. An estimated 50 million people were killed, millions injured and maimed, estimates as high as 20 million people were displaced from their homes and unimaginable destruction of property took place. Entire cities were destroyed. I walked the streets of one such city, Schweinfurt, Germany, after the war. The city was bombed twenty-two times by 2285 aircraft destroying the industrial and almost the entire residential district. I hope I never have to witness such devastation again. I could almost hear the non-combatants crying for help from their crumbled buildings, innocent children buried alive in their graves.

I have served my country during three wars starting in WWII when I was little more than a teenager, flying P-47 fighter-bombers in Europe, killing people and causing great destruction. By the time I finished a tour of duty in Vietnam, where 58,000 valiant American soldiers died in vain, I was totally disillusioned by war. Seeing the continuing carnage wrought by the unjust and unnecessary wars in Iraq and Afghanistan, it is quite clear to me that war is not a good, and certainly not a permanent, solution to the world's problems. Violence begets violence. War fosters hatred. War is an abomination and has been called the ultimate stupidity. One of my favorite philosophers and poets is George Santayana who wrote, "Oh, world, thou choosest not the better part. It is not wisdom to be only wise and on the inward vision close the eyes. Tis wisdom to believe the heart." My heart, and I believe yours as well, tells us that human beings purposely and brutally killing and maiming one another, sometimes by the millions, as a way to settle their differences is absolutely wrong and indeed, an abomination.

We also need to get our collective heads out of the sand when it comes to the issue of human rights. We continually castigate other governments, such as China, over their violations of human rights. Yet, we are blind to the obvious, that the U.S. record is just as bad if not worse, only in a different way.

One of our most precious rights is the right to be secure in our person, home and possessions. It is government's responsibility to ensure that right of its citizens. Yet, millions of Americans suffer violation of that right every year in the form of murder, robbery, rape, theft and child abuse. China executes about 1700 people each year, most being for murder, drug dealing or child molestation. China has little in the way of drug problems. The U.S. judicial system executes about 50 people every year. However, 10,000 Americans are "executed" by other Americans every year with the gun. Gun crimes, including murder and robbery, are rare in China, fewer than 100 annually.

There are about three million cases of child abuse reported annually in our country. Twelve hundred children die each year from that abuse. About 15,000 cases of child abuse occur annually in China, most being from harsh discipline. Death from child abuse there is rare. As to abortion, in China it is forced, in the U.S. it is voluntary, yet China's rate is only slightly higher than ours. We have the highest homicide rate of all industrialized countries. We top the list of the top ten countries with the highest crime rate. Our incarceration rate dwarfs that of other countries. China, with an overall population four times greater than ours, has a prison population of about 1.5 million. We have imprisoned 2.5 million of our citizens, many of them unnecessarily and some wrongfully. The overall crime rate in China is 85% less than in the United States. It is the old problem of sins of commission and sins of omission. In some countries, the citizens cry out against violation of their rights and the state imprisons them. In our country, we cry out over the government's failure to protect us against the criminal and our pleas fall on deaf ears. The result is the same; the people suffer.

Concerning judgment and criticism of others, the scriptures tell us, "Hypocrite, first cast out the beam from your own eye and then you will see clearly to remove the mote from your brother's eye." When we get our own house in order, then will we have the right to criticize other countries about their violation of the rights of their citizens.

We suffer another illusion, that global terrorism is a threat to our national security. The threat to the security of our nation's existence from terrorism is almost nil. We will examine this in more detail in Chapter 6 on National Security. Put in perspective, the risk to individual security from terrorists is relatively insignificant. You are many times more likely to be killed in an automobile accident than in a terrorist attack. You stand a much greater chance of dying from a visit to the hospital as a patient than from terrorism; about 100,000 die every year in the hospital from mistakes or infectious contamination.

Let's put things into perspective when it comes to getting killed. About three thousand people were killed on 9/11. Well over 3000 children die every day in the world from starvation and the effects of malnutrition when there is plenty of food to prevent that. That is tragic, outrageous, and indifference at its best. The world is killing those children through neglect, just as surely as those terrorists have killed because of warped ideologies. We kill over 400,000 of our own people every year from a drug that we grow and distribute; it's called tobacco. No matter the rationalization--warnings on the cigarette package and people choosing to smoke (people choose to use heroin and cocaine, too)--it is absolutely wrong. Tobacco is addictive and kills. We have condoned this purveyor of suffering and death because of politics (the power of the tobacco lobby) and greed. The government derives and loves the huge tax revenues it gets from the sale of tobacco. The states relish the income from taxes as well as billions they are getting from the tobacco industry as a result of the lawsuit settlement. That's the height of hypocrisy, an absolute travesty and a national shame.

Let us look at it from a different aspect. Why are we so afraid of dying? Death is part of the life cycle; we are born, we live and we die. The vast majority of us believe that death of our physical body is not the end of our existence, but rather, our spiritual self moves on to a different and better kind of life. Scripture tells us not to fear those (read terrorists) who kill your body, they cannot kill your soul and that when we die, we become as angels in heaven. Christ said to the thief on the cross, "Today you will be with me in paradise." It is mind-boggling that we often fight like hell to keep from going there.

I've always liked what the Hindu scripture, The Bhagavad Gita, in beautiful prose says of our spiritual self. "It is ancient, constant, and eternal, and is not slain when this its mortal frame is destroyed. The weapon divideth it not, the fire burneth it not, the water corrupteth it not, the wind drieth it not away...for it is eternal. Knowing it to be thus, thou shouldst not grieve." Life is a gift and precious. It should be respected and protected, but whenever or however death comes, we should not fear it. There is something better beyond.

We need to debunk the myth of hell. We believe that God is loving, just and forgiving. It is not only totally illogical, but disrespectful of God, to believe that he would create such a place as hell where he sends people for simple disobedience or because we don't hold certain religious beliefs. We will discuss Heaven, Hell and the Devil in more detail in Chapter 19, The Joy of Death. If we hold the belief that God is just, we cannot believe in the concept of hell. Hell is simply a condition that we create for ourselves or for others. What if we held those beliefs, as we should? With no concern about hell and the threat of death gone, terrorism would have no influence over us.

There is one more issue concerning terrorism that we need to confront before we examine the solution. We seem to have forgotten or we ignore our own sometimes-grim history of terrorism. Such as the U.S. Army Cavalry's raids on the Native Americans' villages, burning them to the ground and massacring every man, woman, and child with the sword and firearms as we stole their land from them. How do you think the Africans felt as they were ripped from their homes, confined under terrible conditions to the dark holds of the slave ships and then sold into an often harsh life of servitude to their white American master, sometimes living under the threat and use of the whip and death?

But that is "ancient history," these are modern times, we are enlightened, we don't do that sort of thing anymore, right? Wrong. Out of misguided zealousness and unwarranted fear of communism spreading in South East Asia, we invaded Vietnam and rained tons of bullets, bombs, napalm and that deadly toxin Agent Orange down upon the heads of the Vietnamese people, killing an estimated 1.5 million of them, including women and children. Staggering damage was done to the land and the economy. Agent Orange, containing Dioxin, one of the world's deadliest poisons, was responsible for 400,000 deaths and 500,000 children born with birth defects as the "children and grandchildren of the farmers lifted their faces to the gentle rain of the poison cloud." Perhaps you remember My Lai, where 504 women, children, babies and elderly were massacred by U.S. ground troops; some tortured, sexually abused and maimed before they died. Can you even imagine the terror that they felt? Or the picture sent around the world of a young nine year old Vietnamese girl, running down the road, naked, screaming in pain and terror, having torn off her clothes ablaze with the clinging burning napalm that had been dropped on her village. We seemed to have totally lost our moral compass.

In 1989, an estimated 2,000 Panamanian non-combatants were killed, parts of Panama City burned to the ground and 20,000 people displaced from their homes as we invaded their country, in a hypocritical and deceitful operation called "Just Cause," under the pretense of protecting Americans living and stationed there as well as saving the Panama people from their drug-dealing dictator Noriega. The ulterior motives being to ensure our control of the Panama Canal and to silence Noriega from revealing secrets about the CIA and our government that he learned from his twenty years on the CIA payroll. It has been called, "The war of lies and shame." By the standards of our reaction to 9/11 and invasion of Afghanistan seeking the perpetrators, the Panamanians had a right to invade the U.S. and bring the perpetrators (U.S. troops) and their leader (the U.S. President) to justice for what they did to them.

Very few people knew of or understood the reign of terror that the British and we helped unleash in Iran, which led to the Iranian Revolution and the hostage-taking of our Embassy people. In 1953, the CIA and British Intelligence agents, along with Iranian collaborators, organized a coup unseating the popularly elected Prime Minister Mosaddeq because he had nationalized the Iranian oil industry, which the British had exploited, and because he was friendly with the communist Soviet Union, which we did not approve of out of an unwarranted fear of communism. Shah Pahlavi, the self-proclaimed "King of Kings," was restored as ruler (read dictator) who then proceeded to oppress and terrorize the Iranian people through the CIA-trained secret police SAVAK, who tortured and executed thousands of political prisoners and suppressed all dissent.

Our continued support of the Shah, "sowed the seeds of anti-Americanism which manifested itself in the revolution against the monarchy" and the taking of the hostages. The anti-Americanism continues today. Hostage taking is not acceptable, however the Iranians' demand that the Shah be returned for trial, that we apologize for our interference in their affairs, our actions against Mossadeq and that Iranian funds frozen in the U.S. be released, were perfectly legitimate. Had we rightly done so, the hostages would have been spared their 444-day confinement ordeal.

In the aftermath of our invasion of Haiti, to remove the military dictatorship and install a democratic government, the plight of the people in Haiti degenerated into some of the worst living conditions in the world. "People were digging through garbage heaps looking for food as starvation stalked the land. Disease, due to shortage of medicines, was rampant with children the worst victims. Over 250 children were dying each week in Haiti." We are responsible for that, in the name of democracy.

Over 400 civilians, overwhelmingly women and children, sought safe haven in a bomb shelter during our bombing of Baghdad. It was designated as a civil-defense shelter and used frequently by large numbers of Iraqis during the war, which was known by our forces attacking the city. But because it was *suspected* as being used by Iraqi Intelligence, stealth aircraft using smart bunker busters bombed it. Those in the upper level were incinerated. The intense heat brought the water in the shelter's watering system to boiling, bursting the pipes and scalding those in the lower level to death.

Think of the "shock and awe" we wreaked in Iraq as we destroyed much of their country's infrastructure and killed thousands of innocents. U.S. terrorism in Afghanistan was widespread; we called it collateral damage. Although we do not deliberately target non-combatants as the terrorists did on 9/11, the result is the same, innocent people suffer and die.

So what is the answer to terrorism, war and violence in general? Every time we pledge allegiance, we announce ourselves as a "nation under God." We consider ourselves a Christian nation. In reality, we are neither. We not only do not listen to God, we outright defy him. We may accept Jesus Christ theologically, but we certainly do not live by his teachings. Don't you think it would be wise to hear what God and Jesus Christ have to say about how to deal with enemies/

terrorists? Their instructions are very clear. I like to think of it as the God Option and it goes like this: "Live in peace and the God of love and peace shall be with you. Seek not vengeance. *Love your enemies and do good to those who persecute you.* If your enemy hungers, give him to eat; if he thirsts, give him to drink. Forgive seven times seventy. Thou shalt not kill. Turn the other cheek. Do not fear those who can kill your body, they cannot kill your soul. Requite evil with good. The command from the beginning is that you must all live in love."

There are those who cite the scripture "an eye for an eye" as justification for killing the enemy. Obviously, that is diametrically opposed to "seek not vengeance." One, therefore, has to be suspect, does it not? If we closely look at the context, it is quite clear which one it is. That eye for an eye is from Exodus, where other diverse laws are also spelled out, such as, if a man curse his mother or father, he shall be put to death, witches shall be put to death and anyone who worships idols shall be put to death. It's quite clear those are the words of men and not God. So it is with other scriptures such as "those who live by the sword shall perish by the sword," which obviously is an untruth.

It has been said that in the Sixth Commandment, "Thou shall not kill," God really meant thou shall not murder. Recent versions of the Bible already reflect that change in wording. However, if we look at the entire context of the Bible, concerning this issue, it is quite clear that God meant we humans are not to *kill* one another. If we can reasonably accept that the translators were diligent and consistent in their work, we would have to conclude that wherever the word kill is used in the Bible it has the same meaning. The word murder is used in other parts of the Scripture, so obviously different words for kill and murder would then be reflected in the translations accordingly. "Thou shalt not *kill*" was an accurate translation. Life is a gift from God. It is not our prerogative to take it from another.

By such as our excursions into Iraq and Afghanistan and continued course of actions there, we are saying, God, you are all wet; you do not know what you're talking about. We know better, we are going to kill our enemies. A pretty serious breach of faith in God and his commands, would you not say? To show love to enemies and forgive them is a radical and hard concept to accept, but God's wisdom is faultless. But rather than listening to it, we concoct our own rules living by such man-made philosophy as there will always be evil in the world and we must be prepared to battle it with the strength of military force. That is a flawed philosophy and false assumption. Scripture speaks of the "peaceable kingdom that is to come, nation will not lift up sword against nation; neither will they learn war anymore, and that God's will is to be done on earth as in heaven." There is no evil in heaven nor terrorism or violence or war.

But until then, the evil that is in the world, spawned by our defiance of God, should indeed be met with force; love being the most powerful force in the world. As Rosemarie Carnarius says in her great work *Armageddon or Awakening*, "Help ignite the world with the light of love instead of the fire of bombs."

We tend to use the word evil too loosely, especially in applying it to persons. An individual may commit an act, aggravated by circumstances, which would be considered evil yet, under normal circumstances, is a good person. Those soldiers at My Lai committed malevolent acts yet, outside the terrible influence of war, most all are likely decent people. Osama bin Laden was considered an evil person. Rather, I believe he was a misguided, fundamentalist Muslim zealot. He incorrectly saw the western civilizations as totally corrupt and evil. His goal was to impose his rigid Islamic values on them by means of the Jihad, a holy war, until they saw the error of their ways and agreed with him. Obviously, he was wrong and didn't succeed.

He did have one redeeming value--he was a human being. No one is totally evil; no one is immune from the power of love to bring about change. Everyone has good in them, sometimes smothered by hatred and false beliefs. It just has to be brought out. God's way of kind, forgiving love is the best way to do it.

What if we implemented the God option? What if President Trump addressed the world at the UN, renouncing war, all violence and retaliation, ordered an immediate cease-fire by all American forces and asked the nations of the world, as well as al Qaida and ISIS, to commit to the same? Further announcing that there has been enough death, destruction and suffering. For the sake of our children and a better world, let us resolve our differences peacefully. We forgive those who have attacked us and ask forgiveness for the suffering we have caused. God makes forgiveness mandatory for both the Christian and the Muslim. Then, stating changes in our foreign policy, such as a reduced military presence around the world with complete withdrawal from and near Muslim countries. We would never tolerate a foreign military base on or near our soil, so why should they? I have no doubt the people of the world would flock to the streets and cry out for joy. The world longs for and is ready for peace.

If the terrorist organizations refused to make a commitment to nonviolence and continued to attack us, they would be the pariah of the world, even a vast majority of the Muslim world, especially if we refused to retaliate, continued to forgive them and vicariously did good to them ("do good to those who persecute you"), such as helping the starving children of the world. Every act of violence anywhere in the world would be met with an act of kindness. Promoting human well-being such as freedom from violence and freedom from hunger is of the utmost importance in resolving conflict, a powerful antidote to hate and violence. The World Health Organization has estimated that world hunger could be alleviated at the cost of $15 billion per year. That is a pittance in comparison to world expenditure on war and preparation for war. Think about what that would do for poverty around the world, as well as the positive effect it would have against conflict and violence.

Another action toward implementing God's instructions to love our enemies and do good to those who persecute us would be to close Guantanamo, give each detainee $5,000 and send them home first class at airline expense. It would be the best $720,000 the government has ever spent on anti-terrorism.

There are those who would say such actions would be a sign of weakness. I believe most of the world would see it as a tremendous act of courage and wisdom. Some would insist that all the perpetrators of 9/11 be brought to justice; how can they be forgiven for the murder of almost 3000 Americans? Looking at it from a retribution standpoint we are more than even. We have caused tremendous destruction to the Afghanistan infrastructure and killed thousands of Afghans, including women and children, in pursuit of terrorists.

We need to gradually embrace a "swords to plowshare" mentality. When we do so, the world will be a much better place in which to live and we will have greatly improved our economic well-being. Not only are we spending ourselves into financial insolvency with those massive and unnecessary "defense," war and counter-terrorism expenditures, we are harming ourselves economically by funneling such huge amounts into the military industrial complex. Military spending creates fewer economic benefits than would be created by equivalent spending in the non-military sector. According to the Congressional Budget Office, every $10 billion spent on defense creates 40,000 fewer jobs than if it were spent in the civilian sector. Military spending is also inflationary in that it consumes resources from the private sector but produces nothing to meet private sector consumption. It pays wages to workers who consume, yet it produces no goods or services to meet that consumption demand.

President Eisenhower warned us about the military industrial complex, the formidable union of defense contractors and the armed forces, which would get us into trouble. He was certainly right about that. It is the biggest, most powerful and harmful special interest in our country. It has its tentacles everywhere, locking in support from all the politicians, with its unwarranted influence on government in the guise of national security. It is a major threat to our financial security. It takes resources from other more essential functions of government. It has helped arm the world to the teeth, only serving to heighten international tensions, making us and other countries less secure. The best that might be said is that it was unsought, brought about by misguided zealotry in the false way of aspiring for world stability through military power.

We were not meant to live in a militaristic world. We are meant to live in peace. We need to open our eyes and minds to that truth. But what is the truth? Jesus Christ said, "Live as I tell you to live and you will know the truth and the truth will set you free." So how did he tell us to live? "Love your neighbor as yourself. A new commandment I give you, that you love one another as I have loved you. Do unto others, as you would have them do unto you. Forgive seven times seventy. Do not fear those who can kill your body, they cannot kill your soul. Love your enemies. Do good to those who persecute you."

LOVE is the truth. Love is kindness, caring and forgiveness. Love is uniting and healing. Love creates well-being, contentment, happiness and joy. Hatred divides and destroys all those things. Only love can conquer hatred. Love is the true panacea that can solve the problems of the world, if only we would listen to God and trust in his perfect wisdom. When we change our thinking and actions from hate and revenge to love and forgiveness we will have won the struggle against terrorism and will be free from it, violence and war. You know the scripture, "Hope, Faith and Love, but the greatest of these is Love." Humanity never ceases to hope for a peaceful world. Hope springs eternal, Faith (belief) keeps it alive, but it is Love that will bring it to fruition.

That philosophy is the solution to the Palestinian/Israeli struggle. Beloved Israeli Rabbi Hillel said, "No Jew can love God unless he is in a loving relationship with his neighbor." Islam dictates that, "None of you is a believer unless he wants for his brother what he wants for himself." Surely, the Palestinians and Israelis are neighbors and brothers to one another. This needs to be forcefully "brought home" to both parties. Neither will ever realize their goals through their present actions. The suicide and missile bombings perpetrated by the Palestinians and the violent destructive and oppressive tactics by the Israelis are detestable and to be condemned. They only foster hatred and more violence.

Both claim to own the land in contest; the Palestinians because they lived on the land for hundreds of years. The Israelis believe that God gave them the land. Neither is valid. In reality, the land was originally owned by others such as the Midianites and Canaanites. Allah/Yahweh is a just God; he could not take land from one and give it to another. Lands all over the world have changed ownership over the centuries. The two parties have to get over this previous ownership mantra and deal with the situation as it exists today; that is, share the land. After all, in the past they shared it and lived in peace for hundreds of years.

Instead of spending billions of dollars on the weapons of war and killing one another, use those funds to make more land fertile and habitable. Water is a vital issue there. Build desalination plants and make the desert a veritable green pasture on which both can live and enjoy. Both Palestinians and Israelis need to open their minds and their hearts and make a "quantum leap" in their thinking. From the hatred and violence that they are both consumed by to love, kindness and forgiveness that their God requires of them. Want for the other what you want for yourself and live in a loving relationship with one another. Think of how wonderful life can be for yourself and your children when you do that. That is your purpose in life. It is not impossible. You only need the will to do it. Disregard the foreign minion mediators. Set the example for the rest of the world. Go down in history as the two peoples that made their world safe for their children.

Yes, we humans have a purpose in life and it is very simple. We are here to enjoy it. And there is so much beauty in the world to enjoy. Consider the majestic snow-capped mountains, the source of flowing streams and rivers, which, along with the thirst- quenching rains, bring life to the valleys and plains below, giving us our superb towering forests, green pastures and waving fields of grain. Just think of all the beauty that flowers bring to us--the exquisiteness of the red rose or a bed of yellow daffodils nodding in the breeze. What of the magnificence of our mighty oceans or the brilliance of a nighttime star-studded sky? Even the windswept deserts and snowy white expanses of the Artic have their beauty. How beautiful the laughter of little children at play, or the deed of helping someone in need!

And I don't think it is any coincidence that we have our five senses with which to experience that entire splendor. With our sense of sight we behold all the glories of nature and treasure the vision of our loved ones. Isn't it uplifting to hear the joy and happiness in the song of the birds or the beautiful strains of a soul-stirring symphony? Oh, how sweet the taste of honey or a chocolate kiss as it melts in the mouth. What delight we derive from the aroma of the lilac bush or hot bread fresh from the oven. How wonderful the loving touch of a mother to the babe or the embrace of a loved one. Have you ever walked barefoot in the sand, on an ocean beach, hearing the call of the seagull above, and felt the soft silky touch of a warm summer breeze as it caresses your face? I have. Oh, how exhilarating and what a wonderful sense of serenity it brings. OH YES, so much beauty in the world.

What if, from a very early age, we were taught to believe that our purpose in life is to enjoy it? What if that philosophy were literally ingrained into our very being? Would we not then embrace all the good things in life, love, kindness and forgiveness? And would we not shun the bad---rejecting hatred, cruelty and violence? I truly believe so!

After all, we know that our actions are governed by our thoughts--as we think so are we. That is not only a widely accepted maxim in the secular sense, but is God's word in the Scripture which says, "As a man thinketh in his heart, so is he." Whatever we believe with our minds, and hold with deep conviction, defines the very essence of our being and indeed, the state of our world.

James Allen, in his inspirational book, *As A Man Thinketh*, has said, "A man is literally what he thinks, his character being the sum of his own thoughts. As a being of Power, Intelligence and Love, and the lord of his own thoughts, man holds the key to every situation, and contains within himself that transforming and regenerative ability by which he may make himself what he wills. By the right choice and true application of thought, man ascends to Divine Perfection." Divine Perfection? Everyone knows no one is or can be perfect, right? Here is a surprise for you. Jesus Christ said, "Be perfect as your father in heaven is perfect." Matthew 5:48. Why would we be told that if we did not have the ability to do it? That doesn't mean never making a mistake. We all do make mistakes; God knows, I've made my share. It means we should always show love and forgiveness to one another, of which we are "perfect"ly capable.

We are beings with amazing abilities who can control our own destiny. We need to stop listening to men who tell us that it is only human to err and we are poor miserable sinners. How about listening to God who has told us how great we are, being made in his image. That we have the ability to choose to do right and make the world good.

We need to give thought to all the joyful things that life has to offer, embrace them and enjoy them as our purpose for being. Let's think about how wonderful life can be for our children and us when we shun violence and live in peace according to God's way. Scripture tells us, "The command from the beginning is that you must all live in love." We humans are magnificent beings who have the power to choose, the complete ability to eschew war and violence and "live in love," kind, caring and forgiving love. This is not Pollyanna. It only takes courage and the will to do it.

Those who are aware of Nelson Mandela know that his extraordinary life was evidence that the world can be transformed. I've always liked his words of wisdom, "No one is born hating another person. People learn to hate, and if they can learn to hate, they can be taught to love, for love comes more naturally to the human heart than its opposite." It is time for this old world of hate, sorrow and terrorism to pass away and a new golden era of knowledge of God, of love, peace and well-being to begin. Remember, God's will is going to be done on earth as it is heaven. Let's get on with it! Someone needs to lead the way. Why not America? Mr. President, go to the UN. Imagine if we did something different. Go for it!

Chapter Three
HEALTH CARE COSTS

There is a great deal of untold truth about our health care system. It is a major budget buster, contributing significantly and unnecessarily to our annual deficits and national debt. The Affordable Care Act was intended to provide health care to all citizens. Prior to its enactment there were about forty million Americans without health insurance. At the end of the first year, less than seven million had been signed up for insurance. It is far from achieving its purpose. There are both good and bad provisions to the act. The claim that it will lower health costs is very questionable. It does lower the rate of premium increase while at the same time costing the taxpayer for subsidies to those who can't afford insurance and tax credits to the middle class income earners and businesses.

It is not a good act and rather than working together to fix the problems, congressional members played the blame game trying to affix all the fault to the administration or the other party so as to gain political advantage. There was plenty of blame to go around, including the insurance companies, but the primary criticism needed to be directed at Congress. There is that old adage, the administration proposes and Congress disposes. Congress makes the laws, the administration enforces them. The final provisions of the ACA were the responsibility of Congress regardless of the lack of partisan support.

We are spending $3 trillion every year on health care or about $9,500 per capita. In life expectancy, at 78.7 years, we rank 36th in the world. Almost every country ranking higher spends half or less per capita then we do; Canada at $4,445 and Germany at $4,338. Most have health care systems that are on a par with ours. Japan, ranking first with a life expectancy four years greater than ours, spends a third of what we do per capita at $3,035.

Obviously there is something drastically wrong with our health care system. If other countries can provide good health care at $4,700 per capita or less, so can and should we. That and other measures means we can save over a trillion dollars every year in health care costs when we correct the flaws in our system. The individual, businesses, the insurance companies and the government (tax payer) will all benefit.

So why are our health care costs twice as high as they should be? The Institute of Medicine reports that the health-care system wastes $750 billion every year, involving millions of unnecessary and expensive tests, inefficient delivery of care, excessive administrative costs, inflated prices and fraud. The *Arizona Daily Star* reported that about one third of the health care that is provided is not needed or does nothing to benefit the health of the patient. That's a trillion dollars spent unnecessarily every year. As Medicare and Medicaid constitute about 40% of the health care costs, that means that we could save the government (taxpayers) $400 billion every year. Think of what that would do for our annual deficit.

The ACA does nothing to address that enormous waste but rather increases it. The Act requires that insurance plans cover preventive care at no cost, such as free checkups, free mammograms, free immunizations and free other basic services. How naïve can you get? There is no such thing as free medical care. You will pay as the insurance companies raise premiums. Medicare and Medicaid costs will go up as the insurance companies bill the taxpayers for those "free" services.

"Preventive healthcare services," in the way of screening for early detection, are a major factor in the unnecessary care provided. They are incredibly expensive. About 13% of American women will get breast cancer. That means 87% will not, yet they will be tested for it. Of those 13%, preventive screening doesn't always catch it. Further, tests often produce false positive results which then require more expensive testing and sometimes invasive procedures.

Applying that concept to the many other diseases, means that a vast majority of healthy Americans will be tested for diseases they don't have. We are talking about hundreds of millions of unnecessary tests. It doesn't take a math genius to understand the immense costs that will be incurred. The concept of screening, preventive health care services, is a very bad idea. It is especially egregious as we know how to actually prevent disease. Screening is okay where special circumstances exist such as a family history of a disease. Yes, preventive screening will save lives, but many, many more will be saved when we focus on keeping people from getting sick, which we know how to do but give it little attention. We will look at this in more detail a bit later.

Tens of millions of unnecessary medical tests are given to people during checkups and routine visits to the doctor as well as hospitals visits. Millions of older women don't need a bone-density scan for osteoporosis as often as is done. Women under 65 do not need bone-scans at all unless certain risk factors are involved. Yearly pelvic exams are often a waste of time and money, and sometimes do more harm than good, when they show false alarms which can lead to unneeded follow-up care. Cancer screening is greatly overused; mammograms are given too early or too often, prostate cancer tests are in much the same category. Expensive annual EKGs and other cardiac screenings are unnecessarily given to patients who have no heart disease symptoms or family history of it. Cholesterol testing and pap smears are prescribed entirely too often. The Annals of Internal Medicine lists 37 scenarios where testing is overused.

Great costs are incurred in testing because of drugs that have been prescribed. Many drugs have serious side effects and therefore continuous testing is done to check on the condition of a body and its organs. Law requires that one must visit a doctor to refill any prescription over a year old, which then often requires extensive testing to determine any adverse effect the prescription drug may have had. The visit to the doctor and testing happens millions of times each year, contributing unnecessarily to health care costs. That law needs to be modified to apply only to certain drugs.

Testing of children as early as eight years of age for cholesterol and then feeding them statins to control the cholesterol is outrageous. About a third of U.S. children are obese or overweight and it is estimated that 10-13% have high cholesterol. The medical experts that are proposing the testing said not one word about the cause of the high cholesterol which generally is diet. That is the problem that needs to be corrected. Treat the cause not the disease. Statins such as Lipitor and Zocor have many side effects such as diarrhea, joint pain, stomach upset, urinary tract infection, insomnia, muscle weakening, memory loss, liver problems and even kidney failure. Do you want your children subjected to that?

The use of statins by the medical profession to manage cholesterol is out of control and extremely costly. Thirty-three million Americans are on statins when the vast majority of them do not need to be. Statins have become convenient pills that do work while allowing patients to continue their health risk lifestyles. High cholesterol levels are caused by liver dysfunction brought about, for the most part, by lifestyles such as poor food choices, being overweight, lack of exercise, smoking, too much alcohol and stress.

Although periodic tests are no longer required to test for liver damage caused by statins, liver enzymes must be checked one time prior to initiating the drug, or in the event the patient displays any symptoms of possible liver enzyme elevation/failure such as unexplained nausea or loss of appetite, yellowing of skin or whites of the eyes (Jaundice), severe lethargy or abdominal pain. Given the numerous side effects of statin drugs, you can be sure a great deal of testing is going to occur.

Most people can generally get their cholesterol levels back to normal by getting plenty of exercise, eating plenty of fruits, vegetables, whole grains, oats and good quality fats, avoiding foods with saturated fats, getting adequate sleep, bringing bodyweight back to normal, avoiding excessive alcohol and stopping smoking. Additionally, such a healthy diet will have numerous other health benefits.

Steven Nissen, cardiologist at Cleveland Clinic suggests that a new risk calculator from the American Heart Association may drastically overestimate the number of people who should be taking cholesterol-lowering statins such as Lipitor and Crestor.

Doctors and hospitals prescribe extensive testing that provides no benefit to the health of the patient, so as to protect themselves from lawsuits. Tens of millions of unnecessary tests are prescribed every year by the doctors and hospitals having to practice "defensive medicine." Tort reform is badly needed, not only to protect the medical caregivers but also to cap the exorbitant monetary awards often given by juries that want to sock it to what they think of as the "deep pockets" insurance companies. Caps are needed on the plaintiff attorney costs, with usually around 30% contrived fees plus a big chunk of the settlement, often leaving small amounts for the victim of the medical malpractice.

Most doctors are dedicated and honest. But there is a faction that prescribes testing that increases their income through their vested interest in the testing facilities. Medicare and Medicaid fraud by individuals, doctors, clinics and hospitals amounts to $60 billion every year. More intense efforts by HHS and DOJ are required to reduce this.

Prescription drugs account for about 10% or $300 billion of health care costs each year. Drug prices in the U.S. are the highest in the world and rising significantly faster than the rate of inflation. Pharmaceuticals are the highest profit sector in the U.S. The drug companies claim they need to charge high prices to fund their research and development of new drugs which then benefit the health of people worldwide. The fact is that only 14% of their expenditures involve R&D, with much greater amounts going for administration and especially marketing. The industry spends $300 million every year lobbying the government to give them special dispensation such as limits and controls on generic drugs, which are just as effective but cost only a fraction of the normal product.

Prescription drugs are widely and often unnecessarily used. According to a study by Harvard Medical School's Dr. Steffi Woolhandler and colleagues, about "25 percent of all Americans 65 or older are given prescriptions for drugs that they should almost never take; drugs that can produce amnesia and confusion, and others that cause serious side effects like heart problems or respiratory failure." Rx drugs can often be more harmful than beneficial. A University of Toronto study reported that "bad reactions to prescription drugs were the U.S.'s fourth leading killer in 1994, with more than 100,000 dying from toxic reactions to medications and two million suffering from serious side effects."

We have developed a culture that is entirely too dependent on the medical field for our health care. We run to the doctor or clinic for all kinds of ailments such as headaches, backaches, stomachaches, earaches, colds, flu, minor pains, indigestion and depression to name a few. Most of those will eventually go away or we can take care of them ourselves. Our fairly recent ancestors were a hardy bunch that adhered to that philosophy. Now we seem to have become wimps when it comes to taking care of our own health.

So how do we eliminate this one-third of health care given that does nothing to benefit the health of the patient? First, everyone needs to be aware of this problem and its serious effect on health care costs. There has been very little discussion of it perhaps because we like the status quo. Everyone is making bundles of money and the patient is getting his and her health problem taken care of, failing to realize that it unnecessarily costs the government (taxpayers) enormous sums of money, increasing the deficit and our national debt.

This enormous waste, estimated at one trillion dollars every year, is not being seriously addressed. Rather, other questionable cost reduction methods are being proposed such as replacing Medicare with a voucher system, reducing the amount of payments to health care providers (a bad idea as some providers, especially hospitals, are already struggling with their costs versus payments, having to take care of the indigent without payment and doctors refusing to accept Medicare and even leaving their practice), increasing cost to individuals and raising the age eligibility. None of these is necessary when the better and much more cost effective way is to purge the wasteful spending on those unnecessary procedures. Everyone, the patient, doctors, politicians, hospitals, insurance companies, the pharmaceutical industry and government must do their part; the by-words being integrity and responsibility. By eliminating that unnecessary care, profits will decrease but that's okay; a reasonable profit will still be made.

The good news is that elimination of that unnecessary one third of the care will not cost jobs. There is plenty of illness and disease to keep everyone in the medical field busy. Thousands are dying of AIDS. One million people are dying every year from heart disease and 600,000 from cancer in the U.S. Diabetes and arthritis affect a large percentage of the population and are on the rise. Seventy five percent of the elderly population has arthritis to some degree. Asthma is plaguing the younger generation. Seventy five million people suffer from allergies. Depression, high blood pressure and obesity are rampant in our society. Twenty million surgeries are performed every year in the U.S.

There is another aspect of the enormous cost of health care that needs to be addressed. About one fourth of the total costs is the result of irresponsibility, primarily by the patient in the way of a harmful lifestyle involving lousy diets, lack of exercise, drug abuse and smoking. These being the leading causes of obesity, heart disease, cancer, diabetes and other ills that plague us. Unprotected sex leading to sexually transmitted diseases (AIDS is extremely costly to treat) and having children without the ability to care for them are both very expensive. The care needed here for those who do not have the means to pay, constitutes a huge health care cost to the government (taxpayer).

The problem is that we have gone down the wrong road when it comes to health care, the road of CURE! Get the disease and we will cure you with the scalpel and drugs. Or spend billions on research for a pill you can pop to cure or control the disease and still let you go on with your debilitating lifestyle. Research is good but too much money is being expended there when it should go to promoting PREVENTION, not preventive services. The truth is that we actually know how to prevent disease.

According to the National Research Council, "at least eighty percent of cancers are caused by identifiable factors that can be controlled. Thirty percent are attributed to tobacco, but an even greater number--thirty five to sixty percent--are caused by dietary factors." Just think, we have the complete ability to prevent 80 percent of those 600 thousand cancer deaths, 480,000 people, and eliminate the huge costs that are incurred. But little effort is made to do so. The primary effort is to cure by means of the scalpel, chemotherapy and radiation.

Heart disease claims almost one million lives every year in this country. We know how to prevent almost every one of those deaths and again, do away with the immense costs that are involved. Doctor Dean Ornish has scientifically proven that diet and lifestyle not only prevent heart attacks, but actually can reverse the clogging of the arteries. Dr. William Roberts, Editor in Chief of the American Journal of Cardiology, says, "Dr. Ornish is on the right road and we need to get on it also." Why isn't the medical establishment getting on with the non-surgical program for preventing and reversing heart disease, as Dr. Roberts suggested? That the use of bypass surgery, angioplasty and drug treatment for heart disease is a $15 billion-a-year business in this country undoubtedly has a lot to do with it!

Preventing disease is no secret. It does receive attention, but it is mostly lip service, just a token effort. What is needed is a massive education effort, by the medical community and the government, and even the schools and parents in moving from cure to prevention. We need a new paradigm of health care, one in which the individual takes primary responsibility for their own health care; each of us being our own primary care provider. The doctor is secondary.

We must change our lifestyle if we want to enjoy good health and keep it that way. We are eating too much of the wrong kinds of foods and in too much quantity. In the 1970s, the experts on weight control got it all wrong claiming there was too much fat in our diets and put America on a low fat diet. Fatty meats, eggs and all dairy products were the culprits. We needed to consume less of them and more carbohydrates. Thus all kinds of flour products, potatoes, rice and sugar started to dominate our diets. Unfortunately, they are the wrong kind of carbs; they are all very high in starch, *the real culprit in weight gain as well as clogging our arteries and contributing to poor health.*

Mother was right; we need to eat our fruits and veggies, the good carbs. We don't have to give up all the breads we love, potatoes au gratin, rice pilaf, pizza, pasta or cut out all sweets. It's okay to have a donut day once in a while. But as they are a major part of our diets, we need to reduce their use rather sharply. Meats, eggs and dairy products are good for you, but in moderation and of course, eat more fruits and vegetables. Experts say we need five helpings of fruits and vegetables daily. Try that and you will soon get sick and tired of them. Try smoothies two or three times a week. You can blend eight or ten different fruits with a bit of water to give it the right consistency. Using fruit juices improves the taste, but you need to be cautious about bottled juices that contain added sugar. Use vegetable smoothies as well. Add a variety of nuts and seeds to both smoothies; almonds, pecans, walnuts, sunflower seeds and flax seeds are packed with health giving nutrients. You can use water or pure vegetable and fruit juice for the right consistency. Use one of the high-powered blenders that are available; they break down the fruits, vegetables and nuts for better digestion and nutrient absorption.

Meat or veggie omelets with either a smooth cream sauce or salsa are really good for you. Fix vegetables au gratin with a creamy buttery sauce. Seasoned stir fry or roasted vegetables are delicious. How about homemade vegetable soup served with warm buttered French bread? Yummy! Use whole grain products. Brown rice is better than the white and it tastes just as good. Use natural sweeteners. Refined sugar is a major, major contributor to poor health. About 80% of all foods in your grocery store contain sugar to some degree. Some are loaded. Use natural and raw foods to make your meals. Learn to cook instead of buying readymade meals. Use fewer refined or processed foods where much of the nutritive value is destroyed. Use your imagination and enjoy good food and good health.

When you eat the right kinds of food, you can reduce both over-the-counter and prescription drug costs by at least half, saving yourself, the insurance companies and the government (taxpayers) a total of $200 billion a year. The Father of Medicine, Hippocrates said, "Let food by thy medicine." And, indeed, it is. Food contains every nutrient that the body needs for good health as well as having healing properties.

There is another area that is critical to good health; one that you can control as your primary care provider. You've likely never heard of triazinetrione dehydrate. It is classified as a bad character chemical, acutely toxic and a known carcinogenic. Yet it can be found in most households and is used daily as an ingredient in the cleanser under your sinks.

Or how about triethylene glycol? It is a developmental toxicant, causes adverse effects to a developing child to include birth defects, low birth weight, and psychological or behavioral deficits that become manifest as the child grows. Exposure during pregnancy can disrupt fetal development or even cause death! Again found in most households and used daily. It's in the deodorizing spray you use around the house, the bathrooms and in the baby's room.

And that's just the tip of the iceberg. Your bodies are literally being assaulted with toxins. Here is a list of toxins that we are subjected to, some on a daily basis: Poisonous metals such as lead and mercury; asbestos; chemically-laden paints and solvents; corrosives in air conditioning units; radiation; nitrates; radon; alcohol penetrants in colognes, perfumes and after-shave lotions; allergens; prescription drugs and over-the-counter medicines; numerous cleaning compounds found in every home; pesticides and herbicides; soaps; skin lotions; chemically altered substances such as trans-fats; chlorine; hair sprays and dyes; food additives; artificial coloring; artificial flavoring; auto exhaust; carbon monoxide; smoke; industrial pollutants, and more.

These toxins can be ingested, inhaled or absorbed through the skin. They are in the digestive system, the bowels, brain and blood stream. They are stored in the lymph nodes and body organs interfering with the normal functions of the body, deforming cells and causing disease. Is it any wonder that humankind is suffering from disease and ill health? The toxins, folks, are a major factor in making us sick and killing us!

Well, you may ask, doesn't the FDA, the Food and Drug Administration, control and establish limits for the use of those toxic substances? Indeed they do, but only on an individual basis. Little or no research is done on the cumulative effect, which over time can be extremely harmful. Nor is sufficient attention given to the combination effect of ingesting a variety of those substances, which can be lethal. Studies show that certain chemicals, when combined, increase up to tenfold in toxicity.

For good health, it is essential that we be aware of what we are ingesting, that we eliminate toxins from our bodies and then avoid them. Read labels on the food that you buy and the other products that you put on or into your body. Refuse to buy those that contain toxic chemicals. Cosmetics are especially egregious, many containing parabens, a group of compounds and chemicals that can be toxic, some known to be carcinogenic. Avoid foods with preservatives, artificial coloring, artificial flavors and trans-fats. At this time the FDA is considering banning trans-fats; it's about time. Go organic as much as possible and avoid pesticides and herbicides. Clean your veggies and fruits with a veggie wash, organic or not. Put a filter on your water faucet and eliminate chlorine and fluoride. Do deep breathing exercises regularly to eliminate toxins that you have inhaled. A diet rich in green leafy vegetables will help remove toxins that have accumulated in your body. Drink plenty of pure water.

Exercise is important, even vital to good health. Our bodies are meant to be exercised. Without it they deteriorate and are more vulnerable to sickness and disease. You don't need to adhere to the no pain, no gain myth. Modest exercise every day is desirable. In addition to some kind of exercise regimen, don't be a couch potato; get up and move around, it's good for your immune system.

When you eat a balanced diet, low on starches, with moderate amounts of fatty foods and healthy portions of fruits and vegetables, eliminate the toxins from your body, further avoid them and exercise regularly, then you can experience good health and truly enjoy life. You will not have to worry about being confined to a nursing home, perhaps bedridden or hooked up to all that life preserving apparatus in your latter years. The golden years can truly be golden.

We really need to reassess the belief and medical mantra that life must be preserved at all costs. It is not only contrary to the natural cycle of life, but cruel, sometimes incredibly so. This physical life is a gift from God and when this mortal frame is destroyed God gives us the ultimate gift, that of eternal life for our spiritual self. It is interesting to note that, in the ancient Aramaic language, the word for death means "not here, present elsewhere." That elsewhere being what we think of as heaven, a place of awesome wonder and utter glory where we will be reunited with loved ones and reside in the presence of God forever. Since over 90% of us believe in heaven and that we are going to go there, why are we so fearful of death? We need to stop thwarting God's plan for us with all those extraordinary efforts to prolong this mortal life? To be bedridden, hooked up to machines, fed through a tube to our stomach, sometimes for years, denying us the pleasure of heaven, is indeed cruel.

When we come to understand and accept that death is not the end of our existence, but actually a joyous experience where we move on to a different and better way of life, we will find ourselves more content and life less stressful. It would certainly bring about major changes in life. We would cease the extraordinarily expensive and futile folly of transplanting critical organs so as to prolong this often less-than-wonderful life. We would do away with the useless practice of preservative cryogenics, ostentatious funerals and the current way of grieving. There would be no more "code blues" in hospitals or human beings hooked up to elaborate life-sustaining devices. We would stop that other cruel practice of resuscitation, bringing those people back from death and denying them the pleasures of paradise. The medical field's main purpose should not be to keep people from dying but to prevent or relieve suffering so that life can be meaningful and joyful.

There is another intriguing prospect when we look at death as not to be feared. If death is a wondrous and joyful event, and the scriptural and near-death experience evidence certainly supports this idea, then if someone were to kill us they would be doing us a favor, would they not? And an accidental death would be a blessing. That may seem bizarre, but what if we had that perception of death? Most of those who kill think of death as punishment. What if they were conditioned to think of death as reward? With the threat of death gone would there not be a profound change in the violence and killing that exists today?

There is one more factor, perhaps the most important, and that is our attitude about our health; how we think about our health. The human mind is very powerful; we don't understand the affect it can have on our health. We know that we can literally make ourselves ill, even cause death, through the power of negative thoughts that we program into our minds. By the same token, we actually can think ourselves well. Thousands of cases have been documented in confirmation.

Actually the length of our lives is not too important; we are all going to die sooner or later, and move on to something better. It's the quality of life that's significant. So if you want to enjoy good health for whatever years you have, take control of your own health care, eat healthy, exercise, avoid toxins and think positively about your health. And as a result, save yourselves and other taxpayers a hell of a lot of money, reducing our annual deficits by $400 billion dollars.

Chapter Four

DEFICIT SPENDING AND THE NATIONAL DEBT

The truth is that a balanced budget can be easily achieved when Congress eschews politics and acts responsibly in our country's financial affairs. The Democrats generally don't want any cuts in spending and the Republicans stand fast against reasonable increases in revenue, both in opposition to the will of the people who want the problem resolved with both a reduction in spending and increased revenue. As an example, Congressional efforts during 2013 to increase revenue by $60 billion per year and cut spending by $85 billion were disgustingly pitiful. That was a mere $145 billion per year against the annual $1.3 trillion deficit.

Fortunately, due to non-extension of the Bush tax cuts and an improving economy the deficit for fiscal year 2013 came in at about $700 billion. Since those tax cuts were enacted in 2001, it cost the Treasury $3.7 trillion dollars, a huge increase in our national debt. It is interesting to note that prior to the cuts, the economy flourished and the budget was balanced. Further, that subsequent to the cuts, job growth actually declined from previous years.

Succeeding deficits through FY 2017 have been around half a trillion dollars. Even at that rate, in ten years, we will have increased our national debt from $20 trillion to over $25 trillion. The interest on that debt will have ballooned to $600 billion. In another two decades, annual interest on our national debt will be over one trillion dollars, one third of our annual government income, a financial state that cannot be sustained and which will have foreboding consequences for our country. Further cuts in spending and increases in revenue are vital and can be reasonably achieved without serious burden to anyone. The two biggest budget busters are health care costs and defense spending, both of which are out of control.

We saw in the chapter on health care costs how we are spending twice as much per capita on health care costs as other developed countries with approximately the same quality of care. That of the $3 trillion dollars cost per year, about one third or $1 trillion is wasted. With Medicare and Medicaid costs being about forty percent of that total, we are wasting about $400 billion of the taxpayers' money every year. Think what elimination of that would do for the federal and state deficits. As we also noted in Chapter Three, it can be accomplished without serious harm to the economy or jobs.

We can save a $100 billion more by eliminating the abuse of health care costs due to the irresponsibility, primarily by the patient, in the way of a harmful life style involving lousy diets, lack of exercise, drug abuse and smoking. These being the leading causes of obesity, heart disease, cancer, diabetes and other ills that plague us and unnecessarily cost us billions (See Health Care Costs). Providing support to much of this irresponsibility is not helping the patients but rather enabling them. Reform is badly needed in the SSI program that is rife with abuse.

The other huge budget buster is defense, intelligence and counterterrorism costs. It is common knowledge that those agencies are highly bloated. Together, with the expenditures still spent on war, they are costing taxpayers about one trillion dollars every year. That is outrageous, especially when we understand that we have no serious enemies, including terrorists.

Our defense posture is totally out of control. The Department of Defense budget, alone, consists of almost 1.5 million men and women in uniform, 700,000 civilians and another 700,000 private contractors. In 2014, budget overrun for weapons systems was running at $500 billion. The Defense budget is full of congressional "pet" projects, costing billions of dollars and most of which the military does not even want.

We could literally cut defense costs by one third and still be the most powerful nation in the world and just as safe as we are today.

Obviously, it would need to be done very gradually so as not to disrupt the economy. A reduction in all types of personnel should be accomplished by attrition. A shift from military industrial complex production to nonmilitary production will require government and industry working as partners to create new technologies, new products and services, new start-ups, especially in green technologies. There is a great need for infrastructure investment.

The concern about meeting the defense sequestration goals of $500 billion over ten years was ludicrous. That's a mere $50 billion a year. There is easily that much waste every year in the defense budget. The Pentagon can't even account for about 10% of its budget; that's about $60 billion every year. The comments that sequestration cuts will be "devastating," "catastrophic," "hollow the military" and cause "knowing destruction of the U.S. military" are pure unmitigated bull manure. The sources of those comments are either ill-informed or have an ulterior motive. They are obviously protecting the military industrial complex and their own turf, sadly, to the detriment of our country and our deficit and debt problems. That's a damn shame.

Pentagon official, Gordon Adams, has said, "We spend about a third of the defense budget not for national security reasons but because it's in someone's district or state." Elimination of that waste results in reduction of the annual deficit by over $330 billion. We could have saved $70 billion a year by ending the Afghan war a number of years ago as 66% of Americans and 60% of our armed forces wanted to do. The administration was totally deluding themselves to think that anything significant was going to change between then and the end of 2014 when we were projected to discontinue our military efforts there.

There are other unnecessary expenditures that haven't been addressed. Such as our staggering 500 plus military installations overseas, involving about 230 thousand uniformed personnel plus dependents and civilian workers, that are costing us $250 billion every year. We should bring those entire 80,000 troops home from Europe. Those nations can adequately defend themselves, especially as they have no serious enemies.

Why are we sending marines to Australia and exploring a base of operations at Cam Ran Bay, South Vietnam with the announced goal of expanding our military footprint in the Pacific so as to assure dominance? I would hope Vietnam would say not only no, but hell no, you have caused us enough grief. In April 2016, the Administration announced a strengthening of our military posture in the Philippines. Our military expansion in Southeast Asia can only aggravate our relationship with China. What the hell are we trying to do? Start another cold war, this one with China? China is no threat to us either economically or militarily. They need our markets; without them their economy would tank. Their modest increase in military spending is in response to our stated goals of military expansion in their area.

Professor David Vine of the American University, in his study of U.S. forces abroad, says, "Foreign bases also tend to heighten military tensions and discourage diplomatic solutions to conflicts. From the perception of China, Russia, North Korea and Iran, United States bases near their borders are a threat that encourages increased military spending. U.S. bases overseas can actually make war more likely and America less safe."

There is no need for us to be dominant anywhere in the world. Somewhere about equal would suffice. Striving for military dominance is unnecessary, very costly, fosters distrust and sometimes leads to conflict. We learned that lesson from the U.S./Soviet Cold War, but alas, we seem to have forgotten it.

Then there is the waste in our intelligence and counterterrorism agencies. They have ballooned completely out of proportion to what is needed in the way of intelligence gathering and counterterrorism. There is Homeland Security, CIA, NSA, DIA, NIC, NRO and others for a grand total of sixteen. It is estimated that almost one million people populate the many intelligence services at a cost of over $100 billion annually. Outrageous! It is interesting to note that the Mossad, Israeli's elite intelligence service, has about 1200 employees with an annual budget of $350 million. They are considered the best in the world, doing the same exact job for their country. Defense, intelligence and counterterrorism are bloated, indeed!

Now that we have identified where to make serious cuts in spending, let's talk about increasing revenue. Reform the tax code; there is incredible unfairness as we all know. Enormous sums of both individual and corporate income are being sheltered from fair taxation because of politics. Legal loopholes, deductions and other tax breaks have been orchestrated by Congress, sometimes even written by the special interests, in exchange for political donations.

Right now, the people's treasury is giving up over a trillion dollars every year in tax deductions. Eliminate mortgage interest deductions for second homes, boats and RVs that are not a primary residence. Reduce overall deductions by ten percent for everyone. That's an easy $100 billion revenue increase without serious burden for anyone. Surely, every patriotic American would be willing to contribute to alleviating the dire financial dilemma that our country faces. It is in their best interests to do so. It is imperative that everyone, including the business world, understands that we must address the deficit and debt problem right now or face an ominous future.

There is a huge disparity in corporate income tax rates; through the tax loopholes and manipulation of the tax codes some pay no income tax at all. The clamor that we have the highest corporate tax rates in the world and that we need to reduce them from 35% to 28% so as to create jobs and bring manufacturing back to this country is absurd. That's the mantra of those that want to make even bigger profits. Warren Buffet, who has no reason to politicize this issue, said, "It's a myth that U.S. corporate taxes are high. Corporate taxes are not strangling American competitiveness." In the 1950s, the corporate tax rate was 50%, yet the economy was booming and the unemployment rate at 4.5%.

The fact is corporate tax rates are much lower; the Government Accounting Office estimates the overall average corporate tax rate at 13%. The ten most profitable companies in the U.S. paid an average

9% in 2011. One of the biggest corporations paid an average rate of 2.3% over the last ten years. Three large corporations paid no taxes in 2008, 2009 and 2010, some even receiving "tax refunds".

It has been called "corporate welfare." This wrongful and unpatriotic evasion of taxes is allowed by the maze of those "legal" tax shelters provided by Congress in return for political donations. There is much truth to the saying that Congress is owned by Corporate America. This huge loss of duly legitimate revenue causes great harm to our country. Corporate America, especially, needs to be aware that if they don't "pay now" they will really "pay later." They can afford it as they are experiencing record profits. If we don't get our deficits under control, everyone's (corporations', individuals' and government's) financial well-being will suffer greatly. It is the small businesses that need a tax rate adjustment; they do not have access to the loopholes and manipulation available to the big corporations.

There is another huge corporation loophole, created by Congress for the obvious reasons, that allows corporations and hedge funds to shelter enormous sums of earnings from being taxed by creating off-shore identities and tax-haven banks. Those earnings have been reported to be as high as $3 trillion with the tax being evaded, a huge loss to our treasury annually. Think of what that would do toward our annual deficits?

Another good guy, billionaire and investor Carl Icahn, is spending $150 million to promote revision of the corporate tax code so as to stop the above practice by corporations. Another example of a generous patriotic American doing the right thing for his country and the people. Too bad he has to spend his money to do Congress' job for them.

Corporations continue to lobby Congress to give them a "tax holiday" so they can bring those profits home without paying taxes on it, claiming it will create jobs. Congress bowed to them, again for obvious reasons, and gave them a tax holiday in 2004. Subsequent studies showed just the opposite happened. More money and jobs went off-shore. Corporate executive salaries grew, they paid bigger dividends to their stock holders and repurchased their own stock.

Corporations need a "Scrooge Moment." They need to bring those profits home, pay the tax due, and invest the rest, in keeping employees on the job, rehire those they have let go, as well as investing in expansion and more hiring. They need to understand that, just like Scrooge's destiny before his conversion was questionable, the destiny of their business is dire indeed if they do not do their part in getting our financial house in order. It would be the honest and patriotic thing to do.

Unfortunately, the 2017 TCJA, Tax Cuts and Jobs Act, passed with collusion by Congress and the President, supposedly to reform the tax code, actually worsened the country's financial condition. It did not close the loopholes but rather gave corporations and the wealthy more tax cuts, adding $150 billion annually to the deficit and national debt. They deviously claimed the Act would create jobs and boost the economy, when in reality neither was needed. The economy was growing at a healthy 3% rate and unemployment was at 4.1% which is considered "full employment." Businesses were, in fact, often having difficulty in finding both skilled and unskilled labor.

A few corporations announced they would increase their minimum wage and give employee bonuses, which amounted to only a small percentage of the windfall they received. Further some companies were closing a number of their facilities and laying off workers so as to maintain their profit margins. The Act and its consequences was a prime example of Congress and the Administration catering to special interests, to their own benefit, but betraying the people's trust and causing harm to the country and the people. Despicable and grossly irresponsible. Yes, treason!

Revenue can be increased by raising capital gains and dividend taxes from 15% to 25%. Capital gains are mainly wealth increase income rather than a source of living income, therefore readily subjected to a substantial tax increase without harm to anyone. Why wouldn't every patriotic American be satisfied with keeping 75% of their capital gains when it helps save our country from financial implosion and the dire consequences to themselves and their fellow Americans?

Eliminate subsidies to gas and oil companies and big agribusiness; they make reasonable profits without them. A tax on financial transactions, FTT, is long overdue. We pay a sales tax on goods we purchase, why not on stocks and bonds we buy. When structured properly it would be shared by the big bank and investment firm brokers. It has almost no negative effect but huge potential for revenue increase and relief of the tax burden on individuals. Over fifteen countries have an FTT which has proven successful without harm to their financial sectors. The London Stock Exchange has levied a .5% tax on each stock trade with a very positive effect. On a $1000 transaction, the buyer and broker would each pay a mere $2.50. If you purchased a $1000 appliance you would pay about $70. Due to the high volume of transactions, it is estimated that rate would raise $90 billion annually. What's not to like? The only thing standing in the way is Wall Street's political influence on Congress. Do what's right for America, Congress.

Increase the IRS's ability to partially collect the $300 billion annually of unpaid taxes. Unfortunately, Congress cut the 2015 appropriations for IRS by 17% while at the same time keeping the tax loopholes for special interests. That is grossly irresponsible, another example of the politicians "impairing the well-being of a state to which they owe allegiance." It's called treason. None of the above sources for increased revenue will cost jobs.

Now that we have identified reasonable and feasible spending cuts and revenue increases, let's do the math. Eliminating health care, given that does nothing to benefit the health of the patient, saves the government $400 billion annually. Moving from curative medicine to preventive health care primarily by the individual saves $100 billion. Reduce Medicare and Medicaid fraud by $30 billion. Reduce drug costs by $50 billion. These costs are savings just to the government (taxpayers) in Medicare and Medicaid. Savings to the entire health care system, individuals, businesses and insurance companies will be much greater. These savings of $580 billion can be accomplished within two years, when politics are avoided and everyone does their patriotic part in making our great country financially healthy again.

Keeping in mind that a "third of the defense budget is not for national security reasons but because it's in someone's district or state," being spent for political reasons, a reasonable reduction in our overseas forces and a sensible cutback in intelligence costs, we can save a third of the overall defense, intelligence and counterterrorism costs of $1 trillion, about $330 billion.

Add the savings in health care costs of $580 billion and the savings in defense and intelligence costs of $330 and "voilà," we're talking big money savings of $910 billion within two years. It is completely possible when Congress and the Administration cut out the damn politics and manage our country's finances the way they should.

And that's only cuts in spending. Let's look at ways we can reasonably increase revenues. Truly reforming the tax code and closing loopholes, including those off-shore shelters, so that everyone pays their fair share will bring in, let's be modest and say $200 billion. Eliminating subsidies to big agribusinesses, oil and gas companies will net about $25 billion. Increasing capital gains taxes from 15% to 25% increases revenue by $50 billion. That modest .5% tax on financial transactions, would raise $90 billion. Reducing overall deductions by ten percent will raise $100 billion. Increase the IRS's ability to partially collect the $300 billion annually of unpaid taxes, another $100 billion. Now we're looking at a total of $565 billion.

There is another source of revenue that is a sore subject for many Americans. That is those 47% of Americans that pay no income tax at all for a variety of reasons like tax credits, deductions and exemptions. Tax credits are being paid in cash to people who pay no taxes at all. That's not right. Although there are some exceptions, the only people who should be exempt from income taxes are those at or below the poverty level. All others of that 47% can pay something. It's the patriotic thing to do and especially essential if we are to avoid financial calamity.

Unfortunately, with Congressional increased spending and loss of revenue by virtue of the Tax Cuts and Jobs Act, our annual deficits are again zooming toward $1 trillion. Totally reprehensible and treasonous on the part of Congress.

All the above cuts in spending and increases in revenue are reasonable and achievable. They pose no serious burden on anyone. There will be no significant job cuts, people will get the care and services they need, businesses will still make a reasonable profit and we will be as safe as ever from our so-called enemies. All the above figures are optimal and could be achieved, but realistically and tragically will not be. The point being made is that we have the ability to easily balance the budget if everyone involved, especially Congress, would act responsibly in this matter.

Every American and every business entity, from the small businesses to corporations and financial institutions, need to understand that our country is in very serious financial trouble. We simply cannot sustain the current huge deficits and a $20 plus trillion national debt. The day of reckoning will come, and when it does it will make our current economic concerns look like a picnic. Think depression. Think 25% unemployment rate, like the last great depression, maybe higher. Small businesses, corporations (like auto companies) and banks going out of business. There will be no bail outs. Our government, already broke and in debt up to its neck, won't be able to borrow a red cent from China or anyone else. China has already expressed concerns about our dire financial condition. It sure as hell is coming if we don't stop the damn politics and get our act together.

We are in it together and we have to deal with it together. It's called patriotism. Everyone has to do their part, from the individual to the corporation to the government, and especially you, Congress. Being a nation under God, we might do well to listen to what God has to say about all this. Like "Do not strive for material things, but first seek the kingdom of God." The kingdom of God being a way of life. Like "loving your neighbor as yourself" and "doing to others as you would have others do unto you." Being kind, caring and forgiving of one another. Like being responsible and *living within our means.*

Not the way we live now, being so uncivil and rude to one another like the politicians. Not killing one another when we should be taking care of one another. Not being greedy without any thought for the consequences down the road. Not paying a fair share of taxes. Not achieving great wealth while 16 million little children go to bed hungry every night here in the U.S. and thousands of other little ones worldwide die of starvation. It is okay to gain wealth, when it is used properly. It's okay to live very well, provide for your future, your children's and grandchildren's education and future and even sock away some for a rainy day, but it is not okay to hoard enormous sums of money. As Christians, what do you who are billionaires and multi-millionaires do with Christ's admonition not to store up riches for yourself here on earth, but rather store up credits for yourself in heaven?

How about answering this question? Is it okay to store up great wealth when little children, anywhere in the world, suffer from the effects of malnutrition and starve to death? It is happening every day to over 3000 of those little ones. I think we all know that the answer to that question is no. I am reasonably certain that God would say it is not okay. I am reminded of a picture I saw of a small child in Africa who had laid down to die, skin and bones, too weak to lift a hand to shoo the flies that crawled upon his face. And the story told by a reporter who had witnessed a scene where a young girl, who was thought dead of starvation and was being prepared for burial, opened her eyes and a tear rolled down her cheek. God, how tragic. And totally inexcusable as there is plenty of food to prevent that. We Americans, alone, waste enough food to feed the starving of the world. Do you think God would bless a country that unnecessarily spends hundreds of billions of dollars every year on the ability to make war instead of feeding those little children? C'mon America, we are better than that! We are a marvelous country, warts and all. We are a beautiful nation with immense potential that we have not realized. We have gone astray because of political malfeasance and greed. C'mon Congress, straighten up and fly right. C'mon Corporate America, pay your fair share. C'mon Americans, let's everyone do our part and save our country. Our best days are ahead of us. And when we right ourselves, we will be making the world a better place.

It's not a matter of literally taking money from the rich and giving to the poor. That sucks. That is not fair to the rich nor good for the poor. As well, there are too many unscrupulous freeloaders who would take advantage. Nor should we demonize the wealthy, "tax it to the rich," so as to resolve our deficit problems. That won't get it. But the wealthy can give to organizations and programs that help people better themselves. Invest in education. Invest in people that want to start a business. Provide micro-loans or better yet, outright grants. Make sure the food bank shelves are fully stocked so that those 16 million little children here in the U.S. don't have to go to bed hungry every night. Contribute generously to international hunger programs. It must be noted that there are wealthy people who are doing so. That remarkable fellow and good guy, Warren Buffet, has pledged to give away 99% of his wealth. He and Bill Gates have encouraged others to give 50% of their wealth, with about 100 responding to the challenge so far. Extraordinary! Marvelous examples of patriotic and compassionate Americans willing to help their country, their fellow Americans and, indeed, all of humanity.

Congress, your performance in this matter of balancing the budget is completely unacceptable. Do your homework; go back to the drawing board. Eschew the damn politics! All the above cuts in spending and increases in revenue may need some tweaking but generally are reasonable and achievable. They pose no serious burden on anyone. The people will get the care and services they need, businesses will still make a profit and we will be as safe as ever from our "enemies."

Clearly, we can balance the budget rather quickly when we shun the damn politics and everyone pays their fair share of taxes and acts responsibly in spending. What America really needs to cure all its ills is a good dose of patriotism and the golden rule.

Chapter Five
JOBS AND THE ECONOMY

The primary reason for anemic economic growth and a stagnant unemployment rate after the "great recession" ended is that businesses, mostly big corporations, were experiencing record profits and sitting on huge cash reserves, yet refusing to rehire or expand out of an unjustified uncertainty of the economic future, including that of Europe. That's an excuse not a valid reason. The business cycle hasn't been repealed. We always recover from downturns and so would Europe. There were positive signs that it was happening for us and Europe would eventually follow. The housing market, a leading indicator of economic conditions, was on the rise with increased sales, improved housing starts and higher prices. Manufacturing showed positive growth, the airlines were making a profit and consumer confidence was improving.

Congress was and continues to be the source of that uncertainty due to their dysfunction and failure to get our financial house in order. As to the corporations, how about a little faith in the great American economic machine and its workers? The Administration, especially the Prez, needed to use the "bully pulpit" to convince the corporations to get off their duff and lead the way to job creation and a robust economic recovery, to their own benefit and that of the American people.

As of 2014, overall corporate profits were still at an all-time high, yet jobs and economic growth were anemic for a number or reasons. The do-nothing, dysfunctional and irresponsible Congress was still busy playing politics, arguing over the deficit, closing down the government and in general not taking care of our country's business. Corporate America was still hoarding their cash, boosting executive salaries, paying out bigger dividends to stockholders and maximizing profits all at the expense of jobs and economic growth.

Both the Administration and Congress needed to address that old bugaboo, "red tape," the myriad of rules and regulations that hinder small business start-up and growth. Many of the rules and regulations originate out of Federal agencies, either out of over zealousness or to justify their existence. The paperwork, time and money expended in compliance stifles small business growth and hiring. That has to stop. According to the Small Business Administration, small businesses are facing annual regulatory costs of up to $10,000 per employee. That's outrageous. Much of this problem is politically driven. So, damn the politics, get your asses in gear Congress and Administration, cut the damn red tape and let good old American entrepreneurship do what it does well, create jobs and grow the economy. That is one of the good things President Trump has done, get government off the backs of business. But he has gone too far, for instance, gutting some of the provisions of the Environmental Protection Agency that protect the safety and health of the American people.

Another hindrance to job and economic growth is the pessimism and negativity fostered by those "nattering nabobs of negativity" that William Safire so eloquently and accurately penned for a speech given by VP Spiro Agnew. It is often done deliberately as a political ploy against a political opponent or party. For example, the unemployment rate, by numbers, is often highly inflated: at one time during the recession, cited as 25 million Americans out of work. That's grossly overblown and nonsense. The U.S. workforce is about half the population at just over 150 million people. Full employment is considered at about 5%. So with an 8% unemployment rate at that time, we had 3% of the workforce or about 4.5 million people who wanted and needed jobs. That's a serious problem for them, but to claim, at one time, that 25 million Americans were out of work is baloney and irresponsible. How about looking at it positively that 97% of our work force was employed.

Then there was the pessimistic chatter about the "fiscal cliff" and sequestration cuts that were going to occur. The politicians, financial "experts" and pundits decried the cuts claiming it would devastate defense and non-defense programs, costing millions of jobs and sending us back into recession. Nonsense, it's reminiscent of the Y2K scare when the Millennium bug was to crash all computers around the world at midnight, December 31, 1999, and nothing happened. There was a clamor for Congress to repeal the sequestration and implement smaller more sensible cuts toward reducing the deficit. We know damn well Congress would argue forever on how to cut the deficit and just kick that can down the road. Why in the world would we want smaller cuts when, in reality, the sequestration cuts were disgustingly pitiful and inadequate, leaving us with an enormous deficit again the next year and for years to come. Now that's really devastating and damn scary.

Sequestration cuts could have been accomplished readily and without loss of jobs or harm to the economy when done properly. Elimination of some of the waste in defense plus spreading cuts across thousands of contracts and agencies throughout all three military services would have a negligible effect on jobs. Reduction of both civilian and military personnel through attrition without rehiring would add to the cutback in costs.

Bringing half of our troops home from around the world as well as from Afghanistan, and keeping them on the payroll, would benefit the economy as they spend their money here, preserve if not increase jobs, and save billions of dollars.

A $60 billion decrease in non-defense spending without cutting jobs or harming the economy would have been a piece of cake. A great place to start would be subsidies to big agribusinesses, coal, gas and oil companies, most of whom are highly profitable and do not need the subsidies. The five largest oil companies had a banner year in 2011 with $137 billion in profits. The $40 billion gifts to those companies every year are the result of Congress's largesse in exchange for political donations. In plain language, that's called bribery.

Having already noted that $400 billion waste in government spending on health care, just eliminating 15% of it would reach the sequestration goal of $60 billion, which could easily have been achieved without cutting jobs, health care services or harm to the economy. Profits would be reduced but that's okay as there is still plenty of health care and necessary medical testing to provide reasonable profits. That profit aspect is largely true for defense spending as well.

Which brings up a common business practice that needs to be discussed and changed.

When it comes to cuts, such as during a downturn or recession, the first action companies take is to lay off employees. Not only is it wrong, but counterproductive. Employees are customers, who are vital to business. Reducing payrolls shrinks revenue and increases costs to the taxpayers in the way of unemployment payments. It's a matter of profits over people. There are other options that should be exercised first. Profit expectations should be reduced, perhaps even to zero until recovery takes hold, maintaining just sufficient so as to keep the company viable. Temporarily suspend dividends to stock holders. As those payments are primarily wealth builders rather than living income, I'm sure the stock holders would be willing to temporarily give them up so that someone can keep their job. It's the golden rule. A temporary reduction in management salaries and employee wage adjustments should be made so as to keep employees on the job. Laying people off should be the very last option.

The corporations need to stop sitting on their profits and cash, the Administration to cut all that business-restrictive red tape and Congress to stop playing politics with our financial house, removing that uncertainty and let the mighty American economic machine go to work. Further, corporations need to stop sending their business overseas so as to increase profits and avoid taxes. That's called greed. Americans, you need to buy American products. Over half of the cars on our roads are foreign made. Sure, you have freedom of choice, but American-made cars are competitive in quality and price. Do what's right for America. It's called patriotism. It's the Golden rule.

Chapter Six
NATIONAL SECURITY

The truth is that our national security is not being threatened either economically, by terrorism or so-called "enemies." National Security is defined as "preserving our nation's political identity, its framework and institutions and its economic well-being." Global terrorism, as it exists today, is no threat to that. Note that even 9/11 had no significant effect on it. Terrorism is a threat to individual security but not to the existence of our nation. Even the threat to our individual safety is vastly over blown. You are many times more likely to be killed in an automobile accident than in a terrorist attack.

Cyber terrorism has been dramatically exaggerated with the use of scare terms like "a cyber 9/11, a digital Pearl Harbor and the cyber domain of warfare." As George R. Lucas Jr., a professor at the U.S. Naval Academy, put it, "Conducting a truly mass-scale action using cyber means simply outstrips the intellectual, organizational and personnel capacities of even the most well-funded and well-organized terrorist organization, as well as those of even the most sophisticated international criminal enterprises." Lucas said the threat of cyber terrorism has been vastly overblown. "To be blunt, neither the 14-year-old hacker in your next-door neighbor's upstairs bedroom, nor the two- or three-person al-Qaida cell holed up in some apartment in Hamburg are going to bring down the Glen Canyon and Hoover dams," he said.

Another Cyber expert said, "There are no cyber threats out there that threaten our fundamental way of life." That is not to say that cyber terrorists can't cause some serious damage such as taking out a power grid or disrupting financial systems, but we have successfully dealt with such past events. Even more severe damage from a cyber-attack will not threaten the existence of our nation (national security). Cyber-attacks on our government and business institutions are occurring all the time but counter technology by the government in coordination with the private sector is able to thwart them, limit the damage or restore operations.

There is some concern about nuclear terrorism. There are those who say we should not be concerned about nuclear terrorism because there is neither "reward nor favorable press" for the perpetrators and there have been no serious threats since 9/11 and therefore not likely to be. That is a false assumption and complacency. The fanatical terrorist has no thought for money or favorable publicity. They are driven by hatred for the "Great Satan" and the perceived wrongs we have inflicted upon them. They believe it is their duty to seek revenge; they are honor bound to exact retribution. They believe they will be greatly rewarded in heaven for killing the infidels. They are much more patient than we, willing to wait for years or even decades to exact vengeance, if that is what it takes.

The FBI has assessed the probability of a terrorist nuclear attack as low. However, if we continue to follow our present course in the struggle against terrorism, which only fosters more hatred and exacerbates the situation, the greater the risk will become. The terrorists have the intelligence, the determination (vengeance) and the funds to carry out such an attack. A terrorist organization could obtain a nuclear device in four ways—be given it, buy it, steal it or make it—all difficult but not impossible. The deployment of the weapon to a large American city, most likely Washington, D.C., is less difficult. Downtown Washington D.C. would be a sea of rubble and ashes. A massive, powerful shock wave would tear 100,000 people to shreds. Beyond the first half mile, some would survive temporarily with their skin burned off or their clothes melted to their bodies. After the shock wave a lethal blast of radiation would penetrate survivors within a few miles who would soon start to hemorrhage through their skin, their eyes and ears. Others, within a few weeks, would lose their hair and their skin start to fall off. With extreme nausea and vomiting they would be unable to eat, and starve to death. Thousands of others would die later from leukemia and lymphoma.

Still, we need to put even a nuclear attack into perspective. The property damage would not be as much as we have caused in Iraq and Afghanistan. The fallout would spread to the east and not be a threat to our "breadbasket." Even with the fallout moving on to Europe, the total deaths would not be as many as we cause year after year to our own population by allowing the distribution of that deadly drug tobacco; over five million since 9/11. A nuclear attack on a city on our west coast is another story. Yet, even that would not be a threat to the existence of our nation (national security). We are a resilient people and would recover from the attack, just as Hiroshima and Nagasaki have recovered from our nuclear attack on them. Both were almost completely destroyed, yet they have risen from the ashes to cities of about one million people, with little remaining effect from the radiation. It behooves us to act swiftly in implementation of the God Option so as to preclude the possibility of an attack.

We must also seriously consider the probability that a terrorist organization, such as al Qaida or ISIS, would not resort to nuclear terrorism. There would be great sympathy for us, hatred for them, immense condemnation by the world and perhaps a world-wide concentrated military effort to bring them to justice, making the use of a nuclear weapon counterproductive to their goal, and actually, a waste of effort, time and funds. All the terrorists need to do is sit back, tweak us with an occasional relatively ineffective terrorist incident and watch us, out of our unjustified fear of terrorism, spend ourselves into financial implosion with enormous sums expended unnecessarily on "defense," homeland security and our multiple intelligence gathering and counterterrorism agencies.

We have grossly overreacted to the threat of global terrorism after 9/11 with our ill-advised invasion of Afghanistan and expensive and unnecessary security measures so as to ensure our national security. In addition to the $700 plus "adjusted" billion annual defense budget, we were spending $100 billion each year on unnecessary and unjust wars. The Homeland Security Agency is a $40 billion a year unnecessary effort that contributes little to our safety. It justifies its existence by promoting an unwarranted fear of terrorism, ever increasing invasion of our privacy with expensive high tech surveillance and ridiculous procedures such as intense airport passenger screening. No country in the world goes to such extremes. Counting the additional costs of operating the $45 billion a year CIA, numerous other intelligence agencies, "black" operations and other contingencies, it is estimated that we are expending close to a trillion dollars each year to "keep us safe." We need to ask from whom? Terrorists are not a serious threat to us. None of our "enemies" is going to mount an invasion. None is going to attack us with nuclear missiles. They are fully aware there would be swift retaliation with massive destruction to their country. They value their skin as much as anyone. It is that massive, unbridled military, intelligence and counterterrorism spending that poses the real threat to our national security.

Put into perspective, our fear of terrorism is totally unjustified, having been fostered by government fear-mongering, terrorist "experts" and the media. Since 9/11, a number of terrorist attacks in the U.S. have been thwarted (the number varies depending on the definition of terrorism). Many of them foiled by agencies other than Homeland Security, such as the FBI, local police authorities and even foreign country authorities. Since 9/11, about 300 people in the U. S. have been killed in incidents attributed to terrorism, the perpetrators almost all "home grown." In that same period, 130,000 Americans have been murdered by guns and over 5,000,000 killed by tobacco. Good God Almighty, doesn't anyone see the monstrous inconsistency in our concern about terrorism? Or how foolish our response to it is, especially the expenditure of billions of dollars on counter terrorism measures?

We have gone astray when it comes to the security of our nation. We suffer the delusion of, and are besieged by, a "military-might-equates-to-national-security" mentality. Nothing could be further from the truth. The opposite is true. It should be obvious that the more the world has armed itself over the years, the greater the danger has become.

President Eisenhower got it right when he said, "Every gun that is made, every warship launched, every rocket fired, signifies, in the final sense, a theft from those who hunger and are not fed, those who are cold and are not clothed. This world in arms is not spending money alone. It is spending the sweat of its laborers, the genius of its scientists, the hopes of its children. This is not a way of life at all in any true sense. Under the cloud of war, it is humanity hanging on a cross of iron." By our continued manufacture of weapons of war, huge expenditures on a military posture and relying on that to kill our enemies and solve problems of the world, we are indeed crucifying the world!

I am also reminded of the words of General William Tecumseh Sherman, spoken during the Civil War: "Many of those who have neither fired a shot nor heard the shrieks and groans of the wounded, often cry aloud for blood, more vengeance and more desolation. War is hell." Those words are just as true today as they were then. Many of us, who have served our country in war, know of what he speaks. What terrible torment, grief and hell the families of those brave soldiers killed in battle must endure. Even more so for the families of those soldiers who have taken their own life. Yes, hundreds have committed suicide for reasons aggravated by the hell of war. Their minds have been so torn asunder by the ravages and horrors of what they have seen, experienced or done, that they opt for the oblivion of death. That is a terrible tragedy brought about by the false belief that military power and retaliation equate to national security.

War is indeed hell! It is incredibly costly in lives, destruction, suffering and money. The United States is spending almost $700 billion annually to maintain a military force and fill our arsenals with bigger and better weapons of destruction so that we can conduct war and be victorious over our enemies.

As asked recently in a *Time* Magazine article, "Do we need eleven aircraft carrier strike groups, when no other country has more than one?" "Do the services really need $400 billion in new jet fighters when their fleets of F-15s, F-16s and F-18s give them vast air superiority for years to come?" "Does the Navy need fifty attack submarines when America's main enemy hides in caves?" "Does the Army still need 80,000 troops in Europe 66 years after the defeat of Adolf Hitler?" The resounding obvious answer is NO!

We are spending $250 billion annually to maintain a military force abroad, most of it unnecessary. Since its inception, our nuclear program alone has cost us about $5 trillion. It has been estimated that in the last fifty years the world has spent over $50 trillion on the ability to make war. Obscene, tragic and disgusting are a few adjectives that come to mind. The great tragedy of it is that little benefit has been derived but rather a more dangerous world has emerged. Just put your imagination to work and think how the world could have been changed for the better by applying those funds, or even half, to humanitarian efforts.

The plan for the U.S. to build a missile defense system to protect Europe, supposedly from Iran, is ludicrous and a total waste of our money. Iran has no good reason to attack a European nation. Any attack on Europe or Israel would result in retaliation that would effectively destroy Iran. The Mullahs, who control the missiles, are well aware of that and have no desire to see their country laid to waste.

A similar situation exists with North Korea. Kim Jong-un is not stupid and perfectly understands the consequences should he attack us or any of his neighbors. He has recently threatened the U.S. with "nuclear catastrophe" *in case of aggression from us or South Korea.* He is showing resolve in the face of our threats against his country. Who can blame him?

We have bungled badly in our relations with Iran and North Korea. We have provoked them by designating them part of the axis of evil. We conduct joint war games with South Korea near the coast of North Korea, which the North Koreans rightly perceive as a prelude to a possible invasion. We have threatened them with our policy of pre-emptive strikes against any country that might pose a threat to our security and way of life and then done exactly that to Iran's neighbor Iraq, when, in fact, Saddam was never a threat to our national security or even Israel's. What are Iran and North Korea to think? Are we next? President Trump has irrationally threatened to destroy North Korea. Kim wants nuclear weapons to protect his country from us, as does Iran.

During and immediately after the 2018 Winter Olympic games in South Korea, there were signs of thawing between North and South Korea with invitations by both sides to hold talks, with Kim indicating the possibility of discontinuing his nuclear program. The U.S. should immediately extend the hand of friendship, offering to remove our forces from South Korea and helping him economically.

Why is there so much concern about Iran's nuclear program? Whether they were developing it for commercial power or to attain nuclear weapon capability is irrelevant. They have as much right to the latter as their neighbors Israel, Pakistan and India, or for that matter, any other country in the world. They want it for defense and prestige, as do other nuclear powers. No country in the world, especially Iran, is going to use nuclear capability for aggression. MAD (Mutual Assured Destruction) still works.

Russia and China are also considered existing threats. The "experts" say Russia represents the greatest danger. Cited are Russia's annexation of Crimea and insertion of forces into eastern Ukraine. That they pose a similar threat to the Baltic States. They are modernizing their military forces and exhibiting aggressive behavior by conducting military exercises inside their borders. The statement has been made that their behavior suggests they would even be willing to use nuclear weapons.

Those concerns do not constitute a valid threat to our national security for the following reasons. The Crimean people wanted to be a part of Russia. The separatists in Eastern Ukraine prefer an alliance with Russia, and the western Ukrainians with the EU and the West. Let them work it out themselves. Putin says he has no intention of attacking the Baltic States. The general consensus of world countries (except US) is in agreement. Putin knows it would result in a mandatory military response by NATO that would be very costly to him both militarily and economically and with no guarantee that Russia would prevail.

The Russian military had been in steep decline since the end of the Cold War, becoming only a shadow of itself. Putin saw the need to correct that condition so as to protect his own national security as well as to restore stature and respect in the world. Still, current modernization of their military forces will not enable Russia to conduct successful aggression against western forces. Western forces are still vastly superior to those of Russia.

Putin has said that their military exercises along their western border are in response to U.S. and NATO expansion and aggression in Europe. He has a point there. We have expanded NATO troops and weapons into the Baltics all the way up to within artillery range of St. Petersburg. We are selling cruise missiles to Poland and planning a missile defense system there, supposedly in the guise of protection from Iran. The U.S. has established the ERI, European Reassurance Initiative which places 30,000 more troops and weapons into Europe. NATO holds war "games" in Eastern Europe and the Baltic sea. We have imposed sanctions against Russian corporations which only inflame the adversity. Too bad Russia hasn't the ability to put some sanctions on U.S. oligarchs.

The statement that Russia would be willing to use nuclear weapons is totally irresponsible, inflammatory rhetoric. Neither is Putin's recent announcement about their possession of a "doomsday" weapon a threat to us. For Russia to use it would spell "doom" to them as well. The reality is that Russia fears the west and perceives us as the aggressor and a danger to their national security. Russia is not a threat to our national security. Much of the rest of the world holds that perception, and that the U.S. is the major threat to world peace.

China has no significant expansionist goals. They would like to be the dominant power in their region of the world but not at the expense of their or their neighbor's well-being. Their modest increase in defense spending is in response to the United States' "irresponsible" goal to increase its military footprint in their region. The U.S.

markets are critical to China's economic needs. China is no threat to us either militarily or economically.

Isn't it strange that there is so much concern about the proliferation of nuclear weapons, especially by the nations that possess them, and nary a word is voiced by them about their manufacture and widespread distribution of conventional weapons that have been and still are killing and maiming millions of people throughout the world?

Our excursion into Iraq was completely unnecessary and in the long run proved disastrous. Saddam Hussein was a bad guy and needed to go, but he was never a threat to our national security and certainly not to Israel. I remember reading the statement from a senior Israeli general who said, "Israel doesn't lose any sleep over Saddam Hussein." Israel would not have hesitated to drop the big one on Baghdad if Saddam had seriously threatened them, and Saddam was acutely aware of that. Conservative columnist George Will has called that 2003 invasion of Iraq "The worst foreign policy decision in U.S. history."

We were deluding ourselves to think we could be successful in Afghanistan. Our government claimed that we had made progress, but the military concedes that it was fragile. We have been there fourteen years and made "some" progress? Let's get real. We apparently learned nothing from our experience in Vietnam or the Russians' in Afghanistan. Nine years and 15,000 dead Soviet troops later, the Russians gave up and withdrew. That's what we face there; they will outlast us just as they did the Russians. A corrupt central government could never stabilize that nation with their centuries old tribal culture of warlords. The Afghans will never be able to stop al Qaeda from operating in their country and Pakistan. In reality, they have little will to do so. The Afghans don't like us, don't trust us and consider us as occupiers. There are those in Afghanistan who would have liked us to stay to support their corrupt and divided government. And those who wanted us to protect them from their own warring factions. We should never have any part of that.

Even with Osama bin Laden gone and the decimation of al Qaeda in Afghanistan and ISIS in Iraq and Syria, we are far from winning the struggle against terrorism. Terrorist cells are active elsewhere in the world and will continue to be in the Middle East. We may kill many terrorists and their leaders but others, out of hatred, will forever step forward and take up the cause. They would most likely be even more violent because of their belief in and desire for retribution because we have killed their fathers, sons and even their women and children. The threat of bringing them to justice and death does not frighten them; most, especially the fundamentalists, welcome it. Our "drone" program for attacking and killing terrorists is badly flawed, if not outright counterproductive. We kill a few leaders and their followers. Yet, other perfectly capable leaders step forth. Because of the collateral damage, killing of innocents, especially women and children, more and more followers are created. And greater hatred is fostered.

Another anti-terrorism program run amuck, out of an unjustified fear of terrorism, is NSA's data mining (read spying and snooping). Their global surveillance and collection of emails and telephone calls has proven more harmful than beneficial. Listening to communications in other countries, including that of their heads of state, has harmed relationships and caused distrust. It has sown the seeds of distrust of our government, and anger among the American people, as well as abroad. It has harmed our economy, causing foreign markets to back away from American technologies and products out of a lack of trust. One example is the $4.5 billion Boeing contract lost to a foreign aircraft company.

The irony, yes, even tragedy, of it is that it is unnecessary, as the threat of terrorism to our national security and, in perspective, to individuals, is negligible. Further, the program has not been effective, there being "no evidence of a single instance in which analysis of collected data actually stopped an imminent attack."

It is extremely expensive, in that billions are being spent in gathering that mostly useless data. As NSA is considered a "black" program, it is impossible to say what their annual budget is, but it has been estimated as high as $20 billion, with the majority of that expended in data gathering. Now they are spending $2 billion to build a 1.2 million square foot facility in Bluffdale, Utah to store that data. The electric bill will run a million dollars a month. The question has to be asked, why are they storing all that useless data? By their own admission, only a small amount of the data is analyzed. Further, the intelligence people know that even good intelligence data quickly becomes inert and of no use as the terrorists frequently change their "modus operandi."

To think that we can defeat terrorism with our current efforts is totally delusional. There is that better way--The God Option.

There are places in the world where danger lurks, but in perspective, not seriously for us. Our national security is not at risk. Those who claim otherwise, refusing to cut a bloated defense budget and even wanting to spend billions more on defense are ill-informed and doing a great disservice to our country. One candidate for political office wanted to build 15 more ships and 3 submarines for the Navy, when we already have those 10 carrier groups and adequate nuclear attack submarines. We are spending twice as much on defense as Russia, China and North Korea combined. President Trump wants to significantly increase defense spending, including production and upgrade of more nuclear weapons, when our current military force is by far the most powerful in the world. Grossly irresponsible.

All this seems so obvious that it would seem there is some ulterior motive in calling for an increase in our already formidable military capability. Are the proponents of that ill-informed? Are politics involved? Could it be paranoia? Is it greed for power and profits? I'm reminded of a Pentagon official's statement that we spend about a third of the defense budget not for national security reasons but because it's in someone's district or state.

The threat to our national security is not from outward enemies but from within. Those trillion dollar annual deficits and the soaring national debt will be our downfall. The politicians who are responsible for that are the real enemy. "We have met the enemy and he is us." It's almost as if foreign agents have infiltrated our government and are determined to bring us to our knees.

Chapter Seven
IMMIGRATION REFORM

How often have you heard the politicians of both parties talk about the need for comprehensive immigration reform. But they do nothing nor explain what the comprehensive reform might consist of. And for good reason, because honest reform will alienate some people and that isn't good politics.

Immigration reform must be honest, fair, practical and compassionate. Let's talk about those requirements. You who have come into our country illegally have broken the law. That's dishonest. And by definition, a crime. Further, by definition, you are a criminal. But do we brand you as a criminal and imprison you as some countries might? That would be impractical and harsh. Of course not; if you're caught, we just send you home at our expense. I'd say that's quite compassionate.

You have not come here in desperation or as a matter of survival. You could have survived in your own country, but you chose to come here so as to better yourself. That's admirable, but wrong, and not fair to those who want to come here legally, who follow the proper procedures and then wait in line for their turn. You, in effect, have jumped to the head of the line, an action that everyone abhors. You are good decent people but what you have done is simply wrong.

Many of you then compound your illegal entry by obtaining false records such as Social Security cards and driver's licenses. That too is unlawful and a crime, but we do not punish you for that either. You then use those illegal documents to obtain services such as medical care, food, housing and education for your children and without paying your fair share of their costs. That is dishonest and not fair to others who have to pay part of your share. Even without documents you get free education and medical care; the latter cannot be denied to you. That is compassionate and the right thing to do, but still not fair to others who have to pick up the tab for the costs.

Yes, you do pay some taxes such as sales tax, property tax if you have acquired property and sometimes income tax when you used your false identification to get a job. But for most of you, that income tax withheld is returned to you because of your low income earnings. With those false documents, some do pay Social Security taxes and few ever collect. But overall, your contribution to pay for the services you use only covers part of their cost, which is over $100 billion each year. That is not fair.

You purveyors of false documents are, of course, breaking the law, committing a crime that is punishable, if you are caught. But you compound your dishonesty, taking advantage of the immigrants by charging exorbitant fees. You employers, in hiring illegal immigrants, are also breaking the law, often with the ulterior motive of paying low wages so as to make greater profits. That's dishonest. In some cases, it is taking jobs away from American citizens. That is not fair. It's certainly unpatriotic.

You who have come here illegally have no grounds to complain about the treatment you receive such as "asking for your papers" or being deported, for you have been treated with compassion, despite your unlawful activities. We citizens must show our "papers" quite frequently, so why shouldn't you? Your demonstrations and demands that we pass immigration laws that will give you what you want takes a lot of gall, is arrogant and offensive.

So, what is to be done about all this? Practically, we cannot find all of you and send you home. But we can stop any further illegal entry. Not by building fences and walls, increasing border patrols or even using our military forces as some have suggested. Those former efforts have proved very costly and have not gotten the job done. We would have to build a wall completely across both our south and north borders and still they would come. As the saying goes, build a sixteen foot wall and they will build a seventeen foot ladder. There would be a booming business in smuggling by boat; easy access via our long open shorelines.

There is an easy and efficient way to control entry, it's called E-Verify. Simply put, it is a system that allows businesses to determine the eligibility of their employees to work in the U.S. It works; the problem being that it is only a voluntary program, although some states make it mandatory. Being voluntary, it leaves those unscrupulous employers an out to hire illegal immigrants, which they do despite the law of the land that prohibits their being hired, and which is weakly enforced.

The simple solution is to make E-Verify the law nationally and *enforce* it. Employers can be convinced to comply by stiff fines and jail sentences for repeated offenses and a good dose of patriotism. C'mon man, do what's right for your country. When illegal immigrants cannot get a job, they won't come. Many of those who are already here and unable to get a job will leave.

Establish a comprehensive guest worker program for seasonal workers. Establish a date for full implementation of the E-Verify law. After that date no undocumented worker will be eligible for work, welfare or education benefits in the U.S. Require those illegal immigrants who can prove they held a job prior to that date to come forth and register with the ICE. Issue them a work permit, making them eligible for services and who would then be required to contribute fully via all appropriate taxes in support of the services they use. Require them to learn English, monitored by their employer. They can stay but must get in line for citizenship via the established procedures. Give priority to families. Citizens must be given priority over illegal immigrants in the job market.

As to those with fraudulent documents, who are subsisting on welfare, without contributing to the costs at all, give them the choice of full prosecution for violating our laws or leaving the country. We might even help them with the latter. Surely, they can be identified by checking the validity of their documents when they apply for benefits. Why has ICE not put the fake document peddlers out of business? Offer illegal immigrants, who have been caught with false papers, immunity from prosecution and a reward, of say $5,000, to identify the providers, money they can use to start anew in their own country. It would be money well spent. Raise the stakes for the providers with stiff fines and prison time.

With that problem under control, few illegal immigrants coming in and those already here, temporarily documented and holding jobs, paying their fair share of costs, we will have arrived at a fair, practical and compassionate solution to the illegal immigration problem.

There are a couple of other aspects of our immigration policy that need to be changed. We need to make it easier for skilled immigrants to enter and for foreign students here on visas, getting an education, to stay. Right now many of those students, now skilled, go home. Because of 9/11, and an unjustified fear of more terrorism, we have tightened our entry requirements for tourists who wish to visit our beautiful country and its many splendid attractions. As a result, we have lost one third of our tourism share, costing an estimated one million jobs. A shame and completely unnecessary.

Immigration reform is not difficult when we eliminate politics from the equation.

Chapter Eight
SOCIAL SECURITY

The truth is that the solution to the Social Security problems is a no brainer. First, we need to stop referring to SS as an entitlement that is costing the government (taxpayers) money. SS benefits are paid for from FICA taxes paid by employers and wage earners throughout their working years, in advance of receiving any benefits.

Secondly, we need to get Congress' grubby hands off the Social Security funds. In the 1980s the SS Trust Fund was running large surpluses. Congress eyed all that green cash sitting there and arranged to borrow it to help pay everyday government expenses and make it look like they were balancing the budget. They continue to do so today. In return they give the Trust Fund paper IOUs, in the form of treasury bonds. There are 2.7 trillion dollars worth sitting there in the Trust Fund today. They are perfectly good bonds but they do not constitute a surplus.

The problem being that the SS Trust Fund can't pay benefits with bonds. They have to be redeemed by the Treasury for cash. But the treasury no longer has any of the money it borrowed, it has been spent by Congress on everyday government expenses such as war. Right now the Fund is solvent, taking in more than it pays out, but when the ratio of wage earners to SS retirees narrows and then tips to more retirees than earners, it will have to dip into the surplus, but there isn't any cash there. And as the Treasury is spending more than it takes in, they will have to borrow the money to redeem the bonds.

That supposed $2.7 surplus in bonds is in reality national debt that you can add to the $20 trillion officially announced. That accounting deception is fiduciary fraud at its worst. What is needed is to reestablish a dedicated SS Trust Fund that Congress can't get their hands on.

As to keeping the Fund solvent in the future, there are two simple actions that can be readily implemented that will do the job. Raise the cap on earned income subject to FICA taxes from the current $110,000 to $200,000, adjusting the rate as income increases. Those making that kind of money can certainly afford it and those employers paying that kind of salaries likewise. The Golden Rule. Congress refuses to do it because it represents increased taxes on the well-to-do.

The other action is means testing. If you don't need it, you shouldn't get it. Or the amount you receive is adjusted to your other retirement income. The moral concept of social security is to insure a sustainable standard of living for people over sixty five. Just because you have paid into it all your working life should not entitle you to receive benefits from it if you have no need for it. It's the Golden Rule. Social Security should be considered income insurance much like automobile insurance. You pay your car insurance premiums for as long as you own a car. If you have no accidents, you don't receive any benefits. So it should be with SS. We are our brother's keeper.

Chapter Nine

THE U.S. POSTAL SERVICE

The U.S Postal Service has fallen on hard times financially due to a decline in the volume of delivery mail as a result of the public using email and because Congress has mandated that the USPS prefund employee retirement benefits, a policy that no other government agency is required to do. Although USPS is an independent agency and does not receive taxpayer money for its day-to-day operation, it is subject to control by Congress. Therein is the problem, that being control (read meddling) by congressional factions for political reasons. They are reluctant to support closure of facilities, reduce delivery days or raise rates due to fear of voter disapproval.

The one move that would solve all the problems for the USPS would be to remove it from congressional control and let it operate like any commercial business. With proper management, it would soon be profitable. That is not likely to happen for obvious reasons, yet there are other solutions that can solve the Post Office financial problems.

The U.S. public is spoiled. We don't need residential mail delivery six days a week. Monday, Wednesday and Friday are sufficient for the vast majority. Businesses and special needs like medicine delivery are exceptions or can use other delivery systems. We will save big bucks in vehicle and fuel costs. Don't lay off employees; reduce the force through attrition. Raise the rates; other countries charge more. All developed countries charge from 50 to 90 cents for first class mail. Raise ours from 49 to 65 cents. If foreign country citizens and businesses can afford it, so can we. It's the damn politics folks; Congressional failure to do the right thing for political reasons. More dereliction of duty.

Chapter Ten
A MIDDLE EAST SOLUTION

The truth is not spoken, common-sense has flown out the window and politics abound when it comes to the United States foreign policy in the Middle East. It is badly flawed if not outright disastrous. Much of it is based on the philosophy of bringing democracy to every country. We need to cease this hypocritical horse hockey about democratic values. Stop preaching to other countries that they should be like us. To start with, we are not a democracy. We do not have a democratic government but rather a representative one in which our representatives often go their own way, not serving the people but their own interests and that of others, at times to the detriment of the country and the people. The ability of the "powerful" congressional committee chairmen to keep a bill from leaving committee and the leaders of the House and Senate to refuse to bring a bill before the membership is a travesty of democracy. It sounds more like petty dictatorship to me.

Secondly, who the hell in their right mind wants a dysfunctional, dangerously debt ridden, corrupt and irresponsible government like ours? We have already discussed judgment and criticism of others and what the scriptures tell us, how hypocritical it is, that we need to get our own house in order before we start preaching to others. Telling others how they should live is offensively arrogant.

As noted in Chapter 2, the United States has been the major perpetrator and supporter of terrorism in the Middle East. The invasion of Iraq and Afghanistan and full blown war against their governments and people, created terror that you can't imagine unless you have lived in a war zone; the most powerful war machine in the world raining terror down upon the people, many of them innocent women and children. All three of those wars violated the Rules for Just War as spelled out in Chapter Two.

The tragedy is that we have received little or no benefit from those wars but rather incurred incredible costs. Financial costs are currently at $4.3 trillion and rising. The eventual cost is estimated at $6 trillion, which includes the cost of taking care of our injured and maimed soldiers as well as the interest we must pay on the money we have borrowed to conduct the war. Over 6,500 soldiers have died and about 60,000 were injured; many of them maimed for life. Hatred, enmity, the terrorist ranks and distrust of the United States as well as instability in the region have all increased. We have destroyed Iraq as a country. It is effectively divided into three entities, the Kurds in the north, the Shiites in the south and the Sunnis in the middle, with the latter two at each other's throats, as well as providing fertile ground for al Qaida and ISIS activity. War is, indeed, an abomination; the ultimate stupidity.

Our meddling in the Middle East affairs for geopolitical reasons has been totally unjustified. Our concern over the flow of oil from the Middle East was never warranted to the point that we need a heavy military presence there to insure it, and whose presence is offensive and destabilizing. The oil exporting countries want to sell their oil and were not going to take actions that jeopardize their financial well-being. The U.S. Navy could surely keep the sea lanes open and don't need to be based there to do that. Further, we are rapidly gaining independence from ME oil and becoming energy independent. Our concerns about communism and Russian influence in the ME was never justified.

We helped overthrow a democratic government in Iran, replacing it with a dictator who oppressed, tortured and killed the Iranian people. We backed Iraq during its invasion of Iran out of an unjustified fear of Iran after the Iranian Revolution. According to Iraqi documents, they received materials from the U.S. and other western nations giving them chemical weapons capability which they used against Iran. We also provided intelligence that helped Saddam effectively use those weapons on the Iranians. The U.S. was the only nation that voted against the United Nations' condemnation of Iraqi use of chemical weapons.

We, in effect, gave Saddam the "green light" for his invasion of Kuwait. In the two weeks before his invasion, the U.S. State Department issued the statements that the "United States has no commitment to defend Kuwait," and that "We have no opinion on your Arab conflicts, such as your dispute with Kuwait, that the Kuwait issue is not associated with America." The United States may not have intended to encourage the invasion, but that is effectively what it did.

In the second Gulf War, for ulterior motives, we invaded Iraq under the false pretense that Saddam possessed WMD. He was never a serious threat to us or his neighbors, including Israel, even had he possessed nuclear weapons. Israel had no serious concern about Saddam Hussein. Had he mounted a serious attack against Israel, they wouldn't have hesitated to make Baghdad and much of Iraq a nuclear wasteland, and Saddam was well aware of that. And we know that he certainly had no desire to become a martyr. Now an almost identical situation exists with Iran, and the warmongers are clamoring for war with Iran, both those in this country and in Israel. God help us from making another stupid mistake.

Then there was the utter disaster in Afghanistan. Fourteen years later, over 2,000 American soldiers dead, 17,519 wounded and maimed, tens of thousands of Afghan civilians, including women and little children, killed and maimed, and hatred multiplied many fold. Other than killing bin Laden, we still haven't accomplished our goals of bringing all the perpetrators to justice and making sure al Qaeda will never operate from Afghanistan again. Both being dubious and unrealistic goals, as other terrorist leaders and recruits will step into the breach because of their hatred and determination, and as al Qaeda and other terrorist groups continue to operate in places like Iraq, Libya, Somalia, Yemen, Mali and yes, in Afghanistan after we are gone. We are totally deluding ourselves to believe that we are on the verge of defeating al-Qaida, ISIS and terrorism. There is that better way, The God Option.

I was astounded when I recently read that a U.S. general responsible for training Afghanistan's security forces was relieved of his duties for criticizing Afghan President Karzai and saying the country's leaders were "isolated from reality." How unfortunate that he was relieved for telling the truth. The commanding general who relieved him said, "Such comments will not keep us from accomplishing our most critical and shared mission: bringing about a stable, peaceful and prosperous Afghanistan." He and our other military and civilian leaders who believe that are the ones totally isolated from reality. Given their corrupt government and warlord culture, we will never bring about a stable, peaceful and prosperous Afghanistan not in twenty or two hundred years. Further, that is not and should not be our mission there.

We have never really addressed the reasons behind the attack on 9/11. There is no excuse for it but there are reasons. They did not attack us just because they wanted to kill a lot of Americans or because they resent us and our economic well-being. It was because of our meddling in Middle East affairs, especially our lack of even-handedness in the Israeli/Palestinian issue. Because they see us as an arrogant power who tries to impose our ways on them. And to a huge extent because they resent our military presence there. That is very offensive to them, and rightly so.

That animosity continues today and we need to, and can do, something about it. A good start, and the easiest, would be to "mend our fences with Iran". The Iranians are a proud Persian people of an old, venerable and non-aggressive country. We have treated them badly. We were on the wrong side when we supported Saddam in his war against Iran. We shouldn't have been involved at all. Our role in dismantling democracy in Iran and installing a dictator who oppressed and murdered the Iranian people is inexcusable. Now we provoke them, falsely labeling Iran as an axis of evil and parking our naval nuclear military power on their doorstep.

How do you think we would react if some country did those things to us? We would be mad as hell and raring to go to war as we did in Afghanistan. Is it any wonder that they hate us and call us the Great Satan? That needs to be restated. The Iranian people do not hate the American people. It's our government and its unwise, political and unwarranted meddling in Mideast affairs. Yes, it is governments and a handful of misguided zealots who usually cause the trouble. Rosemarie Carnarius, in her must-read work, *Armageddon or Awakening*, shows how governments and organizations, with their machinations and big lies, deceive and divide, keeping our world in turmoil.

Let's look at who have been the aggressors in the Middle East. Certainly not Iran, but Israel and the Palestinians in their bloody, destructive and useless attacks on each other. The futile Arab/Israeli wars. The Iraqi war against Iran and U.S. support of that aggression. And then there are the three full-blown wars of aggression by the United States, all of questionable justification, but clearly contributing to the destabilization of the area. Good God, people, don't you see the incredible hypocrisy in our and Israel's ranting concern about a "dangerous" Iran. The Iranians do.

During the negotiations toward preventing Iran from obtaining nuclear capability, there were detrimental comments by some U.S. uninformed and closed-minded congressional members to the effect that Iran cannot be trusted, they are a terrorist country and support terrorists in the region.

But who is the terrorist? One man's terrorist is another man's freedom fighter. When Israel was fighting to establish their country out of the land on which the Palestinians lived, Israeli groups like the Stern Gang and Irgun committed heinous acts of terrorism in their efforts to drive both the British and the Palestinians out of the territory that the UN had designated for the state of Israel. They blew up the King David hotel where the British had their headquarters. They massacred the Palestinian village of Deir Yassin. They called themselves freedom fighters.

Iran supports the Palestinian groups Hamas and Hezbollah in their cause to resist Israeli continued expansion and occupation of Palestinian land outside the boundaries that were designated by the

UN. Who is the terrorist and the freedom fighter there? Most of the world condemns that illegal Israeli expansion and occupation and looks upon the Palestinians as the freedom fighters.

Given our Mideast foreign policy and actions there, it is the U.S. who has the trust issue. We have fostered and committed more terrorism in the Middle East than all the parties there combined.

As to supporting terrorists in the region, our support of Israel in their brutal oppression of the Palestinians ranks right up there in the history of terrorism. In Israel's illegal occupation of current Palestine territories, kids throwing stones at tanks are gunned down, homes and schools bulldozed, clinics ransacked, tank shells lobbed into marketplaces, missiles hurled into crowds, Palestinian leaders assassinated, orchards nurtured over generations have been wiped out and civilian infrastructure everywhere trashed. Palestinian land continues to be confiscated to build Israeli settlements; Israel thumbing their nose at us and much of the rest of the world who have condemned that encroachment. The shame is that U.S. authorities are well aware of this and ignore it because of politics: the power of the Jewish lobby in Washington.

The concern over Iran's nuclear program is highly exaggerated. Whether they are developing it for commercial power or to attain nuclear weapon capability is irrelevant. They have as much right to the latter as any other country in the world. They want it for defense and prestige, as do other nuclear powers. No country in the world, including Iran, is going to use nuclear capability for aggression. The consequences are too great. Nor is Iran likely to do it through the proxy of a terrorist organization, for they would still be the primary suspect, and as well, nuclear weapons leave a signature. Further, they would be killing tens of thousands of their Palestinian brethren who live in very close proximity to Israel. The Ayatollahs, who have the real power, are not insane and you can be sure have no desire to be martyrs.

Foreign policy experts agree that Iran wants respect and to be a reasonable power in the region. That's not compatible with self-destruction by nuclear exchange. Iran would be the pariah of the world. The price is simply too high to pay. The concept that Iran is willing to accept total destruction of their holy city Qom and much of Teheran, massive destruction to other parts of their country, and the killing of ten million of their people in exchange for nuking Israel is quite absurd. You can be sure almost none of the Iranian people would agree to this.

An Israel and/or U.S. attack on Iran with the intent of destroying its ability to achieve nuclear capability would be very foolish and a huge mistake, for Iran would surely retaliate with missiles, and Hamas and Hezbollah would rain rockets upon Israel incessantly. Further, Iran would likely attack U.S. military facilities in the area and support terrorist attacks on us both abroad and at home.

Former Iranian president, Mahmoud Ahmadinejad, had threatened Israel but had never said they should be "wiped off the map." Israeli Deputy Prime Minister Dan Meridor has admitted so. That is a false statement fostered by Israel, as a reason should they decide to attack Iran, and the U.S. politicians who are subservient supporters of AIPAC and Israel. Mahmoud, in an interview with Piers Morgan explained, in effect, that he wanted to "wipe out" the injustices being done to the Palestinians. Iranian general Firouzabadi's recent vow to "annihilate Israel" is fanatical, inconsequential blustering, for he doesn't have his finger on the button. It is clearly hate-mongering, reminiscent of Israel's Ariel Sharon's pledge to kill, burn and eliminate the Palestinians. Iran's basic problem with Israel is with what they consider the "Zionist Regime," its expansionist goals, its atrocious treatment of their Palestinian brothers and its failure to realistically agree to a Palestinian state.

When will we ever learn that the carrot is better than the stick, that an outpouring of friendship, forgiveness, trade and aid are much more beneficial than hate, revenge and blockade? There is a wonderful saying that, "The best way to defeat your enemy is to make him your friend." Iran a friend? Why not? Russia was once our mortal enemy, the big "Red Bear" with its huge nuclear arsenal looking down our throats. Khrushchev once declared that he was going to "bury us." Until fairly recently, when we unwisely started imposing sanctions on them, they were considered more in the friendly column than enemies, thanks to Ronnie and Gorby who made it happen through friendship. You can do the same, Prez, with the now moderate President, Hassan Rouhani.

Ahmadinejad had said in his interview with Piers Morgan on CNN that the hand of friendship should be extended to all the world. Rouhani is even more likely to be amenable to that philosophy. Invite him to lunch. Ask him outright if we can't be friends and then stick out your hand. Explain to him, like you will to Bibi, that he has a chance to make history when he extends the hand of friendship and recognizes the State of Israel, just as Israel is going to recognize and facilitate the State of Palestine, as you are going to convince Bibi to do.

Ali Khamenei is another matter. He is the supreme power in Iran with Rouhani subordinate to him. He won't come to lunch. His policy is not to meet with representatives of Western powers because of what they have done to Iran (especially the U.S. and its wrongful actions against Iran), including the tough sanctions they have imposed on Iran. He had previously nixed talks on the nuclear issue for the same reasons and rightly so. The sanctions that have been imposed on Iran are immoral and unproductive, causing no harm to the government and its leaders, serving mostly to harm the people, foster more hatred and serve as strong rallying propaganda for their leaders. You don't negotiate with governments by making the people suffer.

Still, Khamenei is open to relations with the United States. He has gone on record as favoring a modus vivendi, an agreement between those whose opinions differ, an accommodation between parties to allow life to go on. He is opposed to Iranian aggression as expressed in his opposition to other Iranian leaders who planned to counter-invade Iraq after Iraq had been expelled from Iran after their military conflict. He has stated that Iran is not an enemy of the Israeli people. His problem with Israel is with the Zionist Regime, their expansionist policies, persecution of the Palestinian people and refusal to accept and facilitate a Palestinian state.

Khamenei has shown signs of détente including giving Rouhani the okay to discuss the nuclear issue. During your luncheon with Hassan, ask him about meeting with Ali in Teheran with the purpose of peacefully resolving our differences. Given your pronouncement to the world against war, withdrawal from Muslim lands and the plan to bring Israel into line, Khamenei will be very amenable to doing so. Apologize to him for our lousy actions in supporting Saddam's invasion of Iran and our misguided support of the Shah. That will take a lot of courage, Prez, and you will get some serious opposition from the close-minded hard liners in Congress as well as the military brass, but you are the CIC. Go for it.

But our greatest foreign policy blunder in the Middle East has been not being an honest broker in the Israeli/Palestinian issue, causing great unrest and divisiveness there. To understand the problem we have to go back to 1948 when the State of Israel was formed out of land that the Palestinians lived on. Three quarters of a million Palestinians were displaced from their homes. Naturally, they resented it, resisted, and the conflict started. Who could blame them? Even Ben Gurion, considered father of Israel, said, "We have come and we have stolen their country. Why would they accept that? If we were in their shoes, we would do the same thing, only better."

Still, land has changed hands throughout history and Israel is here to stay, justified or not. Given their persecution, one could say they deserve a state of their own and to live in peace. But then, so do the Palestinians. Israel has given voice approval to a Palestinian state but only on Israeli terms such as accords that give themselves access to water and control of more Palestinian land that they say is needed for their security. They continue to occupy more Palestinian land to achieve that, with the goal of further expansion called "Eretz Israel." That being the restoration of the supposed "God covenanted" lands, to include parts of Lebanon, Syria and Jordan. Menachem Begin stated, "Those who do not recognize Israel's right to the whole

God-covenanted lands, do not recognize her right to any of it."

The Israelis and Palestinians are their own worst enemy. Their strategy and actions so as to achieve their goals of statehood and peace are obviously not working, rather only serving to foster anger, hatred and harden resolve. Israeli bulldozing of Palestinian homes, schools and orchards, occupying their territory and corralling them in camps, as a means of controlling and oppressing them is cruel and abhorrent. Former Prime Minister Ariel Sharon said, "I am willing to do the dirty work for Israel, to kill as many Arabs as necessary, to deport them, to expel and burn them." That's despicable.

Likewise, Palestinian strategy is equally repugnant. The brainwashing of young Palestinians by the elders to become suicide bombers and kill innocent civilians, including women and children is detestable. Rarely, if ever, have we seen older suicide bombers. That's cowardly. Hamas' commitment to the destruction of Israel, to "push them into the sea" is loathsome and constitutes genocide which all of the civilized world condemns. Further, it is totally unrealistic. Given the military prowess of Israel and backing of the United States, it simply will never happen. Give it up, Hamas.

It needs to be noted that the Palestinians have generally backed off their suicide bomber attacks, wisely recognizing that they are counterproductive to the achievement of their goal. Still they threaten Israel and continue to fire rockets at them. It also needs to be noted that Israel has not backed off one inch in their persecution and oppression of the Palestinians, rather continuing to encroach on their land with the building of more and more settlements (Eretz Israel). It is very difficult to understand, almost unbelievable, that the Israelis, given the persecution that they have endured, inflict persecution upon the Palestinians.

There needs to be equal condemnation, by the entire world community, of both Palestinian and Israeli actions over against one another. Unfortunately, the United States has been a major contributor to the instability and violence there by a lack of even-handedness, such as the demand that Hamas and Hezbollah disarm, eschew violence and recognize Israel's right to exist while no demands whatsoever are made for the Israelis to meet similar requirements President Trump's misguided decision to move the U.S. Embassy to Jerusalem, and disapproved of by most world countries, exacerbated the instability there and put another snag in the Palestinian/Israeli peace process.

Further, the United States' unquestioning support of Israel, whatever it does, such as, "The long chain of false incidents (look up The USS Liberty) and hostilities we have invented, and so many clashes we have provoked," as former Israeli Prime Minister Moshe Sharett has said, serve only to inflame the conflict.

That Israel has the power to control America is almost unbelievable, yet there it is. Ariel Sharon said, "We, the Jewish people, control America, and the Americans know it." Our spineless politicians in Congress "quake in their boots" when the Israel lobby AIPAC (American Israeli Public Affairs Committee) is mentioned. As one congressman said, "Whatever AIPAC wants, I'll vote for." AIPAC doesn't just lobby but intimidates and coerces. There is an unwritten understanding in Congress--anyone who supports AIPAC will be rewarded and those who oppose it will be punished. AIPAC has infiltrated every branch of our government, passing information, including classified material, through their embassy to Israel in violation of laws and regulations governing U.S. secrets. Congress is well aware of this but declines to investigate out of fear of AIPAC.

Former Congressman Paul Findley, in his book, *They Dare To Speak Out_*(against Israel's lobby AIPAC), documents all this. He further says, "It is no over statement to say that AIPAC has effectively gained control of virtually all of Capitol Hill's action on Middle East policy. Almost without exception, House and Senate members do its bidding, because most of them consider AIPAC to be the direct Capitol Hill representative of a political force that can make or break their chances at election time."

Former Congressman "Pete" McCloskey puts it more directly: Congress is "terrorized by AIPAC." Conservative Republican Pat Buchanan said, "Capitol Hill is Israeli occupied territory." Every

American should read Findley's book. You will be damned mad at Congress and AIPAC, and think a little less kindly toward Israel.

Professors John Mearsheimer and Stephen Walt in their document "The Israel Lobby and U.S. Foreign Policy" say that the American Israel Public Affairs Committee (AIPAC) in particular has a "stranglehold on the U.S. Congress", due to its "ability to reward legislators and congressional candidates who support its agenda, and to punish those who challenge it." The authors also argue that "the lobby's impact has been unintentionally harmful to Israel as well."

Through the power of AIPAC, Israel is assured of our unquestioned monetary and military support of their brutal oppression of the Palestinian people, expansion of settlements on Palestinian land and refusal to give up occupation of Palestinian land and return to the 1967 borders. The Israelis claim they need the land for security purposes. In reality, it is part of their goal to achieve a Greater Israel, to claim the so-called God-covenanted lands (Eretz Israel). It is a misguided and poisonous path that is counterproductive, causing harm to both Israel and the U.S. It is the major cause of the hatred that Iran and all the Arab countries harbor toward Israel and the U.S. It has been suggested as a major factor behind 9/11.

There is right and wrong on both sides. We do need to understand the concern that Israel has for its security. They are surrounded by "enemies" that continually threaten them and attack them with suicide bombers, rockets and attempted invasions. Those enemies believe they are justified, as Israel has taken land that belonged to the Palestinians, is oppressing the Palestinians, continues to occupy more of their territory and refuses to recognize a Palestinian state. Given that Israel is here to stay, those violent tactics are counterproductive and will never result in achieving the goal of a Palestinian state. Likewise, Israel's violent reaction with their powerful military forces, the devastation and suffering they have caused the Palestinians and their ever-expanding occupation of more Palestinian territory, will never bring them security and peace.

As Israel initiated the instability in the Middle East when they took Palestinian land, as Ben Gurion admitted, it behooves them to take the first steps toward stability. The very first step is to show some contrition, immediately ceasing oppression of the Palestinians. Return to the 1967 borders. Reparations would be in order; one billion dollars, of the four billion they get annually from the United States, for five years would be reasonable. They need to ask forgiveness for their actions against the Palestinians as well as forgive the Palestinians for the harm they have done to Israel and its people. Release all Palestinian prisoners. Announce total acceptance of a Palestinian state and facilitate it. Give up "Eretz Israel," the goal of acquiring parts of Jordan, Syria and Lebanon so as to restore Greater Israel. It is totally unacceptable and unrealistic, as the world will not condone it. Certainly, Jordan, Syria and Lebanon would not agree to it.

The Palestinians need to ask forgiveness for the deaths and injuries they have caused the Israelis, cease all attacks on the Israelis and forgive the Israelis for what they have done to the Palestinians. They must recognize Israel as a state for the Jewish people. There is already an accord, proposed by Saudi Arabia and agreed upon by most of the Arab/Muslim nations, in which they would recognize the state of Israel in exchange for Israel's recognition of a Palestinian state. Israel has declined the offer. They do not want a Palestine state as that would impede their goal of a Greater Israel.

Just as Israel must give up "Eretz Israel,' the Palestinians must forget about the "right of return." It is simply not realistic. Such a huge influx of Arabs into Israel would neuter it as a Jewish country. However, compensation is certainly in order. The demand for Jerusalem as the Palestinian capitol needs to be honored by the Israelis. The Palestinians are willing to share it. The Israelis should move the seat of their government to Tel Aviv, which is in essence their capitol and recognized as such by most of the world. The Palestinians want only East Jerusalem as their capital. The Israelis can retain West Jerusalem as their spiritual capital.

Israel would have nothing to lose, except their unrealistic dream of a Greater Israel, and much to gain. The Palestinians would have no more reason to attack Israel in any way. Hatred by the Arab states would subside. Iran would have no serious excuse for a supposed attack on Israel. Hamas' goal to destroy Israel would pretty much become irrelevant. Will it work? We'll never know if we don't try it. It's certainly better than continuing to pursue the current self-destructive policies.

The United States needs to "persuade" Israel to take these steps. We have the ability to do so. Of course, we need to reiterate our commitment to their existence. But we need to make it absolutely clear that we will no longer tolerate or support their actions against the Palestinians or their goal of Eretz Israel. Congress needs to stop bowing and scraping, get up off their knees, get some collective backbone and rein in the activities of AIPAC, making it clear that as American citizens their allegiance is to America and not a foreign country; that we will no longer put up with their subversive actions concerning the affairs of our government. In numbers there is safety, Congress people, AIPAC cannot punish all of you. Be responsible and do what is right for your country, and, yes, for Israel, as well. Save them from themselves.

The same goes for the Administration. Mr. President, you need to invite Bibi for lunch and reason with him. After some good food and a couple bottles of wine, I think he will be amenable. Despite his stubbornness (that's not a bad characteristic--think perseverance or steadfastness), he is a smart guy and will go along when you explain to him how he can go down in history as the leader who brought peace and security to his people. Explain to him that we are absolutely and totally committed to Israel's existence. But we are not "owned" by Israel and will no longer put up with AIPAC's subversive activities into our affairs, either foreign or domestic. That we will no longer tolerate Israel's brutal oppression of the Palestinians or expansion on to their land. That the goal of a Greater Israel, to claim parts of Jordan, Syria and Lebanon is totally unacceptable and must be abandoned. You need to make him see that agreeing to these points will not harm Israel but rather lead to peace and security for his country. It would probably be a good idea to have the Attorney General send AIPAC a message to cease and desist its subversive activities or some members might find themselves replacing Jonathan Pollard in the slammer.

The validity of Israel's claim to the land by virtue of God's promise to give it to them needs to be questioned. There are words in the Old testament that do support that claim. (God told Moses, "When you have come into the land of Canaan, I am giving you the entire land as your homeland." Deuteronomy 1.) However, if the entire Old Testament context of the issue is examined, it is quite clear that those words are not of God but of men. God supposedly instructed Moses to go into the land he had given them and "Kill all the men, male children and women who have lain with a man, but you can keep the young virgins for yourself." Numbers 31:17. Does God value baby girls more than baby boys? Would he really instruct adults to kill children? He could not, especially as he has commanded in other parts of scripture that we are not to harm the little ones. It is really quite clear that those words are of men, especially when we note the approval for keeping the virgins for themselves. There are also the words, "When the Lord delivers them to you, don't make any treaties or show them mercy, utterly wipe them out." Deuteronomy 7. How could God give such instructions when he had already commanded them "Thou shalt not kill?" He could not!

Further, Judaism maintains that God is just and merciful. It would be an appalling injustice to take land from the Canaanites and give it to the Israelites. And certainly not merciful to instruct the Israelites to murder the little children in the process of taking their land. Those atrocities may have occurred, but any open-minded person of integrity knows they were not at the command of God.

This knowledge about the false "God-covenanted lands" is not going to affect the existence of the state of Israel; it is here to stay. However, the international community and especially the United States must make it absolutely clear to Israel that their expansionist goals so as to achieve Greater Israel will not be condoned. That they must go back to their 1967 borders or come to some agreement with the Palestinians in the way of compensation for the Palestinian land they have illegally occupied. That they must cease their persecution of the Palestinians and make restitution for the original seizure of their land. That they must recognize and facilitate a Palestinian State.

All of the above misguided American policies and actions have led to greater Middle East destabilization, strong anti-Americanism and a rise in Islamic militancy and extremism. The ascendance of ISIS has its roots in the unnecessary and unjustified U.S. invasion of Iraq, which led to the destabilization there. Further, the corrupt and oppressive Shia, Maliki government, which the U.S., in effect, installed and then continued to support, disenfranchised the Sunni population resulting in the rise of the Sunni dominated ISIS.

President Obama was right in withdrawing all of our troops, which the vast majority of Americans supported. Keeping a fighting force there to support the Shiite government would not have prevented the rise of ISIS; but rather resulted in a long-term commitment and the killing and maiming of more American soldiers. ISIS is a brutal extremist organization that even other Muslim organizations (al Queda) and Muslim countries oppose.

ISIS' clever use of the social media has been cited as a major tool to promote their agenda and recruit members. There should be a massive world-wide social media response to discredit their claim that they are "warriors of Allah" doing his will. The response reflecting that they are baby and women killers. That Allah requires forgiveness and mercy. Killing others who do not believe as you do, especially the children, is neither. Islam means peace and the actualizing of good. The actions of ISIS are neither. The political aspect of giving the Sunni population a voice in the government needs to be addressed, however that spiritual aspect should be the major factor in the world's social media response.

ISIS is certainly no threat to our national security. Such an organization will not survive; history dictates the demise of such groups.

There is a great need to change our perceptions about the Middle

East. Now let's take a closer look at how religion presents an obstruction to a better world.

Chapter Eleven
RELIGION:
THE GREAT BARRIER

The truth is that religion has caused humanity a great deal of grief. We would do well to consider the consequences that denominational religion has brought to the human race through its man-made doctrine. Religion is usually considered beneficial but is often otherwise. It has been the source of great enmity and violence in the world. It is a major factor in dividing the human race, when it should be uniting us with one another and with God.

Most religious leaders would say they believe in freedom of religion and often express tolerance toward other religions and beliefs. They probably do, sort of. However, if one were to question or express disbelief of their religious doctrine, one would likely find himself not welcome in their midst. When I questioned the Christian doctrine that only Christians are saved and that God sends everyone else to hell, I was told that I was no longer welcome in my church and was eventually excommunicated. It is interesting to note that in Saudi Arabia on the road to Mecca, as you near the city, there is a road that branches off with a sign that says Infidel Bypass. All non-Muslims are infidels (unbelievers) and are not allowed in Mecca.

More seriously, religious leaders damn other people to a hell of suffering. Most would deny it, but, in fact, they do! When they teach and preach that everyone must believe as they do to be saved, they are proclaiming that those who do not are not saved. They are condemning anyone who is not of their religious persuasion. They do it in absolute contradiction of God who unequivocally tells us in the scriptures that we are not to condemn others.

Attempts to impose religious beliefs through Christian evangelism and Muslim holy jihad only intensify the discord. And even more derelict is the failure of the religions to follow God's basic instruction to teach love, kindness, mercy and forgiveness as the way to peace, harmony and righteousness with him. The source of all this alienation and failure to teach God's truths is flawed religious doctrine--dogma created by men. The religions of the world are by no means evil. They have accomplished much good, albeit at the same time hampering mankind's spiritual development by intertwining false, man-made doctrine with God's truths.

The great commandments that God has given to all the religions of the world are to acknowledge him, love him, and love and care for one another. Almost all religions hold to those tenets. Then they make the mistake of adding man-made doctrine and laws, or interpreting the basic laws and instructions of God to meet their own requirements or beliefs. They require us to follow some great prophet or religious figure such as Christ, Muhammad or Buddha if we are to be "saved."

They declare their religion as the only true one, which must then be accepted and believed in totally if one is to achieve "paradise" or "heaven." Then they have the audacity to proclaim that their loving God damns everyone else to hell! How illogical! What narrow-mindedness! What disrespect for God!

The basic dogma of most religious faiths is the same. We have seen that Judaism requires the Jew to be in a right relationship with his fellow men in order to be right with God.[1] Likewise the Muslim must want for his brother what he wants for himself if he really believes in Allah.[2] And the Christian must love his neighbor as himself.[3]

Surely, our neighbor, our brother, our fellow man means all human beings. But unfortunately, to many Jews it often means only another Jew and, likewise, with the Muslim and Christian. When we look at what is happening in the Mideast, we can clearly see that this is so. To see the hatred that exists between Jews and Arabs and the indifference and intolerance of Christians toward others, we can only conclude that, judged by their own religious doctrine, a great number of them are not believers and certainly are not in a right relationship with God.

There are about two billion Christians in the world today. Most Muslims believe every one of those infidels is damned to hell. There are an equal number of Muslims in the world. A vast majority of Christians believe each and every one of those heathens is going to go to hell. God has perfect, unconditional love and therefore cannot damn anyone.

The religions indeed believe that God is perfect in love and justice, as well as being a compassionate and forgiving God. How then is it possible for God to condemn a child or anyone else who has never heard of, never been taught about, nor understood a Christ or Muhammad or Moses or Buddha? That would surely be unjust!

It should give any reasonable, thinking person cause to wonder that such a compassionate God could condemn so many people to hell because of their religious beliefs. There has to be an inescapable, logical conclusion that all religions cannot be right, which should also give cause to wonder about the validity of their beliefs.

We even become violent and kill each other over religious beliefs. Look at the two great religions Islam and Christianity. History records that the armies of Islam, in the seventh century, spread their belief by aggressive war. Even their fellow tribes were put to the sword if they refused to pledge their allegiance to Muhammad. After Muhammad's death, Islamic armies attacked Syria, India, Africa, Mongolia and Spain in an effort to force salvation upon the world.

Then, for almost two hundred years, in the twelfth and thirteenth centuries, the European Christians mounted eight major crusades in their "holy wars" to repossess Palestine and the "Holy Lands" from the Muslims, which then became, in part, crusades to gain riches and power, and assert religious control over a people. That sort of strife has continued throughout history and even exists today. A recent report showed that, of the 42 armed conflicts that were occurring at the time the report was conducted, over two-thirds were fueled by religion.4 These hostilities are happening because the religions of the world have ignored God's command that we are to love one another, even our enemies, showing mercy and forgiveness. Peace among the nations and people of the world can never be achieved until the barriers of false religious dogma are removed.

Religion is not only a major factor in keeping the human race separated, it is also a significant barrier to our spiritual growth. Every Sunday, in thousands of Christian churches throughout the world, hundreds of millions of people are conditioned to think that they are by nature sinful and unclean; poor miserable sinners. Their minds are programmed with, and their memories have stored the concepts that it is human to err and that they will continue to sin for the rest of their mortal life. As they think, so are they! In that manner, the Christian Church has unwittingly kept mankind in bondage to sin.

Our ability to grow spiritually and improve our relationships with one another is stifled, even thwarted, by much of the religious teaching of the world. We are sometimes taught that it is our nature to sin and create all the hell that often plagues humanity. Those teachings surely demean and suppress the abilities of God's and man's magnificent co-creation: the human being. Such doctrine impedes growth and must be changed, for it represents a formidable barrier to that evolutionary thrust toward a higher level of human consciousness and oneness with one another and with God.

Religion often promotes much of the guilt and low self-esteem so prevalent in the human race. Christianity, especially, depicts man as a groveling, poor, miserable sinner who can do nothing by himself to change that condition. We have been pictured as beings who "don't know how to do good but are rotten through and through" as St. Paul tells us. Or that there is no goodness in man, only "evil and darkness in the hearts of men" as Martin Luther declared.

We are made to feel guilty if we don't belong to a Christian church, if we don't attend regularly, if we don't participate in church activities, if we don't give enough financial support to the church, and if we don't evangelize and bring others into the organized church setting.

We are constantly reminded that we are by nature sinful and unclean beings, sometimes being told that we are totally corrupt, with no redeeming factors. As my brother-in-law, Ronnie said to me, "It has always been a downer for me to go to church each Sunday to confess, to be told and even sometimes sing that I am such a rotten human being when I feel that I'm not that kind of person at all."

We know how the implanting of thoughts and concepts in our minds, especially with repetition and emphasis, brings those things to fruition in our lives. That continual programming of millions of church-goers with the idea that they are poor, miserable sinners who will remain so until the day they die is that ultimate, societal, self-fulfilling prophecy.

Religions must expunge the false man-made dogma from their teachings. This is especially true of Christianity which must look again at what Christ told us. That he didn't come to save the righteous but the sinners, Matthew 9:13. That we will not get to heaven by calling him Lord, but obeying God and doing good works, Matthew 7:21-16:27. That sin is not innate in our character; we can turn from our sins and do what is right and good so as to make the world good, John 8:11, Ezekiel 18:19-32. And that is what God expects us to do so as to be right with him. That we are to love our enemies and do good to them, Matthew 5:44. We are not to seek vengeance. Romans 12:19.

What if we had been taught for two thousand years to believe and live by all those words of Jesus Christ? Imagine what the world would be like! Paradise? That was what was intended for us.

—— *Chapter Twelve* ——

THE NATURE OF OUR WORLD

If we can accept that God, through his intelligence, thought and energy, created this world we live in and that he is therefore omnipresent--that is, present in all things that exist--then it is rational also to accept that everything in the universe is interconnected. Surely, it is a spiritual connection, with God the spirit--the universal field of energy that constitutes all things--as the medium for that link. Scientists John Bell and David Bohm have put forth theories of inter-connectedness.[1] Most physicists, especially those in quantum physics, as well as other scientists, are now leaning toward that concept.

Mankind is indeed a part of God's entire creation, not separate but intrinsically joined to that whole creation. We are a portion of that complete totality just as each cell of our body is part of the entire body. As the state of health of our entire body depends upon the condition of its parts, so the state of the whole world depends on the condition of its inhabitants, including all plant and animal life as well as mineral matter. Just as harm to any part of the body affects the whole, so does harm to any part of creation affect the whole.

Quite often we do not see mankind as the cause of harm in the world, but look elsewhere, even to God, as the cause. When some tragedy or negative circumstance happened to you, did you say, "Oh God, why me?" Or, "Why have you done this to me, Oh God?" Most parents who have lost a child have said that in one form or another: "Why my child, Oh God? How could you let this happen to my poor innocent little girl?"

Have you ever been in a conversation with someone, perhaps an atheist, who asked you, "If there is a God and he is as powerful and as loving as you say, and if he is in control of all things, then why does he let all these bad things happen? Why the terrible wars and killing? Why famine and pestilence? Why the Holocaust? How could

God let that happen to his 'chosen' people? If God so loves little children, why does he allow children to be born with Down Syndrome or deformed limbs or other debilitating diseases?" Do you recall what you said?

Some of the stock answers often given are: "We simply don't know." Or, "It is God's will," or "God has a reason beyond our understanding." The Church has some nice pat answers: "God has never said we won't have trials and tribulations. God is testing you/us. Look at what happened to Job. God took everything away from him, his family, his wealth, his home, everything! But God later returned to Job even more than he had taken because Job had kept the faith. So, too, must we keep faith in God when bad things happen to us." Or, "We must accept the good with the bad because it is God's will." Ministers like to quote St. Paul, who said, "We can rejoice, too, when we run into problems and trials, for we know they are good for us--they help us learn to be patient. And patience helps build trust in God."2

These are nice, theological-sounding answers, but they are foolish, and there is no truth in them because God has no part in them. How can anyone believe that it is God's will, his desire, that terrible things should happen to us. All the affliction and sorrow that happens to mankind is of his own doing. Even the child who is born with deformity. Somewhere along the line, in the conception of that child, man did something to cause that disfigurement. The mother or father may have ingested some chemical or foreign substance, either intentionally or unintentionally, which then caused the deformity. Some distant ancestor in the line may have had his or her DNA altered, for the same reasons, showing up generations later as a deformity in the newborn child. Excepting, for example, a mother who deliberately uses drugs while she is pregnant, no individual should feel guilty for the birth of a deformed child. But, nevertheless, it is certainly the fault of mankind, not God!

Even in accidents in which no individual is considered at fault, the cause is still the doing of man in some way. What about the inhabitant of Africa who lives in proximity to wild animals and is maimed or killed by a wild beast? What of a small child who doesn't know what a rattlesnake is, stoops to examine it, is bitten and dies? How could man possibly be at fault? Yet he is because, out of disobedience to God, man is out of harmony with his surroundings, including all other animal life. And because of that lack of harmony, the behavior of the wild beast and snake over against man is hostile and harmful. If man were in complete harmony with his earth, as God expects us to be, then it may be that the behavior of those animals would be friendly and benign.

It is a hard concept to accept, yet the scriptures lead us to believe it is so. The Old Testament speaks of the "peaceable kingdom"[3] that is to come when we all shall live in peace and harmony in obedience to God's instructions, and when God's will is done on earth as in heaven. "When the wolf and the lamb will lie down together, the cattle will be safe among the lions who will eat grass like the cows, the babies will crawl safely among poisonous snakes without harm and there will be no more harm in all of God's holy kingdom."

What of earthquakes, hurricanes, famine and pestilence? It is possible to acknowledge that man might be responsible for famine and pestilence because of his destruction of the environment, careless disposal of waste and other such actions. But how could man possibly be responsible for earthquakes and other devastating "natural phenomena?" Surely, they are the result of the way that God created this earth, aren't they? Perhaps not! After all, God created this earth to be a paradise for us and his will is to be done on earth as in heaven. Surely, such things as earthquakes, destructive storms, famine and disease do not exist in paradise and heaven. Besides, God has told us that nothing will hurt or destroy us in his kingdom when we are full of the knowledge of God.

Could it be that God causes them to happen now as punishment for our wrongdoing and even the innocent, such as children, have to suffer for the sins of the whole? Then, when we learn to obey him and live in peace and harmony with one another and with our environment, God will cause them to cease? But God has perfect justice and is merciful and forgiving, and, therefore, he could not cause the innocent children to suffer. That leaves only mankind as the source of all earthly distress. Such a precept is almost impossible to accept, nevertheless, it is likely true.

The theory of interconnectedness that dictates that one part of creation responds to another's change is very significant and is the basis of how man causes all earthly distress, including earthquakes! If man were content, happy and at peace with himself, others and his environment, then his earth would be calm, at rest, and, literally, a paradise. When man lives otherwise in a state of anxiety, anger, hatred and violence, the world becomes a hell, as we have witnessed throughout the history of mankind.

In Genesis God says we are to "subdue the earth." Subdue means to tame or overpower. Could it be then that we are to conquer and bring into subjection all forces of the world, including earthquakes, hurricanes, typhoons, tidal waves and winds? But mankind cannot do that until we are in tune with one another, living in peace and harmony according to the instructions that God has given us. We must also have a better understanding of the power of our minds.

The mind and thought are generally considered a field of energy that is active not only within our bodies, but can be projected and remain active beyond the body. A great deal of witnessed and documented psychic data supports this concept. Humans have been known to project and receive thoughts over great distances across continents and oceans. We know that humans project energy and what is known as aura. Most of us have sensed these energies that emanate from others. We feel ill at ease in the presence of certain people, even though there has been no verbal or body-language exchange. On the other hand, there are those people in whose presence we really feel comfortable under similar circumstances. Children and animals are particularly sensitive to those types of energies that people project.

We all have heard of the expression "green thumb" as applied to people who supposedly have good luck in growing plants. Others can use the same fertilizers, watering techniques and so forth, but don't have the same success. It is very probable that something more than physical care caused those with a "green thumb" to achieve greater success in their plant-growing endeavors. That something would involve mental emanations in a real love of what they are doing. Experiments have been done in which seeds and plants respond with increased growth to positive thought, love and even prayer. It also has been shown that plants respond positively to music.

Scientists have studied individuals who, through what is called psychokinesis, can move, bend and break objects with the power of their minds. Uri Geller is a well-known Israeli psychic who can bend objects, such as metal rods, at will, through the power of his mind. Scientists have found and studied hundreds of people with similar abilities. City College of New York conducted experiments with psychic Ingo Swann who, simply by thought, was able to raise the temperature of a graphite block inside a vacuum at the opposite end of a room.4

There are other illustrations of this flow of energy from humans. Kirlian photography, a lensless technique developed by Russian scientists, has photographed the aura of humans. The Massachusetts Institute of Technology has measured electromagnetic energy flowing from the human body.4 It is possible that man is the source of all natural earthly distress, generated by his mental activity. It is also likely that he has the equivalent ability to calm, and to cause that adverse natural phenomenon to end by eliminating stressful mental activity as well by employing use of good, positive, calm and loving thoughts.

The scriptures, as well, tell us that we can change these things if we choose to. Perhaps you remember the biblical story of Jonah, the whale and Nineveh. The people of Nineveh were exceedingly wicked and violent. They and their city were to be destroyed because of it. We don't know the manner in which that destruction was to occur. So God sent Jonah to warn them. After his refusal and supposed adventure with the whale, Jonah finally did warn the people of Nineveh. They paid heed to the word of God sent through Jonah, modified their behavior, turning from their evil and violent ways, and were spared.

It is commonly accepted that God was going to destroy them, but when he saw that they had ceased their wrongdoing, he spared them. The scriptures say, "And God saw their works, that they turned from their evil way; and God repented of the evil that he had said he would do unto them, and he did not."[5]

Can we see the inconsistency there? God was going to do evil to the people of Nineveh? He was going to return evil with evil? That is not possible! Elsewhere in the scripture God says we are not to kill, we are to love our enemies, and requite evil with good. Could God do any less? It might be argued that because the people were so wicked, they deserved to die. But the entire population of Nineveh? All 120,000 of them? Certainly every one of them was not so heinously evil that they deserved the death sentence. Even we human beings are very lenient when it comes to applying the death penalty for wrongdoing. And what of the innocent children and babies? Knowing that God is perfect in love, mercy and forgiveness, it would be absolutely impossible for him to kill those little ones.

What of God's commandment that "Thou shalt not kill?" He forbids killing. But it is okay for him to do so? Surely not! Then there is God's admonition to us, given through Christ, that we are to forgive others seven times seventy for their sins. Christ did not mean literally that we are to forgive another's wrongdoing 490 times. It was a metaphor meaning there should be no limit to forgiveness. That would certainly have to apply to the people of Nineveh. They were to be forgiven, not killed.

Given all these factors, we can only conclude that whatever manner of destruction was to happen to Nineveh, it was not to be the doing of God! It is also a logical conclusion that if the cessation of their wicked and violent behavior and thoughts turned aside or averted the destructive force, then the wicked and violent thoughts and actions were the source of that destructive force.

If one person can bend metal with the energy of his mind and another raise the temperature of a graphite block by the same means, could not the violent energy projected by most of the 120,000 minds in Nineveh cause distortion to the earth, the sea or the air, resulting in some natural disaster that would destroy Nineveh? Then, when they repented, ceasing their evil thoughts, with violent energy no longer emanating from their minds, the sea or earth or sky was calmed and the disaster avoided?

This concept is certainly more conceivable than believing that God could sentence to death and himself carry out the killing of 120,000 people, including little children and babies! If the saving of Nineveh from destruction by some natural disaster was the result of human behavioral change by thousands of people, then millions of people, by their good behavior and loving, kind thoughts, might save the world from catastrophe, subduing even the storms and earthquakes! Perhaps Nineveh is just another biblical myth and, then again, maybe not. We need to keep our minds open, for without that openness there would be little understanding and little progress for humankind--scientific, social or spiritual.

Given the recent increase in violence by "nature," it would appear that the amount of frenzied and violent energy emanating from millions of human minds is on the increase, over-powering the benign thought and behavior. Geologists have reported a significant increase in worldwide seismic activity. A Russian researcher warned that the Koryakskaya Volcano on the Kamchatka Peninsula could explode any time, causing a disaster as catastrophic as the eruption of Vesuvius in 79 A.D. In 1996, damage estimates from the worst flooding in memory across the far western United States reached more than $2 billion in California alone. At least 76 people were killed and more than 42,000 left homeless from floods and landslides in Brazil as storms raged across the area for more than five days.6

Strange weather patterns were being experienced around the world. Bitter cold swept across South Africa, with temperatures plunging to 15 degrees--a record cold in a normally temperate country. On the other end of the scale, unusually high temperatures were experienced in India with record temperatures of 120 degrees F causing hundreds of deaths. A week of torrential rainfall in eastern Cuba caused flooding that killed at least nine people and damaged thousands of homes as well as a great part of the sugar crop. The climate in Kenya changed from a withering drought to unusually heavy rain, causing erosion, flooding and destruction of tons of food and relief supplies that were destined for Somalia. In Vietnam, whirlwinds lashed the countryside, destroying over 600 homes and 5000 acres of rice paddies. In 2004, the Indonesian tsunami, the largest on record, killed 130 thousand people. Super hurricane Sandy, the largest to hit the United States caused $68 billion in damage and killed 286 people. In South Africa, baboons went on the rampage attacking motorists with showers of stones.[7]

Are these just samples of things to come unless mankind gets its act together? Certainly, these types of occurrences are happening to us all the time, and have throughout history; however, their frequency and intensity seem to be increasing. According to scripture there "shall be great tribulation, such as was not seen since the beginning of the world... For nation shall rise against nation and kingdom against kingdom; and there shall be earthquakes in divers places, and there shall be famines and troubles: these are the beginnings of sorrows."[8] If what is happening in the world today is indeed just the beginning of sorrows, then put your imagination to work and visualize the state of the world when these problems are multiplied two or fourfold! There will be "great travail and anguish... men's hearts will fail them; there shall be great distress upon the earth!"[9] Apparently and unfortunately, some of these things are necessary for man to learn. Christ says these things "need be." It seems that it is going to take a very large "two-by-four" to bring man's attention to the fact that he is doing something wrong and must change his ways!

I know it seems a faaaaar stretch to think that humankind could be responsible for earthquakes. Nevertheless, given the evidence, I believe that it somewhat reasonably postulates the ultimate mind power that humankind is capable of. Just a little over 100 years ago it would have been considered insane to think that the mind of man could be responsible for the reality of a fifty-ton metal machine that could fly through the air at 600 miles an hour. The idea that the earth was round was once the thought of crazy people. Some people were put to death when they put forth the idea that earth wasn't the center of the universe.

We have the evidence that man can do amazing things with thought power emanating from the mind--for example, Uri Geller bending metal with the energy of his mind, psychic Ingo Swann raising the temperature of an encased graphite block with mind-thought, the magnificent things that humankind creates with the thoughts of the mind and our ability to either cause illness or heal ourselves by the power of the mind.

If a single individual can do such things by projecting thought energy, imagine the effect that could or would be generated by many minds! The collective power of thought energy from millions of minds would be awesome! Isn't it conceivable then that tens of millions of people who are projecting random waves of frustrated, angry and violent energy could have an adverse effect on weather or even the Earth's crust and tectonic plates, of which they are an interconnected part?

Even that idea of the interconnectedness of all things in the universe was a strange notion just a couple of generations ago. Now it is beginning to be accepted by scientists. Visionary Vaclav Havel believes in it as well as the idea of the earth as a mega-organism. Highly respected scientist James Lovelock, in his work GAIA, puts forth the theory that Gaia (Mother Earth) is a living, super-organism, and that man is a dynamic part of that entity. He even speculates that the human collective intelligence may constitute a Gaian nervous system.

If that is so, then the idea of man causing earthquakes with the bad vibes of his mind isn't that far out at all. Then, if we consider physicist John Bell's theory that "all objects and events in the cosmos are interconnected and respond to one another's change of state," and factor in scriptural prophesy that "God's will is to be done on earth as in heaven"--certainly no quakes in heaven--and factor in the prophesy that when the peaceable kingdom comes there will be "no more harm in all the earth," then the premise of man being responsible for the climatic and geological stability of the earth seems even more reasonable.

Sure it's difficult to accept that mankind is responsible for all the natural disasters that occur on this earth. But shouldn't we keep an open mind to that possibility? Certainly the disasters don't just happen by themselves. There has to be some force that causes them. It wouldn't be correct to say that it's just nature, for God is the force behind nature. It is simply not reasonable to attribute them to God, whom we believe has perfect love and justice. It is neither loving nor just to make innocent people suffer. If we eliminate God and "nature" as the cause, it leaves only man. We should keep our minds open to that possibility and then examine what we might do about it. Exploration and research might be appropriate, such as experimenting with millions of minds coordinated in peaceful mind-wave emanation bringing about a change in human behavior as well as that of "nature."

It could be a monumental but not impossible task. Such attempts have been tried before. Groups with thousands of members have undertaken peaceful mind emanation programs to reduce crime in major cities, including Washington, D.C. Although they have claimed some success, it has obviously been minimal. The reason for lack of any substantial change should be obvious: they were vastly outnumbered. Also, such actions have to be carried out with the sincere belief that they will work.

BLESSING AND PRAYER

There is another misconception about the nature of our world--that God alters world conditions and events through his blessing and in answer to prayer. "God bless you." What does that mean? Or "God go with you?" They are generally thought of as requesting of God the special bestowal of divine favor on a particular person or that he personally look out for and protect a person. Does God really do that? I do not believe so.

A great misunderstanding exists as to the nature of prayer and God's blessings. We tend to think that God blesses some more than others, and we don't understand why. When good fortune comes to a good, religiously devout person, we're inclined to think that God blessed him with that good fortune because of that devoutness. If evil happens to an evil person we think that God saw to it that he got what he deserved. But when evil comes to a good person, we can't comprehend how God could have let that happen. Likewise when a perceived Godless individual is blessed with riches and the "good life," we have trouble understanding the seeming injustice of it.

It would seem that either God has to be biased toward some of us or he is impartial. It surely has to be the latter. He does not interfere in our well-being or our ill-fortune. Being omnipotent he could easily do that, controlling all of our actions, making everything right. But then we would not have free will and would not be made in his image. According to scripture, "God gives his sunlight to both the evil and the good, and sends rain on the just and on the unjust as well."10 That is a quality of our world; it is "user friendly" to all equally. God blesses everyone, both the good and the bad, in like manner. He gives us all the material needs as well as the mental and spiritual attributes necessary for us to live comfortable, peaceful and harmonious lives. It is we who determine the quality of that life and the circumstances around us, or others determine those things for us. God is not involved.

But what about prayer? Doesn't God directly intervene in our lives by answering prayer? Millions pray to God, asking him to bring about some change in their own or other's lives. We frequently ask him to intercede in the affairs of the world, bringing an end to war and other atrocities that continually occur. Then, when that change or circumstance comes about, it is believed that God was somehow directly responsible. If it doesn't happen we rationalize God's seeming refusal to answer in various ways: we aren't worthy or what we asked for wasn't good for us. Or he will answer in his own good time, meanwhile testing our faith or perhaps molding and tempering our character by tribulation. Or the catch-all phrase, "God's ways are not our ways," is sometimes used.

Consider the times we called on God for something in our time of need and didn't seem to get an answer. Most of us know a situation in which a devout person has had to endure difficulties and suffering although many prayers had been offered to God to relieve the situation. How often have prayers gone out to God to stop wars and do something about the senseless slaughter, or to intervene on the behalf of children who are in perilous situations, only to see the carnage and killing continue or the children suffer and even meet with an untimely and unpleasant death? How can we possibly believe that God, who is perfect in love, mercy and justice, could refuse to answer, for any reason, a prayer to relieve the terrible suffering of the children of the world? According to our concept of prayer, he has refused, regardless of the rationalization!

The most common perception is of an omniscient, omnipotent God sitting in heaven, listening to the millions of prayers that are uttered by a few billion people, hearing them all, perhaps categorizing them according to their urgency and validity, deciding which ones he is going to answer, based on we know not what, and then "pushing the right buttons" to bring about a solution to the problem. Or some believe that God answers prayer by sending angels to resolve the issue. That is all a misconception.

Prayer is answered, but not in the way we think. Our not understanding our own nature and underestimating the power of our minds has resulted in this misconception. It is man himself, with the help of God, who brings about change by prayer. The key as to how that is done is given to us in scripture. We are told that whatever we ask for in prayer, *believing*, we will receive it.11 It is something we do, the believing with the mind, that is the primary factor in bringing about results. The thoughts of our powerful mind not only shape our character and behavior but also the circumstances around us to include the bringing to fruition of the things we ask for in prayer.

Belief in prayer is like the placebo effect in medicine. Doctors are puzzled as to why people who are unknowingly given a "sugar" pill, and told that it will help or cure their problem, quite frequently show improvement and are sometimes even cured of their ailment. The answer should be obvious. It is the patient's belief that he will get well that heals. Likewise, it is belief expressed by our powerful mind that brings results from prayer.

James Allen, in his book *As A Man Thinketh*, makes the connection when he says, "The divinity that shapes our ends, is in ourselves, it is our very self. Our wishes and prayers are only gratified and answered when they harmonize with our thoughts and actions."12 The thoughts of our mind in prayer shape our actions, which, in turn, solidify into circumstances. That is how prayer is answered concerning desires for our own welfare. Our prayers aren't answered, and we don't receive what we ask for, for the same reason. While we are praying for something, we are at the same time continually frustrating its accomplishment by thoughts and desires that do not harmonize with what we are aspiring to, the most common being a lack of sincere belief that we will receive it.

Consider the Lord's Prayer, in which millions continually pray for God's will to be done "on earth as in heaven." That prayer is not being answered because there is no belief involved. In the first place, the prayer is a practice in rote; it is most often mindless repetition. Secondly, almost no one really believes that the way things are in heaven, with peace, joy and happiness prevailing, will happen on earth. Rather, they are taught and believe conditions on earth will always be turbulent and continue to get worse until Armageddon finally overtakes us.

Other factors involved in answered prayer are the soul and interconnectedness. That is where the help of God comes in. Our mind, body and soul are intertwined, constituting the totality of our being. Also, the mind and soul are part of the cosmic consciousness, the total field of energy that constitutes everything in the universe. Therefore, all aspects of our being are interconnected with every other being as well as everything. That is how prayer to change "things" occurs. It is how prayer for other people works. The connection is from the thoughts of our mind, through the cosmic consciousness, to the energy, mind and soul that make up other things and people. The soul, the field of energy given from God, can be called upon, by prayer, to aid us in restoring health, growing spiritually, achieving our desires and helping others.

We need to pray properly for it to work. For example, when praying for healing, prayers often take the route of asking God to intervene, then sitting back and waiting for God to take action and the results to occur. That kind of intervention isn't going to be forthcoming. The prayer should be for the healing to take place accompanied by the belief that it will. It is that way of praying, enhanced by continuous and collective use, that will bring results.

Some researchers believe that prayer for others is effective because our minds are non-local--extend beyond our bodies--and are interconnected in some way. But they do not make the jump to say it is done through a universal mind or cosmic consciousness. They think it is too unscientific, preferring to believe that the prayer connection is made through electromagnetic morphic fields of the mind. Of course, that's pretty unscientific, also.

But if we can accept that all of creation is one interconnected, vast field of energy; that we have a mind and a soul that are intertwined yet separate entities of energy; that there is a God, and that he is the creator by reason of his omnipotence and "endless source of energy," then it would seem logical to conclude that the connection is through the universal mind. Further, scriptural testimony that all things are possible with the help of God would lead us to believe that prayer is not accomplished by man alone from one extended mind to another, but through that cosmic consciousness, a universal field of energy created by God.

Controlled research has been performed on both things and people, to provide reasonable evidence of that connection. Two groups of plants in different locations but growing under identical conditions were used in one test. One group was prayed for to the effect that they would thrive and grow rapidly, as well as having thoughts of love directed at them. The other was not. At the end of the test period the group that received the benefit of prayer was taller, fuller and healthier.

Doctor Dean Ornish, in his book *Reversing Heart Disease*, cites research done by Dr. Randy Byrd at San Francisco General Hospital. It was a "Study of 393 patients who were admitted to the coronary care unit during a ten-month period. He arranged for people to pray for 192 of the patients, but not for the 201 others. These two groups were comparable in terms of age and disease severity.

"Doctor Byrd recruited people from around the country to pray for each of the 192 patients. He asked each person to pray every day in whatever form he or she wished. Each patient in the experimental group received daily prayers from five to seven people, although these patients were unaware of this.

"He found that the prayed-for patients suffered fewer complications in three areas: First, only three required antibiotics, compared to sixteen in the control group. Second, only six had pulmonary edema (fluid in the lungs), compared to eighteen in the control group. Finally, none of the prayed-for patients required intubation, while twelve of the others did."13

Doctor Ornish commented that, while this study is small, it suggests that we may be more interconnected than we often realize. Other studies of prayer for things and people show similar findings. Extensive research is currently being conducted, which is already yielding like results. We surely need to change our perception as to the nature of our world.

There has been a great deal of reference to God so far in this text, and even though 90% of the people on earth believe in God or some supreme spiritual being, there is no scientific proof that such a being exists. Is there really a God? Is there any evidence of his existence?

Chapter Thirteen

DOES GOD REALLY EXIST?

At one time or another we all have looked up into the night sky and gazed upon the vastness and majesty of the universe--perhaps pondering the magnificence of it all; perhaps to wonder how many stars there really are. We may have entertained thoughts of the coming morning light, or mulled the concept of night and day.

When we think of this home planet we call Earth and how it rotates on its axis causing night and day, do we really understand the tremendous significance of it? If the Earth did not rotate, one side would be in continuous darkness while the other would always be light, making much of the world uninhabitable. Climates suitable for life would be mainly along the fringes between light and dark.

What makes the Earth continue to rotate at a constant speed without slowing down? Scientists recognize no such thing as perpetual motion. Even if we accept that it was sent spinning into space as the result of some big bang, and even that it is spinning in the giant vacuum of space, it has an atmosphere that causes friction, which would tend to slow the speed of rotation over time. Further, the earth is not a perfect sphere but is irregular, with high mountains and deep valleys and fissures that would result in a wobbling effect, also causing a slowing of the rotation. Obviously some unknown force maintains the constant speed of rotation.

Isn't it amazing that, as we rush through space rotating around that axis at over one thousand miles per hour, we have no sensation of speed? The fact that we are not hurled off into space by reason of the perfect counterbalance of centrifugal force and gravity must surely give you cause to wonder. And what about gravity? We know it exists and what its properties are, such as its force being relative to mass and density, but man cannot create gravity.

More remarkable still is the fact that we are rushing through space in an orbit around the sun, covering 583 million miles each year at a speed of 67,000 miles per hour! Isn't it incredible that the Earth is situated at just the right distance from the sun, creating temperatures and climates suitable to life? Consider the fact that the Earth is tilted on its axis just enough to give us seasons, without which our planet would become vastly different and virtually unrecognizable?

Have you really given serious thought to how this inconceivably ordered universe came to be in the first place? Did it just evolve over billions of years, or was it created? Some say it has always existed and, through evolution, has changed and continues to change over millions of years. Others say it came into existence by chance or accident. Some explain it away with the "Big Bang" theory: "In the beginning, there was not time, no matter, not even space. Then, in some unfathomable way, a universe emerged from a dimensionless point of energy. In the wild first second, the hot, nascent universe inflated to the size of our solar system. At three minutes, the expanding universe became a fusion bomb, synthesizing hydrogen, helium and lithium nuclei from a hot, dense soup of elementary particles."[1]

But these theories raise questions and provide no reasonable answers. Where did the materials, those "elementary particles," come from in the first place? You can't make something out of nothing. What caused that original Big Bang explosion? There was no lightning, no spark. Where did the energy come from? How did that hot, dense soup of elementary particles and the hydrogen, helium and lithium nuclei form into the massive bodies we know as stars and planets, each with its complex composition of gasses, liquids and solids? How did they come to be arranged in those orderly solar systems and galaxies?

Given modern scientific standards, the scientists don't understand the "unfathomable way" or the origin of the "dimensionless point of pure energy" that, they say, caused the universe to emerge. They are getting closer to it though with the Higgs boson "God particle" theory. The Higgs (named after physicist Peter Higgs) being a field that exists throughout the universe. When the boson, perhaps a particle of electrical energy (not matter), passes through the Higgs field, it becomes matter.

Naming that particle of electrical energy the "God particle," they are attributing the creation of matter to God. However, they don't explain how God caused or initiated the particle of electrical energy. I would suggest that the particle is thought (non-matter), the thought of God, which in passing through the Higgs field, becomes matter. The idea of God creating the universe with his thoughts is compatible with scripture, "God only needs to say 'be' and it comes into existence." We humans, created in God's image, can create matter by thought. When we think certain thoughts we create neuropathies (protein molecules). God is much more powerful.

And how do they explain the universal laws of science that hold everything, from the stars to earthly microscopic organisms, in wonderful order and harmony? Explosive creation from nothing and evolution by chance would dictate a universe in disarray and a discombobulation of natural law, resulting in disorder and discord everywhere. When we consider the indescribable magnificence and order of the universe, the marvel of the Earth's rotation, gravity, the Earth's orbit, the changing of seasons and all that these things mean to our very existence, does it really seem reasonable to believe that the universe came into being and evolved by accident or chance?

If we say, "probably not", then was the universe created? And how and by whom? Although it cannot be proved by mathematical calculation or scientific explanation, the evidence of intelligent creation is very convincing. To the scientist as well as the layman, the beauty, wonder and order of the universe seem to indicate a grand design planned by some great architect.

It seems as if there has to be a purpose for everything. Nothing is left to chance. All things are meticulously ordered and intricate in design. We continue to discover how beautifully and mysteriously all things are made, from the magnificent stars to the tiny atom. Scientific laws are universal, controlling and holding together everything in the heavens and on Earth. It not only seems reasonable in our minds, but feels right in our hearts to believe that all things were created by some guiding hand, according to plan.

Consider this marvelous Earth. Where did the oceans come from? What is the unending source of all of that life-giving water which, through the mechanics of evaporation, clouds and winds brings rain to the land on which we grow our food? Did it self-generate from a small puddle? Did all that water appear by accident? Is it just a remarkable coincidence that there is a moon in orbit around the Earth, whose gravitational pull helps create the cleansing tides, without which our ocean shores would be polluted, unattractive and perhaps even uninhabitable?

Think of the amazing symbiotic relationship between plant and animal life. Plants use the carbon dioxide that we exhale and in return help produce oxygen that is essential to sustain all animal life, including the human animal!

Again, is it reasonable to believe that this wonderful congruity and the extraordinarily complex forms of life on earth simply shook out of a dice cup at random? And what of the most complex life form of all--Man? Did we truly evolve from an amoebae to a multi-celled creature, to a fish, to a lizard, to a four-legged land animal, to a two-legged upright mammal, to an ape, and to man in his present form?

Without needing to go into detail about Charles Darwin's *Origin of the Species*, we can say that modern scientists now agree that evolution through natural selection and mutation--the basis of Darwin's theory--is not compatible with evolutionary theories about the earth's beginning. In recent years, the great advancement in knowledge of genes and DNA has caused scientists to estimate it would take about forty billion years for man just to evolve from an ape under the principles of Darwin's theory. And that is many times the Earth's age of 4.5 billion years, as calculated by scientists through carbon dating. So, one part of the evolution theory contradicts another, casting considerable doubt on its credibility.

Further, if we did evolve as Darwin thought, where did the original cell come from? Evolutionists generally say it started from organic molecular materials such as dirt, water, carbon dioxide and perhaps other chemicals. Then through some unknown chemical reaction, caused by sunlight or perhaps lightning (a spark) acting on those chemical components, a molecule was given life.

It is interesting to note that scientists in their modern laboratories under ideal conditions have been trying for years to make life out of organic material and have not succeeded. Even if it were possible to create life from non-living organic material, are we then to believe that a single molecule evolved over billions of years into the incredibly complex form we call the human body?

Let's consider the human body for a moment, particularly the brain, the most complex biological structure known to exist. Among other things, it consists of twelve billion or so neurons or nerve cells, making it a biological computer of awesome capability. Scientists consider it so highly efficient, organized and complicated in design that the latest generation super computers pale by comparison.

Man is unique, and unlike any other living creature. Man is capable of thought, reason, rational choice, love and compassion. Man has a conscience and knows the difference between right and wrong. We possess that ineffable something called "soul." Although the lesser animals possess some of these characteristics, man is the only one who has the capability to develop these traits to the level that allows him to determine his own destiny. Does it seem reasonable that these human characteristics such as soul, conscience, thought and love were produced in the process of evolution?

Evolution cannot be disproved, but neither is there proof that man evolved from an amoeba. The creation and evolution are not necessarily irreconcilable. In reality, it isn't important whether we were made in the process of evolution or created full blown in the form of Adam and Eve. It is only of consequence to those who want to prove their creation beliefs. *How we now deal with our existence as humans is the real issue.* However, as time goes by and man's knowledge increases, in the area of genetics, for example, the evidence does seem to dictate that Darwin and other evolutionists got it wrong about humankind!

If they are wrong, then how did the universe and mankind come into being? When we look upon the splendor and majesty of the universe, the earth's amazingly complex life forms and how they are bound together by order and harmony, it seems logical that such a grand design had to be intentionally created. And if deliberately created, then there must be a creator--a creator whom most of us think of as God.

Most people believe there is a God. Surveys have shown that about 90% of the world's population believe in God, or a supreme being. Some believe through faith, some because it seems reasonable, and some, perhaps, for both reasons. Simple probability demands that the remarkable arrangement of the universe and the awesome complexity of the human body couldn't have occurred by chance in the process of evolution. Our reason and faith tell us that divine order was divinely created.

Faith is believing without seeing. None of us, except perhaps those who have had the near-death experience, has seen God, nevertheless, we believe he exists. We reason with our mind, but some beliefs seem to be instinctive or intuitive. When we see the wonder of a newborn baby, the beauty of a flower, the unsurpassed splendor of the heavens, the power of a storm or mighty ocean waves crashing to the shore, our intuition tells us there must be some supreme being who created all these things. We must almost instinctively acknowledge that somewhere there is something, much greater and more powerful than man, more certain than random chance!

IS THERE A RECORD?

Is there evidence other than the marvelous creation we see with our eyes or what we intuitively feel? Is there perhaps a written record about God and creation? The answer, of course, is yes! We generally call it scripture, any writing or book of a sacred or holy nature. We have the Bible, which includes the Torah, Old Testament and New

Testament. There is the Koran, the Bhagavad Gita, The Tibetan Book of the Dead, The Tao Te K'ing, The Naj Hamadi, the Dead Sea Scrolls and other scriptures, some very ancient. They speak to such subjects as God, creation, life, death, heaven, hell, paradise and salvation.

But are they a reliable record? What is their authority? Aren't they just other books about ancient history? Isn't much of scripture just myth? Scripture most certainly includes history and, likely, myth as well. It also undoubtedly contains the word of God. It is up to us humans to use our minds and common sense to decide which is which. Let's examine the scripture called the Bible. Doesn't it contain stories that couldn't possibly be true, such as Jonah's spending three days in the belly of the whale, then being cast out on the beach, alive and well? Surely the whale's digestive juices would have caused great harm, if not death, to Jonah.

What of Noah and the Ark? The ark was to be 300 cubits (about 450 feet) in length, 75 feet wide and 45 feet high. It doesn't seem likely that Noah and his sons had either the shipbuilding expertise, manpower or time to construct such a vessel, especially one that required special compartmentalization and ramps in a three-story structure, needed to adequately house two of every known species of life. Think of the great animals such as the mastodon, rhinoceros, hippopotamus, water buffalo, polar bear and moose. What of the multitude of other smaller animals and kind within species, such as all the different kinds of snakes? What of the ostrich and all other birds, as well as the insects? It would have been absolutely impossible to house two of every species in such a small configuration as the ark.

What about the matter of food and water for the animals? They were to be in the ark for a very long period of time. Scriptures say Noah, his family and the animals were in the ark for seven days before it started to rain. Then it rained for forty days. After the rain stopped, the "waters prevailed upon the earth for an hundred and fifty days." It took another three months for the waters to recede and another two weeks for Noah to determine that the waters had abated from off the earth.

That would make it about 300 days that they were confined in the ark. That would require a tremendous amount of food. Some of it would have to have been harvested from the animal's original locales. There would have been the need for a large supply of extra animals as meat for the carnivores. Noah would have had to store large amounts of water, as the ark had but one window and one door, which were to be sealed during the deluge, making it impossible to get their drinking water from that source. How did he dispose of the enormous amount of animal waste that would have been created?

Then there are the logistics of gathering the animals from around the world. For example, how did Noah get the Siberian tiger and the polar bear from the far northern regions, the penguin from Antarctica and the ostrich from Australia? How did he determine that he had both a male and female of all the birds and insects?

Where did all that rain come from? God could certainly create more water from his endless source of energy. But he already had established the natural laws of evaporation from the seas and condensation upon the land that brings the rain. As he is immutable, and would not change those laws, it would have been impossible for it to rain enough to cover the earth to a level above the mountains. Continuous rainfall simply would recycle the water from the seas to the land to return again to the sea, never significantly altering the level of the seas. Even if God did decide to change those natural laws, rain would have had to fall at a rate of about 700 feet (not inches) per day to cover the highest mountain! Such a prolonged deluge surely would have pounded and destroyed the ark. How could all that water recede in three months and where did it recede to?

Even if we were to grant that many of the great animals, such as the dinosaurs and mastodons, already had become extinct and God assisted Noah by miraculously transporting the animals from all over the world to Noah's location in the Middle East, and simply created all that water as he created the universe, the logistical impossibility of the rest of the operation renders the story of Noah and the Ark nothing more than myth.

Further, it is unlikely that our wonderfully compassionate, perfect-in-justice God would destroy all of mankind, except for Noah and his family, in such a terrible manner, or in any way at all. Scripture says God did it because the world was full of corruption and violence, except for Noah and his family. But what of the babies and little children? How can a newborn baby be corrupt and violent? It would certainly be unjust for God to destroy them, especially as he says in other parts of the scripture that he places great value on the little children and they are not to be harmed.

Despite these stories and other inaccuracies, the Bible does have credibility. We know it is the biggest selling book in history. It has been accepted by hundreds of millions of people as containing God's word. Despite man's intrusive interference, the Bible's central message remains intact and absolutely trustworthy. It provides us with God's word that shows us how we are to live in this life so as to be right with God and achieve eternal life. Rulers have tried to destroy the Bible. Nations have burned it. Governments have declared it illegal, still it persists. The truths of the Bible are as timeless as they are marvelous. Consider just the one saying, "Do unto others as you would have them do unto you."2 Think of the tremendous impact of that precept if we obeyed God and lived according to it. What a wonderful world this would be!

Intuitive belief, as well as the logic of our mind, tells us that murder, lying, rape and robbery are wrong and that love, kindness and truth are right. That same intuition and reason tells us which words of the Bible are from God and which are of men. We instinctively know that greed, vengeance, killing of people for their land and smashing babies against the rocks are not God's ways, but those of man. We know that showing love, goodness, kindness, caring, compassion and forgiveness to one another, as instructed by the Bible, are truths.

That the effects of living by those truths are good cannot be denied. That message of the Bible can be relied upon implicitly. The Bible does have reliability, authority and credibility. For the reasonable person, it confirms the existence of God. So it is with the other scriptures of the world.

THE NEAR-DEATH EXPERIENCE

We need to examine one more area that provides us with reasonable evidence of God's existence. Although it has existed for centuries, it is only in the last few decades that its study has come to prominence. It is the phenomenon of the "near-death experience."

It is a happening that has provided a great deal of controversy. Extensive research by medical and psychological investigators has resulted in both supporters and critics of the purported encounter with death, an after-life and God. I was among the skeptics. Emotionally, I would have liked to embrace the message of the "experiencers," for who would not want to have "first-hand" evidence of the existence of God and the certainty of an after-life. But intellectually, I had my doubts about people returning from the dead, having met God and experiencing the "ecstatic" joy of dying.

Yet, the idea of it all was highly intriguing, and so I pursued it. After about a two-year period of research--reading all the NDE (near-death experience) literature, attending seminars and talking personally to experiencers--I became convinced of the validity of these encounters.

The experiencers believe in the reality of what occurred to them. They refute completely any other explanation such as hallucination, dreaming, fantasy, influence of drugs, medication, oxygen deprivation, extra-sensory perception, and the like. More and more medical people, who in the past have tended to ignore or disbelieve these stories, are now coming to believe that these happenings are actuality rather than otherwise. Almost anyone who talks to a true experiencer cannot but believe in the validity of what happened to that person.

Researchers found physicians and psychiatrists who, having experienced an NDE themselves, attest to the actuality of the happening. These people are trained and capable of distinguishing dream, fantasy or hallucination from reality. Doctor Melvin Morse, M.D., pediatrician and NDE investigator, and his research team, proved that a person actually needs to die or be near death to have a near-death experience. This finding silenced many skeptics who had said that these events were just hallucinations that any seriously ill patient could have. Doctor Morse went to great lengths to show that "hallucinations resulting from a variety of drugs, psychological phenomena, or physiological stress cannot mimic the powerful experiences of the NDE."3

Doctor Raymond A. Moody, Jr., M.D., Ph.D., and one of the early pioneers in NDE exploration, has said, "If anyone were to research the topic with an open mind, he would be convinced of the reality of the near-death experience."4 In Chapter Eighteen, The Experiencers, I'll provide extensive and more detailed evidence in support of the NDE's authenticity.

Meanwhile, imagine, if you will, a life in which there is no fear of death, life that is serene because death is not a termination of the self, but rather simply a passage from a "here" that is filled with strife, frustration, pain, sorrow, hate and other cares of the world, to a "there" where love is all-encompassing; where joy and love of knowledge are all important.

With the realization of such a future awaiting us, the small concerns of the world cease to be important. In fact, every care and concern becomes a small concern which will be resolved in time, thus allowing a concentration on the things that are truly important: Love of humanity and pursuit of knowing for the betterment of mankind.

People who undergo near-death experiences--that is, a condition that teeters on the brink of permanent death of the physical body-- have returned from that precarious state to report phenomena that are so startling as to present incredible implications.

They have reported being transported out of their body to a point above their corporeal remains, flying up a tunnel of brilliant light, to the presence of beings who emanate light and love. They are then escorted to the presence of a one Being who seems the epitome of all knowledge and love. They are shown every instant of their lives, good or bad, and are made aware of the fact that love of others and pursuit of knowledge for the betterment of this life and eternal life are the two most important things one can do in a lifetime. Then, for a variety reasons, they are returned to this life to continue what is deemed unfinished. They often return with that wonderful sense of complete serenity and a loving spirit.

Hallucination, hoax, mass conspiracy or religious hysteria? How can diverse people of different ages (sometimes children who have no preconceived notion of afterlife), language groups, nationalities, religious affiliation (or lack of it, as some are atheists), all have such consistently similar experiences independently of each other?

It is as if thousands were all to go to a country independently of one another and return to tell you of their journey. No two tales would be exactly alike, but could you, would you doubt the existence of the country just because no two tales matched exactly or because you had no personal knowledge of it, had not seen it and had not been there? Can you see love? No. But do you doubt that it exists? Of course not.

The lives of these experiencers undergo a drastic change. Materialism loses its importance in their lives. They become more spiritual, searching for a right relationship with God and fellow human beings. Almost unanimously they have no more fear of death and express the conviction that there is an after-life and that God does exist.

Critics say that, even so, the near-death experience and the message of the experiencers does not constitute absolute scientific proof of life after death or the existence of God. Technically they would be correct; however, any reasonable person would have to admit that these experiences present very convincing evidence of a life that continues beyond this earthly one as well as the existence of a supreme being. They certainly reinforce that belief already held by most of us and provide food for thought to the doubter! Through the senses of the experiencers, God is almost certainly giving us a glimpse of such wonders as an ethereal world that exists, his ineffable love and the joy of being in his presence.

It is not likely that we will ever "scientifically" prove that there is a God. But what is so sacrosanct about scientific proof? Because we can't examine the evidence under a microscope or prove it mathematically or scientifically, we refute it or ignore it. How foolish to do so! We cannot examine the feeling of love but we certainly know it exists. We can't see gravity, completely examine it or fully understand it, but we are aware of its force and accept it.

To limit our beliefs to only what can be proved objectively is indeed narrow-minded. To paraphrase Shakespeare in "Hamlet", there are more things in heaven and earth than we can dream of. The world, and life, are much more than we can see and prove in the laboratory. Carl Gustav Jung, psychiatrist and psychologist, has said, "We should not pretend to understand the world only by intellect; we apprehend it just as much by feeling."

Besides, it is possible that science has about run its course. Although there are refinements to be made, little of significance may be left to discover that can benefit humankind. Further, a good case could be made that science has adversely shaped us into a materialistic world--a consumer culture in which we strive to gain "things"--thus suppressing our spirituality, that is, enlightenment as to our purpose in life, our true nature, the nature of God and the relationship between God and man. Although science has improved the lot of humankind through convenience, it has certainly caused us considerable grief through such things as the invention of gun powder and weapons. Science has not promoted peace and harmony among humankind, but often strife and discord.

Bryan Appleyard, in his work *Understanding The Present: Science and the Soul of Man,* shows that "Though science has advanced our understanding of the universe and provided us with the toys and weapons of modern civilization, it has failed to answer the ultimate questions: Who am I? Does life have a purpose? Is there a God? What lies beyond death?"5

He argues that "science has changed the world, but not the human condition; that many scientific questions have been answered, but the solutions to life's problems still elude us."5 A better understanding of spiritual matters can answer all of those questions, solve life's problems and change the world for the better! It is time for spirituality to flourish--there is a great deal about it to discover.

Through our "hearts" and minds we need to expand our beliefs, never assuming that we have the ultimate truth, but always searching for knowledge and relying more on the wisdom of the heart--our inner or higher self. We have seen what poet George Santayana has said about that, "O World, thou choosest not the better part! It is not wisdom to be only wise, And on the inward vision close the eyes, But it is wisdom to believe the heart." Unfortunately, we seldom listen to our heart. We are often even hard of hearing when it comes to accepting that which is experienced by our conscious mind.

When we see the wonder and beauty of the universe, the multitude of scriptures that speak of God and hear the extraordinary message of the experiencers, our mind and heart tell us that God does indeed exist. We should believe it! It is important the world acknowledge the existence of God, for a God-less world would be unbearable. If we can conclude that God exists, then what is he really like? What is the nature of God?

—— *Chapter Fourteen* ——
THE NATURE OF GOD

What is God like? Can we really know? Is he a crowned, white-haired, white-bearded, old-looking gentleman sitting on a golden throne somewhere in heaven, as he is often pictured in religious stories? Is he an omnipotent, most-sovereign monarch who rules the universe from on high? Is he surrounded by seraphim and cherubim continually worshipping him, and the angels of heaven singing their never-ending song "Hail to the Chief," as the scriptures imply? Or is he a spirit, as the scripture also says, who can manifest himself in many ways? Is he really omnipotent, omniscient and omnipresent? We can understand that he is all-powerful and all-wise, but how can he be everywhere at the same time?

Is he really a God of vengeance, anger and wrath, as some religions often teach? Or is he a God of love, kindness and mercy? Or can he be both? Are we to believe that all those events of blood, violence and massacre in the Old Testament were either perpetrated by God himself, or by the Israelites because God commanded them to do so? The Christian theologians generally say yes, those are the inspired and infallible words of God. The explanation is that God is just; those people were wicked and deserved to be punished and so God destroyed them, either by the swords of men, or by his own hand.

Did God himself really destroy the Pharaoh and his soldiers in the Red Sea as they were pursuing Moses and the Israelites who were fleeing Egypt, as the Bible records? Is it possible that God told Joshua to go into Ai, a city of 12,000 inhabitants, and "Kill every man, woman and child, but you can keep the cattle and the spoils?" Or that he told Moses to kill all the Midianite males but could keep the virgins? Were the babies and little children in Ai also wicked and deserving of being slaughtered? Is it possible that God would condone all that killing? The Church would say yes, because of the sins of their fathers. What absolute nonsense!

The Church goes to great lengths to try to explain these terrible atrocities. Christian dogma cites Adam and Eve in the Garden of Eden. How, through the "fall"--that is, because of Adam's and Eve's disobedience to God--they became sinners and, subsequently, all their progeny are innately sinful from birth. Hence, all children are sinners, as well as having the sins of their fathers visited upon them. But, in establishing such doctrine, the Church completely ignores God's word in the scripture, which says, "The son shall not bear the iniquity of the father."[1]

The Christian Church also ignores the word of the one they call Lord and Master, Jesus Christ. He said, "Anyone who has seen me has seen the Father."[2] St. Paul, whose writings are the foundation of much of Christian doctrine, also expresses the same likeness between God and Christ when he speaks of the "Glorious gospel of Christ who is the image of God."[3] As an important aside, it should be noted that we also are the image of God, being "made in his likeness." Those two statements by Christ and Paul make it clear that our recognition of Christ, his life and his qualities, is a recognition of God.

Christ was kind, patient and forgiving. He neither killed nor harmed anyone. Some say that isn't so, that Christ was not exactly a "peacenik," citing his whipping and driving the money changers from the temple. When one examines that story, it appears likely that it never took place. The sales in the temple were taxed by the government, an important source of revenue. Government guards were posted at the temple. It is not likely that they would allow a lone person to disrupt the business in the temple.

Christ said, "Not only are we not to kill, but we should not get angry with one another without cause, or we shall be in danger of judgment." He healed the sick, had compassion on the multitudes and fed them. He cared for people and comforted them. He truly loved his neighbor as himself and forgave others. He said that God puts great store by the children, and woe to them that harm the little ones! Therefore, that is what God is like. He is loving, good and compassionate beyond our understanding. How then could God in any way be responsible for those evils portrayed by the Old Testament? He could not be and was not responsible!

A wise man once said that it appears that man has made God in man's image. We have most certainly done that, making God a person with human visage and even implying that he has human frailties such as our often-displayed tendency toward anger, vengeance and violence. That is what our forefathers in the Old Testament surely indulged in. They were cruel and vengeful. They plundered the goods of their enemies and massacred them. So, to excuse themselves, their leaders said, "Our God is a vengeful God, he has destroyed our enemies, or God commanded us to do this." And so it was recorded. Those massacres of men, women and little children indeed may have occurred, but certainly not by or at the command of God!

God does not change; he does not alter the rules as the game of life goes along. Surely his omniscience would preclude establishing rules that needed to be altered at some later date. He is constant and immutable, as most religions teach. God gave his people the Ten Commandments, one of which is "Thou shall not kill." How, then, could God, who is unchanging, do an about-face and tell his people to kill their enemies? How is it possible to justify that Old Testament violence, supposedly at the behest of God, with God's instructions, given in later scripture, that we are to love our enemies, do good to them that persecute us, return evil with good, turn the other cheek, and don't worry about those who can kill the body but not the soul? We cannot make that justification and, therefore, must conclude that the Old Testament characterization of God as angry and vengeful is the errant word of man.

The commandment "Thou shall not kill" has never been qualified by God. There are those who would disagree, quoting the proverb, "He who lives by the sword, shall die by the sword." Obviously, that is an untruth, for we know there are those who lived by the sword but did not perish that way, some even dying peacefully in their bed. It was undoubtedly formulated by men as justification for killing each other. That proverb is often used to support the death penalty. But we should ignore it because it contradicts an unqualified commandment from our immutable God that we are not to kill, which is then reaffirmed by Christ in the New Testament.

Throughout time, religion and men have distorted God's word and gone to great lengths in order to justify killing. St. Paul said "God put all governments in power and their ordinances are to be obeyed without question." That and other scripture, of similar nature, is often used by religious fundamentalists to support the death penalty for criminals, as well as to justify war. Further, Paul says that "those who disobey a government ordinance are disobeying God and shall be damned." He said that "rulers are ministers of God." Did God put Hitler and Stalin in power and were they ministers of God? Clearly, we can see how wrong Paul was.

Martin Luther, who was sometimes referred to as a "second Paul," took the same position as St. Paul, with even more explicit statements of how God is responsible for wars, killing and governments. He said, "For the very fact that the sword has been instituted by God to punish the evil and protect the good and preserve peace is proof, powerful and sufficient, that fighting and slaying and the other things war-times and martial law bring with them, have been instituted by God. What else is war than the punishment of wrong and evil? Why does anyone go to war, except because he desires peace and obedience? Although slaying and robbing do not seem to be a work of love; therefore, a simple man thinks it not Christian to do, yet in truth even this is a work of love. By way of illustration, a good physician, when a disease is so bad and so great that he has to cut off a hand, foot, ear, eye, or let it decay, does so, in order to save the body."[4]

That's rather faulty thinking, wouldn't you say? Even in his own time, the untruth of his logic was clearly evident. No matter how one twists it, robbing can never be a work of love. Slaying can be an act of desperation or self-defense or even self-righteousness, but never an act of love! When one kills in service to one's country, or in defense of one's loved ones, such as an intruder in one's home, it can be an act of self-defense or survival or vengeance, but never love. Killing for any reason cannot be an act of love! To compare slaying and robbing to a physician who cuts off a decayed limb to save the rest of the body, as Luther does, is a poor, if not completely illogical, analogy.

More often than not, in war, it is not the corrupted flesh that is killed, but rather the whole and clean. In many wars it is the leaders that are unjust, yet they survive and stay in power. It is the people, the old men, the women and the children, and many soldiers who were forced, against their wishes, to fight who are the good and just, yet they are the ones who are maimed and killed by the thousands. And often because of the terrible destruction to a country's infrastructure, thousands more of the just and good, the children, die from starvation and disease. What horrible injustice brought about by supposedly "just war." What a terrible desecration of God's creation! Surely, it's blasphemous to say that God institutes war!

Look at the horror of the Civil War in this country--Father killing son, son killing father, brother killing brother, and Christians killing other Christians. Surely, you can see how absurdly wrong Luther was when he said, "What else is war than punishment of wrong and evil? Why does anyone go to war except that he desires peace and obedience?" Neither peace nor real obedience were threatened in the case of the Civil War. And neither side was more or less wicked than the other. What disrespect for God Luther showed when he said that war, killing and robbing can be acts of love and are instituted by God!

Taken in, along with other false perceptions of God, is the mistaken notion that God is in control of this world and causes all things to happen, both good and bad; that he is responsible for all governments, wars, murder, famine and all misery that occur to mankind on earth. Or that he allows these things to happen perhaps as a lesson, perchance as punishment or for some reason unknown to us. None of that is so. God is not in control of this world. You can be sure that if he were, things would be peaceful and orderly.

God created this earthly paradise for us and put us in charge. He gave man control of the earth. He said we are to have "dominion over all the earth."5 We are to "subdue it."6 Yes, man rules the earth, and that is why all the distress, injustice and tragedies occur. That is "why bad things happen to good people." They are the results of man's failure to listen to God and his prophets, or perhaps even his desire to follow false prophets. He gave us all the rules and guidelines we need to live in peace and harmony, making this world a paradise, but we refuse to accept them, obey them and live by them. Instead, we give governments power, such as the power to kill, and follow their ordinances even when they contradict God's instructions. We have organized ourselves into divisive religious sects establishing doctrine that causes suspicion, discord and even hatred, violence and death. We have "trampled the laws of God" for the sake of false religious beliefs and tradition.

We have based the misconception of God being in control of our world on the errant writings of such men as St. Paul and Martin Luther, meanwhile ignoring the fact that God has told us in the scripture that we are in control of this earth! It is surely God who makes the "world go round" and God who is the force that gives life to the earth and its inhabitants, but mankind is the caretaker. We are in charge and we are responsible! Through false, man-made religious doctrine, we have made God what he is not and blocked perception of what he really is.

If God is not a person with humanoid countenance, then of what form is he? We need to think of God in terms of spirit rather than possessing human form and attributes. God cannot be classified by gender, but is simply spirit. The scriptures clearly tell us that, "God is a spirit and in spirit shall ye worship him."7 Spirit is defined as a supernatural being, the breath of life that animates or gives life to all organisms. God is a living entity, the supreme primal being, in spirit form, who is the origin of all that is. He is the ordering force of everything that exists. He is a never-ending source of energy from which the universe flowed and continues to do so!

He forms the stars and planets and places them in their galaxies and orbits. He is the force of gravity and the dynamism that keeps the earth at a constant speed of rotation. Scripture says, "It is only the spirit that gives life."[8] God, the spirit, is the force that gives life from seed, plant as well as animal. It is most certainly true that, "Only God can make a tree," as Joyce Kilmer has surmised in his poem, "Trees." God is the life force that guides growth of all plant and animal life into the innumerable and varied forms that exist in this world. What imagination God has! What beauty God creates!

Most of us believe that God is the creator of the universe and all living things in the universe, but give little thought as to how he creates. Of course, that's understandable, as we are so little able to envision the way in which a universe, containing millions of galaxies, was created, or even how our relatively small world was made? However, through an understanding of quantum physics and awareness of the basic building blocks of all life and material, we can get a glimpse of the process of creation.

A quantum is the basic building block or smallest unit of anything. At the quantum level, matter comes into being out of something that is not matter. Physicists know that matter, such as a molecule, can come into existence from thought or intelligence. For example, neuro-peptides in the human body spring into existence when we think certain thoughts.

When we see a block of cement or steel, we think and speak of them as solid and motionless. But through an understanding of quantum physics, we know that isn't so. They are made up of atoms that are constantly in motion, thereby representing energy. As we know that thought is energy, we can reasonably conclude that matter, such as the basic building block, is the expression of intelligence, thought and energy.

We humans can create matter, such as neuro-peptides, by thought. Surely, that is how God creates matter. Remember, we are made in his image. And, as God is all-intelligent and all-powerful, then it is reasonable to believe that he created the universe by intelligent thought and his endless source of energy. Then we can also understand why he is omnipresent, for his energy, his thought, his intelligence, his being, his spirit is present in every atom of everything that exists. The universe is a physical manifestation of God. That also explains why he is omniscient, for being present everywhere, he is aware of all things. Just as scripture says that "not one sparrow shall fall to the ground without God's knowledge."

Note that the quantum concept of how God creates is supported by Taoist scripture. "Not visible to the sight," which correlates with God as spirit. "It is inexhaustible," means God's energy is endless. "It (Tao/The Way/God) is the Mother of all things" and "It is the beginning of Heaven and Earth" which surely shows that God creates all that is. Koranic scripture is also supportive of God's creative power by means of intelligence, thought and energy. "God only needs to say 'be,' and it comes into existence."

Spirit is thought of as an invisible force such as consciousness or essence. We think of it as the principle that animates the body, giving us life. The scripture declares that "God is spirit,"9 and "only the spirit quickens (gives life)."10 Therefore, we can conclude that it is God who gives life to humans. Is it not also reasonable to conclude that he is the creator of all matter? Although physicists acknowledge that matter, at the quantum level, comes into being out of something that is not matter, they are reluctant to take that last step and identify the something, the intelligence, as God. There is nothing else that it could be!

Quantum physicists also accept the concept that the universe is "nonlocal." That is, all objects and things in the universe, such as people, animals, trees, the earth, the atmosphere, the planets and stars are not separate entities, but are all an integral part of the whole. It is a theory, postulated by physicist John Bell, that "all objects and events in the cosmos are interconnected and respond to one another's change of state."11 British physicist David Bohm speculates, from a scientific viewpoint, that there is an "invisible field that holds all of reality together, a field that possesses the property of knowing what is happening everywhere at once."12 As we believe that God is the creator, then it is certainly logical to conclude that the "interconnectedness," the "invisible field" and the "something" from which matter springs into existence, is simply God the spirit, the intelligence, the thought and the energy that have created all that is and holds it together in perfect order and harmony!

Surely that concept of creation of the universe is more reasonable and credible than believing the universe emerged from a speck of nothingness as the scientists have postulated with their theory of the Big Bang. When we observe the orderliness of the universe with all the natural laws that govern its order, it would seem logical to believe that some intelligence designed and created it. It is certainly more believable than the concept that all that "primordial soup" somehow formed itself into the orderly systems and galaxies that make up the cosmos. The universe may have begun with a "Big Bang" as the scientists have theorized. But it was God that was the "spark," the "unfathomable way" in which the universe emerged. He is the energy source of the hot, dense primordial soup of elementary particles, from whence all of the universe has come.

When the scripture says that God is spirit, it also says, in "spirit shall you worship him."13 What does it mean to worship God in spirit? Are we to bend the knee and bow the head to this God-king in heaven, aggrandizing his name, extolling his virtues and continually giving him praise and compliments? Does our repetitive pious prayer please God? Is God really pleased with that kind of worship? It is not very likely!

Worship means to give honor, respect, high regard, love and obedience. To worship God, then, is to give him deep respect, reverence and love. To worship God is to obey him. As God is spirit, being present everywhere and in all things, then to worship God in spirit is to show respect, regard and love for all of creation. When we love our neighbor as our self, living in peace and harmony with one another, as well as our environment, we are honoring and showing reverence to God and only then is he pleased with our worship!

When we "feed the hungry, give drink to the thirsty, shelter the homeless, take care of the sick, visit those in prison" and generally take care of one another, then are we properly worshipping God, showing him love and respect. For God said, "When you do these things to one another you do them unto me."[14] The Christian Church teaches that those are the words of Christ speaking of himself as king and God. Scripture does attribute those words to Christ, but what we must remember is that Christ said on three occasions that he was not telling us his own words but what God had told him to say.

Because God is omnipresent, then we need to reexamine our perceptions of people, places and things. The lowly, homeless street urchin is just as holy and as much to be respected as any church or government official. Also scripture tells us that "God is no respecter of persons."[15] Status doesn't count with God; none of us is more or less important to him than another. Your home is as sacrosanct as any church; God is just as present in the shack in shantytown as in the greatest cathedral. Ancient relics have no more significance to God than modern things. God cannot be pleased when humans fight and kill one another over places and things that they designate as "holy." Surely human beings, made in God's image, are more precious to him than a place or a thing!

What is the true nature of the human being? Is it truly human to err? Are we flawed, poor sinful beings whose nature it is to cause all the hell that goes on in the world as religion often teaches us? Or are we magnificent, sentient beings who are masters of our own destiny, who can control circumstances along the road that leads to it?

──── *Chapter Fifteen* ────
THE NATURE OF MAN

Are we no more than a bag of water and bones; a mortal "assembly of nerve cells and their associated molecules," as some contend? And when that "assembly" disintegrates in death, is that the end? Or is there more to us than just this physical, mortal body? What do we know about the nature of the human consciousness? We usually think of it in terms of the physical body and/or in abstract terms such as awareness, intellect, thought, mind and perhaps soul or our true spiritual self. One near-death experiencer has said, "Know this, that we are not our body." In that we are more than just the body, that is true. However, our true being is mind, body and soul. They are the sum total of our being.

Most of us believe that we are both body and soul. We know the physical body dies and have reasonable proof that the soul does not. The scriptures of almost all religions speak of this arrangement. For example, the New Testament of Christianity speaks of the body and the soul. It says don't fear those who can kill the body but not the soul. Jesus Christ said to the thief on the cross next to him, "Today you shall be with me in paradise."1 That could only have been possible if their souls separated from their physical bodies which were to die and be buried.

Islamic scripture has many references to the body and the soul. "Do not say that those slain in the cause of God are dead. They are alive, but you are not aware of them."2 The Koran says, "He sends forth guardians who watch over you and carry away your souls without fail when death overtakes you. Then are all men restored to God, their true Lord."3

The scriptures of the Eastern religions such as Hinduism, Buddhism and Taoism are replete with references to the soul of man that does not die but lives forever. It is a belief that is almost universal in the Orient. The Bhagavad Gita, epic scripture of the Hindus, speaks of the soul as indestructible and eternal.4

The Tao Te K'ing, written sometime before 500 B.C. by Lao-tze, the founder of Taoism, speaks of the creator of the heavens and the earth and how all the souls that he also created shall live forever: "There is something which existed before Heaven and Earth. Oh how still it is, and formless, standing alone without changing, reaching everywhere without harm. It appears to be everlasting. Its name I know not. To designate it, I call it Tao. How unfathomable is Tao! All things return to it. Not visible to the sight, not audible to the ear, in its use it is inexhaustible.

"Tao produces all things; its Virtue nourishes them; its Nature gives them form; its Force perfects them....It is the beginning of Heaven and Earth....it is the Mother of all things....He who acts in accordance with Tao, becomes one with Tao. Being akin to Heaven, he possesses Tao. Possessed of Tao, he endures forever."5

Take note of how the scriptures are in agreement. The New Testament says, "Don't fear those who can kill the body but not the soul." The Bhagavad Gita, in beautiful prose, says of the soul, "It is ancient, constant, and eternal, and is not slain when this its mortal frame is destroyed." The Koran says the soul is restored to God, and the Tao Te K'ing tells us that all things return to it (Tao/God).

How is it possible for any reasonable person to deny the existence of man's soul, that it never dies but lives forever and is eventually restored to its creator? Surely we must conclude that man's essence consists of both body and soul! And because man's soul is eternal, then it must be acknowledged that we are immortal. Would not a greater awareness of that result in a change of our ways so that we live and act in accordance with what God expects of us?

THE PHYSICAL BODY AND THE CONSCIOUS MIND

What are the characteristics and qualities of these separate, yet intertwined, entities we refer to as body and soul? We know the physical body quite well, but not completely. Through the medical wonder of ultrasound, we observe it almost from conception, monitoring its progress in the womb. We are well acquainted with the birth process, see the child grow to maturity and then watch the body decline into old age. How familiar we are with death; yet still do not understand it and look upon it with fear and even loathing, when we should not.

One obvious capability of the physical body and the conscious mind is the capacity for incredible wickedness. Throughout history predators, autocrats and tyrants such as Stalin and Hitler, as well as others closer to home, have inflicted terrible cruelty on humanity. Look at the carnage in this country from crime, and the violence in the Middle East due primarily to religious differences. Consider the frenzied manslaughter that took place in Rwanda generated by political and racial differences.

Think about what has happened in Bosnia-Herzegovina. The ethnic cleansing of the Bosnian Muslims by the Serbian Christians is a prime example of the hatred and violence brought about because of religion, as well as vengeance for what the Muslims did to their forefathers five or six decades ago. Of course, the Muslims there are not innocent either, perpetrating similar atrocities against the Serbians.

You could ask both the Christian Serbs and Muslims if it isn't better to be kind than cruel. I'm sure they would all agree. The Serbs would say that they believe in Christian values such as forgiveness. The Muslims would agree their religion teaches that they must do good and forgive, so as to achieve paradise. Most would probably agree that it would be foolish to hold someone responsible for something that their great grandparents did sixty years ago.

Yet, there they were, completely ignoring all those things they say they believe in; killing and maiming one another, even the children. Isn't a person a hypocrite if he or she doesn't practice what they believe? They would probably agree with that, too. The problem is that they, like most people, don't understand the power of the mind. They believe in love, kindness and forgiveness, but those kinds of thoughts are held in the mind only fleetingly. The thoughts of anger, hatred and vengeance are dominant and therefore control their actions. It is those kinds of mental seeds out of which chaos grows.

In Somalia, men greedy for material wealth and power, systematically withheld available food, starving their fellow human beings to death. During one period, one thousand children were dying every day from starvation in Somalia. Around the world, hundreds of thousands of our children are dying every year from the effects of lack of food.

Think of those thousands of homeless children in the streets and sewers of the big cities of Brazil who have to steal from the merchants in an effort to stay alive, and then must evade the gunmen whom the merchants hire to hunt them down and exterminate them like rats! What monstrous human cruelty and injustice! How can governments allow these things to happen?

How do we explain all the evil that humans inflict on one another? Christian Church dogma says it is the result of the innately sinful nature of man. In the 16th Century, the secular and religious authorities of Europe established the Augsburg Confession, which has declared that "Since the fall of Adam all men who are born according to the course of nature are conceived and born in sin. That is, all men are full of evil lust and inclinations from their mothers' wombs and are unable by nature to have true fear of God and true faith in God. Moreover, this inborn sickness and hereditary sin is truly sin and condemns to the eternal wrath of God all those who are not born again through Baptism and the Holy Spirit."

Luther characterized humankind as such, "There is not one iota of goodness in man, but only evil and darkness exists in the heart of man." This is the basis of much of Christian doctrine; that man is corrupt and depraved, and can do nothing by himself to change that condition. It is only through belief in Jesus Christ as Savior and Redeemer and the power of the Holy Spirit that man can do good.

Christian theologians cited the scriptures as justification for the doctrine concerning the depraved nature of man. They began with the story of Noah and the Flood wherein God said he was going to "destroy all living things upon the earth, both man, and beast and the creeping thing," because "all flesh had become corrupt....because of the wickedness of man....every imagination of the thoughts of his heart was only evil continually."6 Can we see the error and contradiction there? If all flesh had become corrupt, there had to be a time when it was not corrupt.

It could not be that God was talking about all men being corrupt since Adam's Fall in the Garden of Eden, for the book of Genesis says that God had "respect for Abel,"7 the son of Adam. Certainly God would not respect him if he were corrupt, wicked and evil continually! What of Noah himself, whom the scriptures say, "was perfect in all his generations," and of whom it is said that God "found no fault with Noah?" Also, what of the animals? How was it possible for them to become wicked and corrupt?

But if all of this is true; if the decree of the Augsburg Confession that all men are full of evil lust and inclinations from their mothers' wombs is factual; if Luther was right and if all the scriptural references to man as abominable, filthy, lascivious and wicked are the literal, infallible word of God, then that explains Hitler, Stalin, Rwanda, Bosnia-Herzegovina, Somalia and all the other carnage that man commits around the world, doesn't it?

But wait! What about all the empirical evidence that supports the ability of man to do good without the benefit of Christian beliefs? If man has only evil and darkness in his heart, as Luther says, is lustful from conception as the Augsburg Confession decrees, and can overcome that condition only through the enabling relationship with Christ, baptism and the power of the Holy Spirit, why is it that non-Christians can live good, decent lives? According to Christian doctrine about the nature of man, non-Christians, being evil and corrupt, without having been baptized, without faith in Christ or belief in the Holy Spirit, can live only wicked and immoral lives. There can be no good, decent people other than Christians!

But we know that is utterly false, don't we? Most of us personally know, or know of, a number of non-Christians, such as Muslims, Buddhists and Hindus, or perhaps even atheists who are wonderfully good, kind, worthy and respectable human beings, perhaps more so than many Christians we know.

Even entire non-Christian societies live in the spirit of God's instructions to show love and do good to one another; sometimes much more so than Christian societies. We all know of the immorality, corruption, violence, killing, child abuse, drug abuse and indifference that is occurring in our country, a nation that counts itself as being 84% Christian. Why do you suppose that is? Most Christians are not aware of the fact that in Tibet, a nation that is almost 100% non-Christian, kindness, goodness, peaceful demeanor, caring and brotherly love have greatly subdued all of these terrible wrongs.

Although most Buddhists have not been baptized, do not believe in the Holy Ghost and know little or nothing about Christ, many live in accordance with his teachings. They believe in and live by the code of love and forgiveness. They believe in living in peace and harmony. They believe in goodness and kindness toward all others. Their philosophy is: "Hatred does not cease by hatred at any time; hatred ceases by love. Let a man overcome anger by love, let him overcome evil with good. If someone curses you, you must suppress all resentment and make the firm determination that your mind shall not be disturbed, and no angry word shall escape your lips. You will remain friendly and kind, with loving thoughts and no secret spite. If then you are attacked with fists, with stones, with swords, you must still suppress all resentment and preserve a loving mind."8

Not only do Buddhists believe these things, most practice and live by them. You may have noticed their credo is remarkably similar to the instructions Christ gave to us: "Love your enemy; do good to them that curse and revile you; don't get angry with your brother; turn the other cheek and love one another." All Christians should ask themselves and their pastors the following question. Given the Christian teaching that all men are evil and corrupt and can only live decent honorable lives through baptism, faith in Christ and belief in the Holy Spirit, how then do the non-Christian Buddhists do so? When you come up with the correct answer, then will you understand the nature of man, comprehending, finally, why Christians can commit atrocities and why non-Christians can do good! You will find that it has nothing to do with the dictates.

What of the preponderance of scriptural evidence that belies Christian doctrine regarding the depraved and innately sinful nature of man? Why were Noah and his sons saved after God had declared that he was going to destroy all men because all flesh had become corrupt?

If we examine the scripture with an honest and open mind, the answer is quite clear. Noah found grace in God's eyes because "Noah and his generations were perfect; Noah walked with God." That can only mean that Noah walked in God's ways and his actions were pleasing and acceptable to God. The Good News Bible says in Genesis that, "Noah had no faults and was the only good man of his time, he lived in fellowship with God."

Farther along in Genesis, God says to Noah, "I have found that you are the only one in all the world who does what is right." In the King James Version of that message, God tells Noah that he "sees Noah's righteousness." This does not mean that Noah had never done anything wrong. It means Noah obeyed God and lived in accordance with his instructions. And, if he did fail, he repented, expressed his sorrow for the wrong he had done, turning again to God's ways. Noah was thus considered perfect in God's sight.

The theologians and ministers like to quote Psalm 51:5 to support the doctrine of original innate sin where King David says, "Behold, I was shapen in iniquity; and in sin did my mother conceive me." They took that out of context, just as they did in the matter of Noah. They completely ignore David's following words which belie the doctrine of original sin and total corruption of man.

After David had sinned by coveting Bathsheba, the wife of Uriah, he said to God, by way of penitence, "You desire truth in the inward parts."9 How could there be truth in the heart if there was total depravity there? David goes on to say, "Purge me with hyssop, and I shall be clean; wash me, and I shall be whiter than snow."9 He asks God for a clean heart and a right spirit.

Clearly then, David expected to be pure in heart again. How was that to be accomplished? He couldn't be washed pure as snow by the blood of Christ, as the ministers like to say, because that blood hadn't been shed yet. He couldn't be clean and pure simply by believing in the promise of a savior and shed blood, because David couldn't possibly have understood the cross and Atonement as it is taught by the Christian Church today. The only possible way for David to be "clean" again would be to have a change of heart, turn from his sin, return to God's ways and obey God. David even says that he will then "teach transgressors God's ways, and they will be converted."9

In saying that man is totally corrupt, the Church dismisses, even denies Jesus Christ when he says "Blessed are the pure in heart."10 They explain those words of Christ by saying we are pure in heart when we believe in and accept the crucified Christ as our savior. But that is not a valid premise, for according to Christian dogma, Christians are still innately sinful even after acceptance of Christ; there is still sin in their hearts. But Christ says there are those who are pure in heart. Where there is purity of heart there can be no sin and certainly not depravity or corruption.

The empirical and scriptural evidence that man has the ability, of his own volition, to do good as well as evil, is overwhelming. From life's experiences, we know that we are capable of extraordinary goodness. Witness the many who have dedicated their lives to helping others. Look how people respond automatically in times of crisis, particularly when another person's life is in jeopardy. In times of natural disaster, wide concern is shown for the welfare of those involved through an outpouring of support in the way of money, food, clothing, medical supplies and prayer. Man is even willing to give up his own life that others might live--his sacrifice not being guided by his religious persuasion.

It is clear that man's wickedness is not innate, but rather learned.

The Church acknowledges that sin is willful disobedience to God. It is not possible for a new-born child to be willfully disobedient to God! To say that newborn babes or little children are lustful, wicked and depraved is ludicrous. The Christian doctrine of "original sin" is badly flawed. The Church teaches that Adam disobeyed God in the Garden of Eden, and as a result of that "sin," Adam caused mankind's great "fall" from God's grace. Because Adam sinned, we as descendants are all sinful from the moment of our conception. Not one of all mankind is righteous. We can only be rescued from that fallen-from-grace condition by God's punishment of Christ for our disobedience. St. Paul claimed that "through one man, Adam, all men have fallen from God's grace and are damned to hell by God; and only through one man, Jesus Christ, are all men saved from God's wrath and condemnation."[11] That philosophy is not only errant but quite bizarre!

This means that all people who lived and died before Christ appeared as a savior were not rescued from their fallen-from-grace condition. They died in their sinful state and are all damned to hell and eternal punishment by God. Are we to believe that our wonderful, loving God condemns his people to eternal hellfire by reason of ignorance of Christ? That cannot be. God certainly wants us to do what is right and good, but he doesn't condemn us to hell and eternal punishment if we fail. Throughout the scriptures, through all the prophets and in the Gospel, through Christ, God continually told the people to cease their wrongdoing, obey him, do what is right and good, and they would become righteous and live in his good graces again.

All the prophets were counted as righteous by God. In Genesis, we saw that Noah was righteous and God found no fault with him. There are numerous references throughout the Old Testament to those who were righteous with God--Abraham, Moses, Elijah and David, to name a few. The New Testament speaks of many a righteous man who longed to see the time of Christ. To declare that all men have fallen from God's grace and that none is righteous even contradicts Christ himself who spoke of the "righteous" and the "pure in heart" and who said that he didn't "come to save the righteous but the sinners."12

Think further about that notion of original sin. According to Christian teaching, God told Adam and Eve they could eat the fruit of all trees in the garden except from one specific tree in the center of the garden. Came the devil in the guise of a snake, carried on a conversation with Eve and convinced her it was okay to eat the fruit that God had forbidden. She partook and gave it to Adam as well. Now God had created Adam and Eve in perfection, but the instant they ate the fruit, they lost that perfection, and sin became innate in their character. Then all descendants of Adam and Eve were born in that imperfection with their character sinful and unclean.

Let's analyze what supposedly occurred in the Garden of Eden. God had created man and woman in perfection and placed them in a garden of paradise. He wanted them to remain perfect. Yet, knowing that his creation was subject to temptation, he planted a tree in the garden whose fruit, when consumed, would instantly turn his creation into an imperfect being. Most of us would have left that tree with its debilitating fruit out of the garden. It's strange that God didn't think of that.

But let's go on with this myth. Then God, who is omnipotent and could have barred the devil from the garden, made another mistake and allowed the devil access to paradise. Perhaps he forgot, or didn't recognize, the devil in that disguise as a snake. Then there is the miracle of a snake that could talk, even though it didn't have the physiological features required to form speech. What about those amazing magical properties of the fruit that, once eaten, could turn a perfect, sinless human being into an innately sinful being?

To top it all off we find that God was negligent and uncaring. Being as powerful as he is, it would have been a simple matter to reverse man's imperfection and start over, rectifying his mistakes with the poisonous fruit and allowing the devil to accost Eve. But he didn't, and thus let the process of "original sin" proceed so that all of humanity would sin, requiring him to damn them all to hell and eternal punishment until he came up with some plan of redemption.

Surely, anyone can see how foolish the concept of original sin is! It demeans God, depicting him as a bumbling, inefficient, even cruel creator. Of course God is none of those things, as we all would agree. Whether metaphorical or reality, the Garden of Eden and the Christian interpretation of the events that transpired there, when seriously analyzed, raise questions about the validity of that Christian doctrine. As God is perfect and could not possibly concoct such a flawed plan, we can only conclude that the Christian teaching of what happened in the Garden of Eden, as well as the concept of original sin, is errant and that man is not innately sinful. It is most likely that the Garden of Eden and the events that happened there were simply a story of disobedience to God, an exercise of free will by man to choose either obedience or disobedience.

Adam was created in perfection, but had the free will to choose obedience or disobedience. He chose to disobey God's instructions not to eat of the fruit of that specific tree. We are all created in perfection without the knowledge of sin, but when we are old enough to understand the difference between right and wrong, we have the free will to choose just as Adam did.

To believe and teach that God created us in the learned image of Adam is to desecrate God's creation--man! It is a denial of God's wisdom and omnipotence. Besides, we all know learned characteristics cannot be inherited. God does not create imperfection! We are created without sin; born in perfection, pure and innocent as little children. Later we learn to sin. Through our own conscious thoughts and subsequent actions we have made ourselves imperfect.

Through that same power of mind and thought we can reverse that imperfection and choose to do what is right and good, thereby becoming, once again, righteous with God. This is what God means when he said to get ourselves new minds and hearts; turn from our wrongdoing, do what is lawful and right, and then we shall be right with him. It is called repentance. This is what Christ meant when he said we must be born again and become as little children. Not childish but childlike, pure and innocent. And we don't have to worry if we should fail again, for God will forgive us, if we forgive others, showing love and mercy to one another. That is the true gospel of Jesus Christ.

The nature of our physical self, our conscious being, is quite clear. We are not the inconsistent, inadequate, poor miserable sinner who is, by nature, sinful and unclean, and unable to do anything by himself to change that condition. We are not rotten and depraved, with only evil and darkness in our hearts. Our physical self is capable of both good and evil, with the power to choose to manifest the good and avoid or suppress any tendency to do evil.

There is a very interesting dialogue in John Steinbeck's *East Of Eden* where Steinbeck, in his inimitable way, reflects on man's abilities when it comes to doing what is right and wrong. Lee, Adam's Chinese servant, was engaged in a conversation with Adam and Samuel, telling them about his study of the Old Testament in a group that included some elderly Chinese gentlemen and a rabbi:

"After two years we felt that we could approach your sixteen verses of the fourth chapter of Genesis. My old gentlemen felt that these words were very important too--'Thou shalt' and 'Do thou.' And this was the gold from our mining: 'Thou mayest.' 'Thou mayest rule over sin.'

Samuel said, "It's a fantastic story. And I've tried to follow and maybe I've missed somewhere. Why is this word so important?"

Lee's hand shook as he filled the delicate cups. He drank his down in one gulp. "Don't you see?" he cried. "The American Standard translation orders men to triumph over sin, and you can call sin ignorance. The King James translation makes a promise in 'Thou shalt,' meaning that men will surely triumph over sin. But the Hebrew word, the word timshel--'Thou mayest'--that gives a choice. It might be the most important word in the world. That says the way is open. That throws it right back on a man. For if 'Thou mayest'--it is also true that 'Thou mayest not.' Don't you see?"

"Yes I see. I do see. But you do not believe this is divine law. Why do you feel its importance?"

"Ah!" said Lee. "I've wanted to tell you this for a long time. I even anticipated your questions and I am well prepared. Any writing which has influenced the thinking and the lives of innumerable people is important. Now, there are many millions in their sects and churches who feel the order, 'Do thou,' and throw their weight into obedience. And there are millions more who feel predestination in 'Thou shalt.' Nothing they may do can interfere with what will be. But 'Thou mayest'! Why, that makes a man great; that gives him stature with the gods, for in his weakness and his filth and his murder of his brother he has still the great choice. He can choose his course and fight it through and win." Lee's voice was a chant of triumph.

Adams said, "Do you believe that, Lee?"

"Yes, I do. Yes, I do. It is easy out of laziness, out of weakness, to throw oneself into the lap of deity, saying, 'I couldn't help it; the way was set.' But think of the glory of the choice! That makes a man a man. A cat has no choice, a bee must make honey. There's no godliness there. And do you know, those old gentlemen who were sliding down to death are too interested to die now?"

Adam said, "Do you mean these Chinese men believe the Old Testament?"

Lee said, "These old men believe a true story, and they know a true story when they hear it. They are critics of truth. They know that these sixteen verses are a history of humankind in any age or culture or race. They do not believe a man writes fifteen and three-quarter verses of truth and tells a lie with one verb. Confucius tells men how they should live to have good and successful lives. But this--this is a ladder to climb to the stars." Lee's eyes shone. "You can never lose that. It cuts the feet from under weakness and cowardliness and laziness."

Adam said, "I don't see how you could cook and raise the boys and take care of me and still do all this."

"Neither do I," said Lee. "But I take my two pipes in the afternoon, no more and no less, like the elders. And I feel that I am a man. And I feel that a man is a very important thing--maybe more important than a star. This is not theology. I have no bent toward gods. But I have a new love for that glittering instrument, the human soul. It is a lovely and unique thing in the universe. It is always attacked and never destroyed--because 'Thou mayest.'"

We can indeed consciously choose our course, making the decision to do what is right   and good, rather than that which is wrong and evil. When we do so, cooperating with the perfect uniqueness of our soul, then all possibilities are opened to us.

THE SOUL OR THE SUBCONSCIOUS

What of our other half, our spiritual self, our soul, that which the "sword cannot cleave and which neither fire nor water nor wind can destroy, but which is eternal, unalterable and incorruptible?" What is its nature? What is its relationship to our physical self? What is its purpose? When do we acquire it? We have concluded, and most people believe, that, in some manner, it emanates from God. We have a preponderance of evidence from all the scriptures of the world that it does not die, but survives the death of our physical body and at that time, in some manner, returns to God.

As it emanates from God and is universal, unalterable and incorruptible, as the scriptures say, then it must have God's characteristic of perfection, to include love, compassion, forgiveness and perhaps omniscience.

When the soul separates from the body at the time of the body's death, it appears to retain all the memories, intelligence and experiences of the physical body and mind. During the near-death experience, those who undergo this phenomenon, find themselves out of their physical body usually looking down at it or going through a tunnel and/or arriving in some ethereal heavenly place. At all these times they are aware of every aspect of themselves and their past life, with the exception that they have a new and different type of body. It may be that, at the time of death of our physical body, the mind --that intelligent field of energy that we create--merges with the soul--the field of energy given from God--to form our new spiritual self.

We can then reasonably conclude that the soul, being intertwined in some way with the body and mind, has undergone and taken on all the experiences and development of the physical body and mind. But that does not mean that it has become changed or corrupted by any wrongdoing or bad things that the physical self has chosen to do. It remains unalterable and incorruptible as scripture tells us.

The soul does have very important and vital functions. As scripture says, the soul is invisible and, as such, is spirit. And as spirit, it is of God. The scripture says, only the spirit gives life. When the soul leaves the body, the body dies. Therefore, it is our soul, which flows out from God, in the form of spirit, that gives us life.

We humans are co-creators with God. Man and woman provide the sperm and egg that are the beginning of a human being. God imbues it with a soul that gives it life and guides its growth. Woman nourishes it. Medical science understands the process of conception and the formation of a fetus. But they don't have the slightest clue as to what makes that embryo grow from a fertilized egg into the incredibly complex human body. They generally accept that DNA is the blueprint, the memory that is responsible for how it grows, but still cannot explain the force that causes the cells to divide and form into organs, limbs, blood vessels and the massive network of nerves that constitute the human form.

There has to be an intelligence that does that. That intelligence is God, Brahma, Allah, Tao, the Supreme One, the primordial Being or however we wish to designate the Creator. It is God within us in the form of an intelligent field of energy called our soul, inner self, the Atman, or often thought of as the subconscious. As the Tao Te K'ing says, "God produces all things, he gives them form, he perfects them. Each human body has its own soul which gives it life and guides its growth." So it is with the fetus. The mind of the mother does not know how to form and perfect the human creature that is growing within her. Nor would it be reasonable or logical to believe that the mother's soul guides the growth of the fetus until the first trimester or until birth, at which time the mother's soul leaves the fetus and God imbues it with its own soul. Surely, the fetus has its own soul which guides its development from the moment of conception. But it is likely that the fetus is not aware--it has not yet developed a conscious mind.

In addition to giving the physical body life, the soul has other functions that are indispensable to our total being. Not only does it direct fetal growth, but growth after birth to maturity. Usually through the mechanism of the brain, the soul controls the heart rate, breathing, hunger, thirst, sleep, wakefulness, sexual drive, functions of the liver, kidneys and all other organs, as well as the entire nervous system. It regulates blood pressure, blood-vessel dilation and con-striction, all senses, chemical balance and metabolism.

The human body is an astounding machine without equal. We are indeed magnificent beings. We simply take our bodies and abilities for granted, not realizing how wondrous they really are. The construction of the human body and how it functions is marvelous. It is made up of trillions of cells, which are continually replaced by new ones. Scientists know that we are constantly renewing our cells, thereby creating new bodies. As we breathe we take in atoms that combine with the food we eat and the water we drink, forming new cells in every part of our body. We are constantly being renewed.

Another marvelous facet of our being is the mind. It has generally been misunderstood; where it is located and what it consists of. It is usually associated with the brain, and thought of as originating there. It is considered one entity, yet with two distinct capacities, the conscious mind and the subconscious or unconscious mind. It has been estimated that the conscious mind comprises about twelve percent of the mind, with the subconscious mind making up the remaining eighty eight percent. How anyone could determine such a statistic is a mystery. It has been thought that the subconscious mind is the storehouse of everything we have ever learned and is the part of our mind that controls our behavior. Although it is almost surely associated with the brain, it is not likely that the rest of the above is true.

We cannot know, for sure. However, through modern research, quantum physics and logic, we can draw some reasonable conclusions about the mind. It is believed that the mind is not confined to the brain, but can affect the cells of the body. Our body is a thinking body; all cells having thought receptors and being cognizant of what is introduced into the body both by thought and by physical or chemical means. Scientists know that there are receptors on all cells that receive messages from the thought process. When we think, we cause chemical reactions.

For example, when we entertain the thought of danger, certain cells in the body immediately spring into action and produce adrenaline, which increases the speed and force of the heartbeat and thereby our ability to react more quickly and forcibly to the danger. Adrenaline dilates the airways to improve breathing and narrows blood vessels in the skin and intestine so that an increased flow of blood reaches the muscles, allowing them to cope with the demands of strenuous use.

This is one of the many wondrous functions of the body that the Creator has designed in order to help ensure our survival. That particular function of producing adrenaline is one in which we participate with our conscious mind. There are others that are automatic and of which we are unaware. The body has numerous mechanisms to measure bodily activities such as blood pressure, temperature and changes in chemical composition, brought about, for example, by the ingestion of food. If the body becomes hot, adjustments are automatically made in blood vessels and skin to provide cooling. If cold, the blood vessels contract in order to preserve heat.

Other protective functions of the body involve the ability of the red and white blood cells. If the intake of oxygen is impeded by loss of blood during injury, or because of lung disease or perhaps due to an ascent to high altitude, the brain, having received a signal from the affected areas that something is amiss, immediately notifies the bone marrow to go into action. The marrow, which is responsible for production of the red blood cells, rapidly increases output in order to boost the number of oxygen-carrying cells in the blood. The normal blood cell count is about 5 million per cubic millimeter. In the situation of ascent to high altitudes, the blood cell count, after a relatively short stay, can be as high as 10 million per cubic millimeter.

In the event of injury, the cells at the site of the injury literally send out a call for help by releasing substances which send signals to other parts of the body. The blood vessels expand, allowing a greater flow of blood to the injured area to increase the amount of clotting agent at the site, while at the same time constricting the blood vessels in the immediate vicinity of the severed flesh in order to assist in the clotting efforts. White blood cells, present everywhere in the body, are called to the injured area and, aided by the increased flow of blood to the area, increase their number to more effectively fight any intruders such as bacteria that cause infection; as well, they clean up the fragments of damaged cells by literally engulfing them.

Obviously an intelligence exists within us that is carrying out all these automatic activities without our cognizance. It certainly isn't our conscious mind, for then we would be aware. When we sleep, or should we be in a coma, our conscious mind is not functioning, still involuntary actions such as heartbeat, breathing and functioning of the organs continue unabated. When the soul leaves the body at the time of our "death," all of these automatic functions cease. We can conclude then that it is the subconscious or soul that is the intelligence, the force that is responsible for sustaining our life.

The conscious mind is generated by the physical self. As our bodies grow and expand from birth so it is with the mind. Clearly the newborn infant does little if any thinking or reasoning, obviously because the conscious mind is undeveloped. The babe survives, compliments of the soul, which keeps the body functioning. An example would be the instinct to cry when it is hungry or, perhaps, ill. As the child grows, the mind develops by experience and learning. It stores knowledge in the memory of the conscious mind.

It has been thought that the subconscious mind is the storehouse of everything we have learned, but it is not. All of life's experiences are stored in the memory, a function of the conscious mind. We experienced them with the conscious mind and recall them with the conscious mind. Neither is it the subconscious mind that controls our behavior, as is popularly thought. It is our memories and the thoughts of our conscious mind that determine our actions. Nor can we program the subconscious, through hypnosis, so as to change our behavior. The subconscious or soul never changes but is unalterable and incorruptible, as the scriptures tell us. It is the conscious mind that we program through experience, repetition and memory. When we program it with new experiences or new thoughts, when we change our perceptions, and when we suppress old memories with new ones, then changes in behavior occur.

We have only one mind, the conscious mind. It is an intelligent field of energy that we create, just as the soul is a field of energy that God has created. After all, we are made in God's image; he creates, and we create. We create such things as offspring, music, literature, concepts, neuro-peptides, mind and thought. Our mind is most likely seated in or associated with the brain, developing from childhood as the brain grows, absorbing learning and experience through all our senses which are connected to and coordinated through the brain. When we receive a blow to the head that renders us unconscious, the effect of the blow on the brain causes the mind to dysfunction. A lack of oxygen to the brain can also result in the loss of consciousness. These are reasonable indications of the association of the conscious mind with the brain.

There is indeed a mind-like intelligence that is in every cell of the body. But it is not the mind, either conscious or subconscious. It is our soul, a separate entity, given from God, indestructible, that gives life, forming and perfecting the body, sustaining it through the constant production of new cells. It is the dynamism behind all these involuntary actions such as heartbeat, breathing and other organ functions. It is the life force that knows how to heal.

Although the soul may influence us by means of its intuitive characteristics, what we call "heart," it cannot dominate our physical self but is generally subordinate to the mind. It cannot override the decisions we make with the mind, such as to do wrong. That is the free will that God has given us. Yet, the soul is the master in controlling the vital functions of the body. Although we can vary our breathing and heartbeat with thoughts of the mind, we cannot cause them to cease.

The mind and the soul are two separate entities that possess and control our bodies. The soul is the constant, always working toward our good. The mind is the variable that causes difficulties in our lives, such as illness and lack of well-being. When we get our mind in sync with our soul, then we can enjoy good health and even bliss. In the chapter on health, healing and medicine we will examine how the mind, working with the soul, can produce perfect health and bring about miracle cures.

With our total being we are capable of amazing things. We can accomplish incredible good or great evil. We can make our lives a complete joy or a veritable hell. Humankind can destroy the earth or make it a paradise. How we think about ourselves determines which it will be.

— *Chapter Sixteen* —
AS WE THINK SO ARE WE

Consider a machine so complex and powerful that it can perform millions of calculations per minute. No, not the human mind, but today's super computer. It was invented by the human mind--a mind like yours. A mind like yours invented the airplane and the submarine, and put mankind on the moon. A mind like yours discovered the vaccine for polio and cures for many illnesses.

The human mind has brought forth many things from nothingness into existence, from an idea to an actuality simply through the creative effort of thought. As a man thinks, so is he. It's true when you consider it. In the same manner that a man's thought concerning flight led to the invention of the airplane, our thoughts concerning our self bear similar fruit. For us to decide then, is whether or not the fruit of our thoughts will be bitter or sweet. As we conceive ourselves to be, so we will become by acting upon our thoughts.

If the human mind can put man on the moon, can it not also do so simple a thing as change the circumstances of one's own life? If we think of ourselves as lacking control over our lives it will come to pass because our actions, reactions and expectations will reflect the attitudes we have implanted in our minds. Similarly, if we perceive ourselves in control of our lives and our circumstances, we will act as if it were true and it will become true through our behavior and desires. As the twig is bent, so grows the tree.

Except when oppressed by others or unusual circumstances, we have the means to control all aspects of our lives. We can choose well-being by the thoughts of our conscious mind. Through the blueprint of the human body, God has endowed us with an incredibly powerful mind. But that latent power of the mind is not understood or used by most of us. We refuse to accept God's statement to us that we are "wonderfully and fearfully made" with amazing abilities; even the ability to do miracles. Instead, we accept and believe the words of men that we are innately sinful, basically corrupt and prone to error, and subsequently those characteristics are brought to fruition in our lives.

The scriptures tell us that, "As a man thinketh, in his heart, so is he."[1] What does it mean to "think with your heart?" Also, we often hear the phrase "listen to your heart." We can't think with the muscular organ in our chest that circulates the blood throughout the body, nor can it speak to us. As we think in our heart, means to hold thoughts with deep conviction and determination. For example, if we originate a thought in our mind to make some change in our behavior, then cling tenaciously to that thought, the change will occur. That seems logical, and we generally accept the idea that how and what we think forms the kind of person we are.

But, how is it possible to "listen to our heart?" If, indeed, we can, then there must be something else in our nature besides thought and the reasoning capability of our minds. It wouldn't be conscience, for that can be conditioned. We often think of "heart" as intuition or feeling. Sometimes it is spoken of as the inner self or higher self. Still, all those terms are vague; where does intuition come from and what is the inner self?

It is likely that the soul--the spiritual field of energy given from God, which gives us life and is indestructible--is the inner self, and provides us with those intuitive characteristics. Whatever "heart" is, it and the power of the mind figure prominently in mankind's behavior, well-being, health and salvation.

If you think you are an inadequate and inconsistent person, if you think you are something less than a good person; and if you think that you must experience unhappiness and failure along the road of life, so it will be. But if you think of yourself as a magnificent human being, wonderfully and fearfully made, as God has told you; if you believe you were created in God's likeness with his qualities of love, wisdom, goodness and compassion; if you believe you have the ability to manifest those qualities in your life; if you think you have the capability to live in accordance with God's instructions, and if you think your life can be filled to overflowing with well-being, so it will be! As you think, so are you!

We have noted that James Allen, in his inspirational book, *As A Man Thinketh*, says that, "As a being of Power, Intelligence and Love, and the lord of his own thoughts, man holds the key to every situation, and contains within himself that transforming and regenerative ability by which he may make himself what he wills."

God has said essentially the same thing about his creation, mankind. "You are wonderfully and fearfully made....You are the light of the world....The Kingdom of God is within you (We possess the godly qualities of love, wisdom, goodness, patience, mercy and forgiveness)....You are created in God's image....Get yourselves new minds and hearts....As you think, in your heart, so are you....Be perfect as your Father in heaven is perfect."

God has indeed created us to be truly magnificent beings of spectacular complexity with fantastically powerful minds. By thought and the power of the mind we can, indeed, make ourselves what we will. We can choose good health, happiness and success. We can choose to let our light shine. We can choose to be good, kind and loving to our neighbor. We can choose to "obey and live by every word of God." He has told us we have the ability to do that. We should not doubt him.

With that God-given power, we can stop others and circumstances from shaping our lives. We can take complete charge of our lives. We can embrace the good things in life that lead to happiness and success; choosing good literature, good television fare, good music, healthy and nutritious food and all the things we know in our heart are right and true.

When we implant harmonious, constructive thoughts in our minds, they will bring harmony and happiness into our lives. We should cease to dwell on fear, worry, anger, superstition and false beliefs. Replace them with thoughts of courage, love, truth and God's instructions and we can move onward and upward to peace, joy and abundance. Through the power of the mind and the thoughts that we implant there, we can change any discord, tumult, sadness and hardship in our lives to harmony, tranquility and success.

Great desire and belief are the basic powers that allow you to attain your goals. Conviction must always be deep-seated and believed with all your heart and mind. Half-hearted belief never gets the job done. Sustain a belief whole-heartedly, never giving up, doubting or wavering and your belief and aspiration will be rewarded. The latent powers of the mind are becoming more and more manifest as time goes by and we are coming to understand the workings of the mind and its capabilities.

Thought is simply the process of programming our mind and memory. Both harmful and beneficial mind programming is happening to each of us all the time. It is done by parents, peers, ourselves, the church, television, and in many other ways. Mind programming is essentially the lifelong implantation of data in the memory of our conscious mind. Its simplest form is basic learning, both what is good for us and that which is bad for us. Sometimes it is done haphazardly through life's experiences. Much of the time it is done deliberately, in a structured manner, as in formal schooling or through advertising.

We know that almost all deviant behavior in a society is caused by societal failure to instill proper values, beliefs and behavior patterns in its members. Instilling those beliefs, values and behavioral patterns is nothing but mind programming and it is obvious that we have done, and are doing, a poor job of it in our society. We allow media, television for example, to program the minds of our children with violence, loose sexual morals and bad habits such as smoking, drinking and the consumption of unhealthy foods.

It is no secret that if a child in his formative years is told or perceives that he is not loved, not wanted, perhaps that he is no good and will never amount to anything, he will most likely turn out that way. On the other hand, the child who is shown a great deal of love, continually reinforced with the encouragement that he can grow up to be anything he wishes, almost always turns out well and is the achiever. All this, again, demonstrates the phenomenal power and effectiveness of mind programming.

Not too long ago, I viewed a television documentary about mentally handicapped individuals with amazing abilities. A young man in his early twenties was severely mentally handicapped. His mother put a piano in his room, thinking it might provide him some entertainment. One day she heard beautiful piano music coming from his room. To her astonishment, her son was playing the piano. He had never touched the keys of a piano before, yet he was playing like a master. She found he could listen to any musical composition, no matter how long or complicated, then sit down at the piano and play it completely and without error. His mind accepted completely what he had heard and, through its fantastic power and capability, was able to transmit that knowledge to his hands, bringing it to reality on the piano.2 What a wonderful and magnificent demonstration of the ability and power of the mind!

Thoughts planted in the mind are like seeds planted in the earth. With care and nourishment those seeds grow and bring forth after their kind. They can produce sweet fruits and beautiful flowers, but they can also produce weeds and thorns. Likewise, thoughts planted in your mind, given constant attention, nurtured and affirmed steadily, will bring forth the essence of your being, be it beautiful or ugly.

The thoughts that you establish in your mind and hold with deep conviction in your heart can produce love, goodness, mercy and forgiveness in your actions. But certain kinds of thoughts can also produce hatred, anger, cruelty and vengeance. The scriptures say, "A good man out of the good treasure of the heart brings forth good things; and an evil man out of the evil treasure of the heart brings forth evil things."3 Whatever we store deep in the memory of the mind, and believe with certainty, is what we will bring to fruition in our lives.

Mankind is capable of both good and evil. We can choose the one we wish to manifest in our behavior by the simple expedient of the thoughts that we fix in our minds. If we put good, positive and godly thoughts in our minds, we will bring forth "good things out of the good treasure of the heart." But should we let our minds dwell on evil, negative and ungodly concepts, we will bring forth "evil things out of the evil treasure of the heart."

Others can plant evil, negative and undesirable thoughts in our minds, but we can choose not to nourish them. By not nourishing them, or by replacing them with good, desirable thoughts, they will die and have no effect on our life. We indeed can exercise complete control of our lives by the power of the mind and the thoughts that we entertain.

Those who constantly dwell on immoral, worldly thoughts are often immoral people who are sunken in depravity and consumed by unrestricted appetites. Their destinies, on earth, are questionable. Those who entertain good, moral, positive and godly thoughts become molded in a way such that their reward is happiness, success and harmonious living.

You must replace all less-than-godly thoughts that have been implanted in your mind with good, positive and godly thoughts. You must supplant any thoughts of hatred, anger and resentment with notions of love, kindness, patience and contentment. Then will your light shine forth. Harmony and peace between your mind and your soul, between your physical self and your spiritual self will prevail. When you attain that peace and harmony, you will enjoy good health, joy and success. You must always concentrate on those good thoughts. It is the conflict between the less-than-godly convictions of your mind and the basic, natural goodness of your spiritual self that saps your energy and causes illness, unhappiness and failure. Get yourself in sync and your life will improve dramatically.

How can we ensure that we store only good treasure in our hearts? Many of us have tried to do what is good and right, even living according to God's word, but seem to do it only half-heartedly or fail completely. We may even completely accept that God's instructions for living are good and realize we should live by them, only to find that the "spirit is willing but the flesh is weak."

God has told us how we are to do it. He says, "Get yourselves new minds and hearts."4 We are to change what we think with our minds and believe with our hearts. For years you have let all manner of computer hacks have access to your mental computer, programming it with all kinds of negative, harmful thoughts.

You need to take complete control of the programming that enters your mind. Use a code for access--Loving, Good, and Positive thought. If it's not compatible with that code, it is to be rejected. Use the power of your mind to promote good health, happiness and success in your life. Use your God-given mental power to promote peace and harmony in the world. Use your amazing mind to search for knowledge and truth. Use your mind to create miracles!

Most of us have read about, heard of, or know someone who has experienced a miracle. Some of us have experienced our own. That is, some situation to which there seemed no earthly solution, was eventually brought to a satisfactory conclusion. One of the most frequent involves terminal illness such as cancer. There are those who have had inoperable cancer spreading throughout the body. The doctors have abandoned hope and sent the patient home to die. However, because the patient had absolute, undoubting and unwavering belief that he would get better, he was healed. The cell structures within the body were deformed, yet they were returned to normal.

Doctor Gerald G. Jampolsky has written a marvelous book called, *Teach Only Love*. He practices mind/body healing at his Center for Attitudinal Healing in Sausalito, California. He talks about the case of a young woman of 23 who was legally blind. She had a small amount of close vision, but could not function as sighted. As a premature infant, she had been placed in a high-pressure oxygen tank, which resulted in her blindness.

She was active, with the help of her seeing-eye dog, attending college and working at part-time jobs. Having been told, later in life, the cause of her blindness, she felt, as would most people, a certain amount of rage and resentment at the world. She had heard of the Attitudinal Healing Center and became involved with an attitudinal healing group there.

One day she asked Dr. Jampolsky if he thought it was possible for her to regain her eyesight. He told her anything is possible; the mind knows no boundaries. She began to grasp the idea that the thoughts we put into our minds determine our perceptions. She began to work on positive mental pictures. She began to practice peace of mind, peace of God, unconditional love, forgiveness and listening to her inner voice. Her bitterness began to dissolve and her attitude about herself began to change. Where she had always treated herself as a blind person, she now began to think of herself as normal and whole.

And the miracle happened; her vision improved so that she was legally sighted during the daytime. She became involved in helping and being of service to others with her new attitude about the holistic approach to health. One day she called Dr. Jampolsky and told him she would like to take him for a drive. He exclaimed, "What do you mean?" She then told him she was licensed to drive and was now sighted for both day and night. Doctor Jampolsky later said it was the happiest time he ever had in a car, even though he cried.

What an extraordinary and wonderful story of love, caring and the miraculous power of the mind. If we can do such things as put cancer into remission by returning deformed cells to normal and restore eyesight by attitudinal healing and the thoughts of our minds, surely we have the power to change and control the behavior of our character. Surely, we have the power to obey God and follow his instructions. Assuredly, we have the ability to manifest the godly qualities of love, goodness, mercy and forgiveness in our lives, and to live in peace and harmony with our fellow human beings and all of creation.

We do all those things by getting ourselves those "new minds and hearts," as God has told us to do. We get them by changing our way of thinking. We do it through the power of the thoughts that we implant in our minds. We do it through the power of love!

To love is the greatest commandment of all. That commandment has been given to all the religions of the world in one way or another. Yet that caring, kind and forgiving love that we are told to show one another is generally not taught in the churches, the schools or our homes. Most unfortunately, we do not teach it to our children, but more often teach them hatred, violence and materialism.

The simple truth is, that mankind can live in harmony with all of creation simply by following God's instructions concerning love. Granted, it can be difficult, particularly as we have been conditioned all our lives to believe we cannot live harmoniously. We are continually bombarded with such notions that it is our nature to sin and it is human to err. We are often programmed from cradle to grave to believe we are poor, miserable, inadequate creatures who can't help ourselves. As we think, so we are!

But it is not difficult to follow God's instructions when we change our way of thinking and get ourselves new minds and hearts. We stop thinking we are those poor miserable creatures; that it is our basic nature to do wrong and live in discord. We start thinking that we are magnificent human beings, created in God's likeness with good qualities and with the ability to live by and keep God's commandment to show love to one another.

Think about it! Isn't it just as easy to love as to hate, to be compassionate rather than being cruel and to forgive instead of bearing resentment and seeking retribution? In fact, it's much easier! I'm reminded again of Nelson Mandela's words, "No one is born hating another person. People learn to hate, and if they can learn to hate, they can be taught to love, for *love comes more naturally to the human heart than its opposite.*" And the reward is marvelous! Do you remember the wonderful feeling you enjoyed when you showed love, were kind to, or forgave someone? Try it again and again! Deliberately practice it!

A few years ago, Ann Herbert, of California, saw some graffiti that read, "Random acts of Violence." She decided that kindness was better and coined the phrase, "Random acts of kindness and senseless acts of beauty." It received wide media attention and led to the publication of a book, *Random Acts Of Kindness*, by Will Glennon. The publishers, Conari Press, held a "random acts of kindness party" where guests told stories of kind deeds that had touched their lives. Will Glennon said, "It was almost magical, the impact it was having on people was extraordinary. People were crying."[5] Actually Ann, acts of beauty are not senseless, but we know what you mean.

To practice acts of kindness and beauty is a marvelous thing to do. Those who do so understand the reward of showing love to others. It makes you, as well as the recipient, feel good and promotes harmony in the world. Difficult as it may seem, we can and should always think love, kindness, mercy and forgiveness and practice these qualities in our daily living and actions toward all others. No exceptions! Let that be your new habit, your new way of life! And when you live like that, think of the effect it has on humanity and the world! God says, "A little leaven leavens the whole loaf." God's wisdom is impeccable!

Through the power of our minds, God has given us the capability to implant righteousness in our hearts and live as he desires us to. He has given us the ability to promote peace and harmony on earth. There is an old Chinese proverb that says:

> If there is righteousness in the heart, there will be
>   beauty in the character.
> If there is beauty in the character, there will be
>   harmony in the house.
> If there is harmony in the house, there will be
>   order in the nation.
> If there is order in the nation, there will be
>   peace in the world.

By the creative effort of thought, we get new minds and hearts, and shape all aspects of our lives. By the effort of thought we create goodness, peace and harmony in our character, our homes, the nation and the world. Yes, as we think, so are we!

Chapter Seventeen

MATERIALISM AND SPIRITUALISM

Much of the world's trouble has its root in the striving for materialism with little attention paid to spiritualism. The scriptures tell us that we are to "Seek first the Kingdom of God and his righteousness and then these things (material needs) will be added unto us."1 The Kingdom of God is a way of life. It is loving your neighbor as yourself, doing unto others as you would have them do unto you, it is forgiving seven times seven (meaning there should be no limit to forgiveness), it is taking care of the poor and sick, it is living in peace and even showing love and goodness to the "enemy." To be righteous with God means to practice all the above. When we do so then all the things we need in life will accrue to us.

We are also told that "The destiny of those who do not listen to God is destruction. Their god is their stomach and their glory, their shame."2 This aptly describes much of the world! Yes, materialism is the god of many. It is certainly a "look-out-for-number-one" world.

We admire and envy those who are affluent and live in opulence. How often we hear, "Oh, how nice it would be to be rich or win the lottery." And when wealth is achieved, it is often hoarded, rather than used to help those who are less fortunate. Acquiring wealth is not wrong. It is the storing up of more than we can possibly use while others are in need that is inappropriate.

That is what the scriptures mean when they admonish us not to "store up treasure for yourselves here on earth rather than in heaven."3 We are indeed our "brother's keeper." We must not be indifferent to those who are poor and in distress. We are to use our means to help them, and when we do, we store up treasure for ourselves in heaven.

A message basic to all religions is to love, care for and be of service to one another without thought of remuneration. And that service is to be directed to those in need who cannot pay, rather than those who can. Scripture tells us, "When you put on a dinner, don't invite your friends, relatives or rich neighbors for they will repay you in turn, but instead invite the poor, the crippled, the lame and the blind for they can't repay you and then you will receive your reward in heaven."4

But we don't do these things. Materialism is our first priority rather than spiritual values. We do store up treasure for ourselves here on earth while others are homeless, sick and starving. We concentrate on making it in the world of materialism, and if we have time along the way we might look into what God is about and what our relationship with others should be. Our priorities are completely out of whack. We pay exorbitant salaries to people who can bring in the big bucks, but won't spend adequate funds to properly educate our children. We spend billions of dollars on weapons of war and space programs, but often do not feed the hungry, shelter the homeless or take care of the sick. How can we possibly defend the expenditure of hundreds of billions of dollars spent on space exploration when tens of thousands of children here on earth are dying each year from starvation and sickness? It is unconscionable that we have so misplaced our priorities!

In February 1997, our space agency spent an additional $347 million to install a more powerful camera in the orbiting Hubble telescope, which will enable the scientists to see farther into space, exploring more of the universe. It is incredible that such tremendous amounts of money are being expended, just to observe more of what they already know. The latest Mars venture cost over $300 million to determine if there is or had been water there. Since 1965 there have been 43 missions to Mars costing over 30 billion dollars, with two thirds of them having failed. Why are we spending such huge sums of money on exploration of a dead planet when the children here on earth are starving to death. The administration, Congress and the space agency need to be asked this question: "What is more important, to explore space or relieve the suffering of the children?"

To peer through a multi-billion dollar telescope that has been hoisted into orbit, thinking we are going to "see the beginning of the universe" is foolish. It is not likely that the scientists will ever "scientifically" discover how the universe was created. They are wasting their time and our money trying to detect its origin. To indulge our hobby of astronomy and aspire to "go where no other man has gone before" is okay and perhaps even admirable if funds were left over after we have taken care of the needs here on this earth. We try to justify all these actions by claiming free enterprise, prestige and national security. I doubt that God has acceptance of those excuses! When one really analyzes all the scriptures, it is clear that indifference to the plight of others is the great sin in God's sight. God's question to the people who have had a near-death experience is, "What have you done to help others?"

Scriptures tell us that God puts great store by the children. We are admonished that mistreatment of the "little ones" will bring dire consequences. We have been told not to deny the children, but to "bring them up in the nurture and admonition of the Lord."[5] Nurture means to raise them with unconditional love, teaching them God's admonition to love others unconditionally, forgive our fellow human beings and help those who are in need. We have failed miserably in that. In raising our children, we need to de-emphasize materialism and teach them spiritual values such as love, compassion and forgiveness, by example. It has been rightly said that if we could "raise one generation with unconditional love, we could empty the prisons."

Most people do not understand what spiritualism is. We are told in scripture that God is Spirit. So to be spiritual would mean to be like God and spirituality or spiritualism would be to exhibit God-like characteristics in our way of living. Those being loving, compassionate and forgiving. After all we are told that we are made in God's image and to be perfect like God.

When we let materialism be our priority in life bad things happen in the world. Greed and its consequences raise their ugly head.

Poverty, hunger and starvation abound. Corruption, crime and violence thrive. War happens. People suffer. But when we let spiritualism be our goal, all these things will fade and well-being, goodwill and peace will flourish.

There is a phenomenon that is occurring every day that gives evidence that God is not pleased with our materialism but rather expects us to exercise more spiritualism in our lives. It is called the Near-Death Experience.

Chapter Eighteen

THE EXPERIENCERS

"In the middle of one circle was a most beautiful being. It was neither a man nor a woman, but it was both. I have never, before or since, seen anything as beautiful, loving and perfectly pleasant as this being. An immense, radiant love poured from it. An incredible light shone through every single pore of its face. The colors of the lights were magnificent, vibrant and alive. The light radiated outward. It was a brilliant white superimposed with what I can only describe as a golden hue. I was filled with an intense feeling of joy and awe. I was consumed with an absolutely inexpressible amount of love. I had the overpowering feeling that I was in the presence of the source of my life and perhaps even my creator. In spite of the tremendous awe it inspired, I felt I knew this being extremely well. With all my heart I wanted to embrace and melt into it as if we were one."[1]

Another experiencer said, "I was aware...of my past life. It was like it was being recorded....There was the warmest, most wonderful love. Love all around me...I felt light-good-happy-joy-at ease. Forever-eternal love. Time meant nothing. Just being. Love. Pure love. Love. The Light was Yellow. It was in, around, and through everything....It is God made visible. In, around, and through everything. One who has not experienced it cannot know its feeling. One who has experienced it can never forget it, yearns for its perfection, and longs for the embodiment of It."[1]

Here are a few excerpts from the narratives of other experiencers: "It was really like a homecoming. It was beautiful, it was magnificent. And it was so warm."...."Oh, God, I'm dead, but I'm here! I'm me! And I started pouring out these enormous feelings of gratitude. My consciousness was filled with nothing but these feelings of gratitude because I still existed and yet I knew perfectly well that I had died."..."You are shown your life, and you do the judging. Had you done what you should do? It's the little things, maybe a hurt child that you helped, or just stopped to say hello to a shut-in. Those are the things that are important...You are judging yourself."1

Speaking of the life review, an experiencer said, "What occurred was every emotion I have ever felt in my life, I felt. And my eyes were showing me the basis of how that emotion affected my life. What my life had done so far to affect other people's lives using the feeling of pure love that was surrounding me as the point of comparison. And I had done a terrible job. God! I mean it. You know, I'd done a horrible job, using love as the point of comparison....Lookin' at yourself from the point of how much love you have spread to other people is devastatin'. You will never get over it. I am six years away from that day (of his NDE) and I am not over it yet."1

Extensive research reveals that those reports of journeys to another world, apparently a spiritual world, have been with us for ages. Carol Zaleski in her work, *Other World Journeys*, gives accounts of near-death encounters in medieval and modern times--from a soldier named Er, whose experience Plato detailed, to Carl Jung to all the NDEs that present day researchers have reported.2 These reports now seem to be more frequent and, in our world of modern communication, the message is being spread throughout the world.

In the past, the stories told by the experiencers carried no credibility. They were usually dismissed as hallucinations, fantasy or the work of the devil. Even today they are sometimes labeled as such by critics and would-be debunkers. However, since 1975, when Dr. Raymond Moody, Jr. published his *Life After Life*, the first book on the near-death experience, many other researchers have gathered a large amount of evidence that supports the reality of these experiences.

Doctor Melvin Morse, pediatrician, has conducted an extensive study of the near-death experience. In his book, *Closer To The Light*, he relates the case of Katie, a nine year-old girl who died in a swimming pool accident. She experienced passing through a tunnel and meeting a guardian angel who helped her. She met relatives, a Being of Light and then was returned to life. During her NDE, Katie visited her home. "She saw her brother playing with a GI Joe, her sister combing the hair of a Barbie doll and her mother preparing a meal of roast chicken and rice. Later, when Katie mentioned this to her parents, she shocked them with her vivid details about the clothing they were wearing, their positions in the house, even the food her mother was cooking."[3]

Doctor Morse probed Katie's religious beliefs. He "wanted to see if she had been heavily indoctrinated with belief in guardian angels and tunnels to heaven. The answer from her mother was an emphatic no." Doctor Morse said his "deepest instinct told me that nothing in Katie's experience was 'taught' to her before the near drowning. Her experience was fresh, not recalled memory." He said that "Katie told her story in such a powerful and compelling way that he believed her implicitly."[3]

The term "near-death experience" was coined by Dr. Moody. It refers to people who have been pronounced clinically dead, having no heartbeat, nor respiration and, in some cases, a flat-line electro-encephalogram. But, because of heroic efforts by medical personnel, and in many cases for reasons unknown to medicine, these people have returned to temporal life. They are now popularly known as "experiencers."

Calling these events "near-death experiences" could be considered somewhat of a misnomer, for the physical bodies, by our medical standards, did indeed die. Yet, because they are alive today, they obviously have not died. It is somewhat a matter of semantics. To be technically correct, they would have to be called "near-final-death-of-the-physical-body experiences." Even more correct would be to call them "resurrection experiences." Researchers and writers may have been reluctant to use such a term, for it would likely offend those who believe there has only been one true resurrection, that of Jesus Christ. They believe there will be no other resurrection until Judgment Day when all those in the grave will be "resurrected" as was Christ. Yet that is precisely what happened to these experiencers. The soul that sustains life in the physical body departed, leaving it in a state of death, but later returned to the body and gave it life again.

The clinically dead condition has lasted, in some cases, up to a known one hour. When the brain is deprived of oxygen, usually for five minutes or more, at room or body temperature, brain damage begins to occur. After an hour there would be extensive, irreversible damage to the brain. In some cases, C-scans showed massive swelling of the brain; however, when these people recovered, no damage had occurred and they were perfectly normal.

In describing that case of Katie, Doctor Morse said, "I stood over her lifeless body in the intensive care unit...A few hours earlier she had been found floating face down in a YMCA pool...An emergency CAT scan showed massive swelling of the brain...Three days later she made a full recovery."[3]

Doctor Morse also documents the case of an eleven-year-old boy who had a cardiac arrest, "He was without a heartbeat for at least twenty minutes. During this time, several cardiac medications were given, with no success. One of the nurses present remembers saying, 'I wish we didn't have to do this,' meaning that she thought the life-saving attempts were useless.

"As a last resort, the physicians tried the cardio version paddles again. They pressed the devices against his chest and pushed the buttons that sent electrical current jolting through his heart. Miraculously, the boy opened his eyes and said, 'That was weird. You sucked me back into my body."[3] He made a complete recovery.

Phyliss Atwater, researcher and experiencer, is unique in that she died three times and is still living today. Her encounters with death led her on a quest to find and question other experiencers. She located over two hundred other survivors. She said, "I often asked the question, 'How long were you dead?'" She said, "The average time 'out' was thought to be five minutes. Many were 'gone' longer, one for over an hour."[4] These people having made complete recoveries is scientific evidence that some supernatural force was at work and this evidence supports the validity of the experience.

During that period when they were clinically dead, these people encountered consistently similar experiences. The following sequence is a compilation of happenings that occur during the near-death experience, although all do not experience every one of these events. They often hear the doctor pronounce them dead. They find themselves out of their bodies, usually hovering above or nearby. Pain and physical distress are gone being replaced by a great sense of peace. They have another type of body, often described as a spiritual body, with unusual abilities.

Time and distance are irrelevant. They travel distances in an instant. They can pass through walls. During the sequence, most, but not all, pass through a long tunnel at very high speed entering into what has been described as a heaven-like place. Others come to meet them, usually deceased relatives or friends.

Communication is by thought rather than word. They encounter a Being of Light who radiates unconditional love, peace and joy. The Being shows them a sort of panoramic review of their life. They perceive it as taking place in seconds, yet it is inclusive of all things they have done, and they fully understand it. No judgment or condemnation is pronounced by the Being.

They are sometimes asked if they wish to return, or told that they must return. Most do not wish to because of the overwhelming peace and joy they are experiencing. But they find themselves reunited with their earthly, physical body, sometimes suffering the pain they may have been experiencing just before death.

Doctor Kenneth Ring perhaps best articulates the meaning of the near-death experience, basing his conclusions on empirical research, medical data as well as the narratives of the experiencers. In his work, *Heading Toward Omega,* he documents the events that occur to those who encounter death: "All pain and fear had vanished, warmth and comfort permeated my being and a feeling of solitude and peace surrounded me....I was floating in the air above my body. Not only was I floating, I could also fly at a terrific rate of speed....I thought it was some sort of tunnel and immediately entered into it and flew with an even greater sensation of the joy of flight....Friends and relatives came to help me and were very pleased to see me, exhibiting total love and acceptance....There was this most gorgeous living light; entering it was a wonderful, joyous feeling, an ecstatic experience....It was a great sense of freedom; it was like coming home. There are no words in the human language to adequately describe it."[5]

Doctor Ring relates one experiencer's encounter with the Being of Light: "Instantly my entire life was laid bare and open to this wonderful presence, 'GOD.' I felt inside my being his forgiveness for the things in my life I was ashamed of, as though they were not of great importance. I was asked--but there were no words; it was a straight mental instantaneous communication--'What had I done to benefit or advance the human race?' At the same time, all my life was presented instantly in front of me and I was shown or made to understand what counted. I am not going into this any further, but, believe me, what I had counted in life as unimportant was my salvation and what I thought was important was nil."[5]

Ring believes the lessons that the experiencers learn will help humankind evolve to a higher level of consciousness. For instance, experiencers have said, "We learn to share more love, to be more loving toward one another. To discover that the most important thing is human relationships and love and not material things. And to realize that every single thing that you do in your life is recorded. The little things that are recorded that you don't realize at the time are really important."...."One of the things that I discovered that is very important is patience toward other human beings and realizing that you yourself may be in that situation."...."I realized that consciousness is life. We will live in and through much, but this consciousness we know that is behind our personality will continue."...."And that death is not to be feared, because if death is anything, anything at all like what I experienced, it's gotta be the most wonderful thing to look forward to, absolutely the most wonderful thing."[5]

It is interesting to note that young children do not receive a life review. It is perhaps significant in that the Being does not find little children in need of a review because they are not considered deliberate sinners. That would fit in with the scriptural view of little children being innocent. Nor do all adults undergo a life review. Perhaps because they have met the criteria for non-judgment such as having shown mercy or much love to others.

The out-of-the-body part of the near-death experience has been proven without doubt. When these events occur in a hospital emergency room, those who were resuscitated from their clinically dead condition were able to give elaborate, detailed accounts of the resuscitation procedures, equipment used, people present, their dress, and what was going on in other areas such as waiting rooms and halls outside the emergency room. These detailed accounts have been absolutely verified by doctors and nurses who were in attendance.

Doctor Morse documented the case of Jimmy, who "fell from a bridge when he was fishing and hit his head on a rock in the water below. The doctor's report says that Jimmy had stopped breathing and was without a pulse when a police officer pulled him from the deep water in which he had floated face down for at least five minutes. The policeman performed CPR for thirty minutes until the hospital helicopter arrived, but he reported that the boy was dead on the scene when they started the rush to the hospital where he was revived.

He described, to his physician, his entire rescue in vivid detail, including the name of the police officer who tried to resuscitate him, the length of time it took for the helicopter to arrive on the scene, and many of the lifesaving procedures used on him to revive him in the helicopter and at the hospital."[6]

Doctor Michael Sabom has done some fascinating work on out-of-body experiences, reporting the results in his book, *Recollections Of Death*. "Sabom asked twenty-five medically savvy patients to make educated guesses about what happens when a doctor tries to get the heart started again. He wanted to compare the knowledge of 'medically smart' patients with the out-of-body experiences of medically unsophisticated patients.

He found that twenty-three of the twenty-five in the control group made mistakes while none of the thirty-two near-death patients made mistakes in describing what went on in their own resuscitations."7

Doctor Moody reported that several doctors told him they were "utterly baffled about how patients with no medical knowledge could describe in such detail and so correctly the procedures used in resuscitation attempts, even though these events took place while the doctors knew the patients involved to be dead."8

If the out-of-body experience has been proven to be true, then it is likely that the rest of the near-death experience is also authentic. Further proof that the rest is also authentic is provided by the following event that occurs while the experiencer is in that "spiritual otherworld."

They encounter a relative such as a distant uncle, a great-grandparent, or a friend of another member of the family of whom they had no prior knowledge. That relative or friend identifies him or herself by name and relationship. Later when they tell living family members of the encounter, those family members confirm that such a person did indeed exist and that the experiencer was never told about and could not have had prior knowledge of that person.

Doctor Morse relates the experience of a young man named Cory who "told his mother that he had met an old high school boyfriend of hers who had been crippled in an automobile accident. She had never mentioned the man to Cory, not to hide her relationship, but simply because she had not seen him in many years. Cory said to his mother, 'don't worry, he said to tell you he can walk now.'"9

Although the near-death experience cannot be proven "scientifically," sufficient evidence exists that something very unusual has occurred to these people and that a lesson is to be learned from their encounters. It seems rather clear that God is sending us another message or reminder of his existence and what he expects of us.

What is the message that these modern day messengers bring us? There is absolutely no doubt in the minds of the experiencers that man has a soul, a spiritual self, that is released from the physical body when the body dies. From the proven out-of-body experience, it is apparent they are right. If we can conclude that the rest of the NDE is real, and it seems reasonable to do so, then we are being told there is a life hereafter in a paradise-like world different from this one we know. We come to understand that it is a spiritual world, the location of which we know not, but perhaps parallel to this physical world.

We are being told of the important things in this life. People come away from these encounters with the belief that love and knowledge, in that order, are most important, both in this life and the one to come. When they encounter the Being of Light they perceive the Being as having perfect understanding and perfect love, love that is unconditional. The Being asks, "What did you do for others because you loved them; how have you learned to love?" It further questions, "Are you able to love others in the same way?"[10] They take this to mean, "Do they love others in the same unconditional way that the Being loves them."[10]

They also perceive that the Being of Light is not interested in theology, religious dogma, denomination, or even particularly what they believe. The thrust of their non-verbal conversation centers on the spiritual aspects of their life and their relationship with their fellow human beings.

Dr. Moody related the account of a man who had studied at a religious seminary before his NDE: "My doctor told me I had 'died' during the surgery. But I told him that I 'came to life.' I saw in that vision what a stuck-up ass I was with all that theory, looking down on everyone who wasn't a member of my denomination or didn't subscribe to the theological beliefs that I did.

"A lot of people I know are going to be surprised when they find out that the Lord isn't interested in theology. He seems to find some of it amusing, as a matter of fact, because he wasn't interested at all in anything about my denomination. He wanted to know what was in my heart, not my head."[11]

Ring reports a woman in her mid-twenties who, after her NDE, told him, "Yes, I'm quite more religious than I was but I don't exactly believe in what the churches do. I don't like their methods.

They're into scaring people. Everything they preach I don't feel is exactly true, so I have my own beliefs."12 Another said to him, "I don't think it (church-based religion) has anything to do with what Jesus was about."12

Moody says, "People who undergo an NDE come out of it saying that religion concerns your ability to love--not doctrines and denominations. In short, they think that God is a much more magnanimous being than they previously thought, and that denominations don't count.

"A good example of this is an elderly woman in New Hampshire who had an NDE after a cardiac arrest. She had been a very religious and doctrine-abiding Lutheran since she was a child. But after the NDE, she loosened up and became a more joyous person. When members of her family asked her to account for the change in her personality, she said simply that she understood God after her episode and realized that he didn't care about church doctrine at all."13

Love seems to be the key to everything--not romantic, sentimental love, but caring and forgiving love. As one experiencer put it, "Love that is unmotivated, unequivocal, spontaneous, overflowing and shown to others regardless of their faults. The kind of love that makes me want to know if my neighbor is fed and clothed and makes me want to help him if he is not."14

Those who have the NDE undergo a spiritual awakening. They have a great desire to seek knowledge, particularly spiritual knowledge. What is their purpose in life; what is God's will for them; what is God's plan for mankind? They become much more avid readers.

They bring a message concerning the fruitlessness of materialism. Their materialistic views change drastically. Their lives are no longer possession-oriented. They in no way take a vow of poverty or disdain material things, but rather rearrange their priorities. The first priority now becomes spiritualism--understanding and gaining a right relationship with God and their fellow man. They are less judgmental against others, and they always try to look for the good in everyone.

Their message is very much in accordance with the teaching of the scriptures. God exists and is spirit in nature. Doctor Ring reports the case of Janis: "I was raised Protestant...I gave it up in my early teens...I researched Catholicism. I found that was worse...Essentially, at the time of my accident, I was a ranting, raving atheist. There was no God...He was a figment of man's imagination...Now I know that there's a God. And that God is everything that exists, that's the essence of God...Everything that exists has the essence of God within it. I know there's a God now. I have no question."[14]

Their message that love and knowledge are the two most important things in this life is also very much in accordance with the scriptures. To show love to others is the dominant message of the gospel of Christ. Elsewhere scripture says, "And now abideth faith, hope and love, these three; but the greatest of these is love."[15] "Owe no man anything, but to love one another: for he that loveth another hath fulfilled the law."[16] "The greatest commandment is to love God with all your heart, soul and mind. The second is like the first: Love your neighbor as much as you love yourself."[17]

Concerning knowledge, the scripture says, "Knowledge is pleasant unto thy soul, apply your heart to understanding, cry after knowledge, ask for understanding, seek knowledge, happy is the man who gets wisdom and understanding and seek knowledge as you would seek hidden treasure, then you will understand the might of the Lord and find the knowledge of God." Clearly God puts great emphasis on the pursuit of knowledge about him. As scripture also says, "When the world is full of the knowledge of God then there will be no more harm in all his Kingdom."[18] Given the terrible violence and harm that is present in the world today, it would appear that the knowledge the religions offer as to the nature of God, is far from the truth.

The Bible tells us not to worry about or take pride in material things, but "Seek first the Kingdom of God and his righteousness"[19] and then the necessary material things will accrue to us. Scripture says, "Judge not that you be not judged."[20] All of that philosophy is very much in accord with the attitude and actions of the experiencers after their return from the "hereafter."

That latter admonition from God to judge not, and on which the experiencers place a lot of emphasis, is very important. It is a command from God that we all violate many times every day because we do not really understand its meaning. We judge when we criticize others. We do it constantly over many things. Stop and think of how often we criticize the people around us. We criticize how they dress, how they drive their car, how they perform their work, their looks, their tastes, and on and on. Judging others is a major factor that prevents harmony, peace and goodwill in our lives and throughout the world. When we judge others, it causes anger and animosity. It seldom brings about a resolution to the matter, but rather fosters resentment. It brings disruption and discord into our own lives. We often get angry and frustrated when others won't change their ways to suit us.

Instead of judging or criticizing, we should always look for the good in others, for it is there. We can help bring it out by showing love, patience and forgiveness toward others, rather than criticizing them for the things they do that irritate us or wrong us. It is part of our purpose in life to look for the good in others and through our own actions, help to manifest it in them. Each of us needs to do his part to change the world for the better. God has commanded us to do these things, and when we obey him, harmony and peace come into our lives and are promoted on earth. When we realize all these things, we come to understand God's wisdom in telling us not to judge others.

The experiencers understand this very well and practice God's adjuration. NDE researchers report that tolerance of, compassion for and acceptance of others as they are is a common result of the near-death experience. As one experiencer said, "Now I find that everyone that I meet I like...I very rarely meet someone I don't like. And that's because I accept them...I don't judge people."[21] Another said, "I try not to be biased, and not to judge people."[22]

You might ask about all the apparent criticism in this text; the criticism of the politicians, the theologians, the religions, government and the Church. How can that be reconciled with God's admonition not to judge? Surely we aren't to remain silent when we see obvious wrong being done. But then that requires man's fallible determination of what is right and wrong. Perhaps judging is different from criticism; judging having to do with condemnation and forgiveness in respect to sins and salvation. Perhaps we should not do it on a personal basis, but rather institutionally. There has to be some basis for rendering criticism of actions that seem wrong. After all, Christ was very judgmental of others. He was extremely critical of certain people, such as the self-righteous Pharisees. He called them some pretty strong names such as "hypocrites," "vipers" and an "evil generation." He called some "fools!"

The scriptures give us a clue as to how we are to reconcile this seeming conflict. Christ said, "Don't criticize, and then you won't be criticized. For others will treat you as you treat them. And why worry about a speck in the eye of a brother when you have a board in your own? Should you say, 'Friend, let me help you get that speck out of your eye,' when you can't even see because of the board in your own eye? Hypocrite! First get rid of the board. Then you can see to help your brother."23 When we get our own "house in order," doing what is just and right, then we will see clearly what we should do and say about others. And any criticism should always be given in a kind, loving and tactful way without anger or bitterness.

Researchers into near-death experiences have been criticized for delving into that matter, even denounced by some of the clergy who say it is the work of Satan. The Bible says to "Beware of false teachers. You will know them by their fruits. You can detect them by the way they act, just as you can identify a tree by its fruit. You need never confuse grapevines with thorn bushes or figs with thistles. Yes, the way to identify a tree or person is by the kind of fruit produced."24 Applying that standard then to those who have had the near-death experience and the message they bring from the spiritual world can leave no doubt that this phenomena is not the work of Satan but of God.

There can be no doubt where the experiencers fit in. Their own lives are changed for the better. They radiate energy, love, kindness and contentment. They have an "overwhelming, burning and consuming desire to do something for other people." Those whose lives are touched by these people are better off for it. The fruit they produce is love, kindness, confidence, compassion, patience and forgiveness.

There is one problem with the research that is being done in that field of NDEs. The researchers are in danger of doing to the message of the experiencers what the theologians have done to the truths contained in the scriptures of the world. The theologians have reasoned so much over the scriptures that they have lost sight of the scripture's basic message, thus causing great confusion among the people about the nature of God, their own nature, and what God expects of them. So it is with the researchers and the near-death experience. When one reads the NDE literature, it is obvious that some of it is written by psychiatrists and psychologists for like readers, with language that is not conducive to learning by the average reader.

One encounters such phrases as "amorphous structural-functional framework defined neither etically nor emically," "noumenon underlying phenomena," "primitive archetypal interpretation," "psycho dynamical concepts," "neurobiological models," "veridical out-of-body perceptions" and other Freudian and Jungian-type language. Researchers speculate on the validity of the NDE and its similarity to experiences when the Sylvian fissure of the brain is electrically stimulated, or theorize about such things as the nature and complexities of the intangible astral world in which the experiencers find themselves. They argue about the type of society or culture that exists in that world. Is it a transcendent, Cockayne or Utopian one? There is discussion about the dimensional analysis of that world, derivative predictions and the nature and composition of the spiritual body.

Surely, all research is good, but care must be taken by the researchers not to minimize or even forget the basic message of the experience, which is that God exists, has unconditional love for all mankind, and is what he expects us to show to one another, in order to be one with him. That is the knowledge and understanding that researchers and NDE organizations should promote and teach to the world.

The evidence provided by the near-death experience is sufficiently valid for any reasonable person to conclude that man does have a soul, a spiritual self that does not die, but continues on to eternal life in a paradisiacal world where there is total love, joy and contentment. The evidence strongly suggests there is a powerful Being who sends the souls of the experiencers back into their earthly bodies for two reasons. First, the experiencers believe they have been returned to this mortal life to complete tasks which have been deemed unfinished, such as taking care of their children or straightening out their own life; secondly, to bring humanity another message of the assurance of God's existence, his love for us and what he expects of us.

The scripture provides support for the experiencer's claims that God exists, that there is an afterlife, and that we take on new spiritual bodies when our physical bodies die. Christ addressed the question of what happens to us after our physical body dies. He said, "God said to Moses, 'I am the God of Abraham, and I am the God of Isaac and I am the God of Jacob.'" God was telling Moses that those men, though dead for hundreds of years, were still very much alive, for he would not have said, "I am the God of those who don't exist!"25 He also said that after we die and our "spirit rises to heaven, we neither marry nor are given in marriage; but are as the angels in heaven."26 It is quite evident that when we die, we immediately take on our new spiritual bodies.

St. Paul was partly right when he said, "First then, we have these human bodies and later on God gives us spiritual heavenly bodies. I am telling you this strange and wonderful secret, we shall not all die, but we shall all be given new bodies. It will happen in a moment, in the twinkling of an eye, when the last trumpet has blown. All the Christians who have died will suddenly become alive, with new bodies that will never die and then we who are still alive shall suddenly have new bodies, too."27

But it will not happen all at once, at the sounding of the last trumpet, as Paul thought. It happens to each of us individually at the moment our physical body dies. What Christ said about Abraham, Isaac and Jacob shows that. They were alive and well in their new bodies at the time of Moses, hundreds of years after their "death." They still live today, not having to wait until some future date when the "last trumpet has blown." The testimony of the experiencers also gives evidence that this is so. It is not only Christians who receive new bodies, as Paul supposed. Certainly Abraham, Isaac and Jacob were not Christians. They knew nothing of Christ. They lived and died under the law of obedience and still got to heaven. Also we know that the experiencers come from all religious faiths. Some are without a religious affiliation, yet they all received new spiritual bodies at the time of their physical death even though they were sent back into their old bodies.

Although the experiencers are told that love and knowledge are the two most important things in this life, as well as the one to come, they are not told everything that is going to happen in the next life. They encounter total peace, indescribable joy and the presence of a Being who radiates unconditional love, compassion and understanding. But they find a border beyond which they do not go. It is the border of not knowing completely what is going to happen to them in that new spiritual world. They are given glimpses of beautiful places or cities--perhaps the "mansions prepared for us." But some also encounter frightening NDEs where they witness people in great anguish, or even experience it themselves.

When we transition to the next life, we will know and understand many things. That is one message of the near-death experience. We will be made aware of all things we have ever done in this lifetime; that is the life review that many experiencers undergo. We will understand the good we have done, as well as the wrongdoing we have inflicted on our fellow human beings. We will be aware of the love we showed to others, as well as the hatred, indifference and cruelty. That is the Judgment. It will be of our own doing. This belief is common among those who have undergone the near-death experience.

The Koran speaks of it in saying, "They will testify against themselves....."28 The Day of Judgment is the day that each of us dies! That is why scripture speaks of it as being like a thief in the night that comes upon us unexpectedly.

The "life review" that experiencers undergo could explain Christ's statement that he is going to "come with the angels and judge us according to our deeds." A "being" is present when they have the life review. Some experiencers identify that being as Jesus Christ and others perceive it as an angel or even God. Still, it is not Christ, an angel or God who is doing the judging, but we ourselves by witnessing and understanding all things we have done in this lifetime.

But if we have shown love and forgiveness to others, no judgment will occur. God has told us in the scriptures that if we have been merciful to others, his mercy will win out over any judgment of us--the life review will not take place. Scripture also tells us that if we have loved much we will be forgiven much. But if we have loved little, we will be forgiven little and punishment of some kind will follow. If we have been indifferent, unkind, cruel and vengeful to others, we will feel great guilt, remorse and anguish. That is the punishment, or hell, we will endure. There will be "weeping and gnashing of teeth."29 One experiencer said that after her life review, in which she saw and re-experienced all the terrible things she had done in her lifetime, it was as close to experiencing "hell" as she could imagine. Can you imagine the incredible agony and sorrow that tyrants such as Hitler and Stalin must have experienced during their life review, watching and feeling the terrible cruelty they inflicted on their fellow human beings?

Therefore, it behooves each one of us to search for the knowledge that will enable us to wind up in the wondrous presence of our Creator. Understanding this will allow us to escape judgment and provide us the wisdom that will give us the confidence and surety that we will enjoy the presence of God forever.

The Torah, Gospel and the Koran, as well as other scriptures all contain this information, a message of love, mercy and forgiveness, the requisites for being right with God and achieving victory over death.

Chapter Nineteen

THE JOY OF DEATH

We treasure life highly and its enjoyments such as love, family, the beauty of nature, friends and food--they make life worth living. As death threatens to take away all these things, we look upon it with loathing, fear and even anger. Although about 90 percent of all people believe that this earthly life is not the end and that there is some kind of heaven where they expect to end up, there is still that unwillingness to consider death as anything but distasteful and so it is generally ignored. Even strong religious beliefs of an afterlife do little to assuage repugnance toward death.

Our perception of death, for too long, has simply been erroneous. It is thought of as the time when our life comes to an end and we go to a dark, dank grave. It conjures up visions of the grim reaper, a black-hooded figure with a scythe, who cuts our very existence out from under us so we cease to exist. Or it is thought of as complete obliteration of our consciousness. It is often spoken of as going to sleep to awaken at some later time. Or it is decreed that we go to the grave to await the judgment day when we shall all come forth, at the sound of a trumpet, to be judged either fit to go to heaven or down into the fiery pits of hell.

Death is none of that! It is most certainly not the end! The evidence of this is overwhelming. Most people believe that we have some future beyond the cessation of this mortal life. We should not even think of it as death. It is the beginning of another stage of our being. Therefore, rather than call it death, it would be more appropriate to call it by another name such as transition or perhaps graduation. What happens to us at the time of the death of our physical body is no longer the "great unknown." We know a great deal about it. It is that knowledge that should be taught instead of the myths and false beliefs that are generally espoused today. We, our higher selves, do not go to the grave, but find ourselves in a heavenly other world. It is interesting to note that, in the ancient Aramaic language, the word for death means "not here; present elsewhere." We do not leave loved ones forever, but are reunited with those who have "died" before us and will be again with those to follow.

The evidence shows that death is not unpleasant, but rather a joyous experience. Scripture upholds that proposition of death as an exhilarating and blessed event. We learned from Christ that both he and the thief on the cross were going to be in paradise the same day that their physical bodies were to die. Also that, when we "die" we become as the angels in heaven. The Koran repeatedly speaks of the joys and pleasures of being in paradise after we leave this mortal life.

The testimony in the previous chapter, of those who have died and returned to tell us about it, clearly supports this premise. Another experiencer explained her encounter with death in this way, "This enormously bright light seemed almost to cradle me. I just seemed to exist in it and be part of it and be nurtured by it and the feeling just became more and more ecstatic and glorious and perfect. And everything about it was--if you took the one thousand best things that ever happened to you in your life and multiplied by a million, maybe you could get close to this feeling."[1]

The scriptural evidence along with the testimony of the experiencers should give us incentive to examine and then discard the archaic, false beliefs about death that are generally held today. Even without that, we have had a great deal of knowledge available to us concerning death, yet that knowledge has been ignored or distorted by the philosophers, theologians, those who would profit from death and even our own imagination.

We know we cannot scientifically prove what happens to us at the time of death; however, a preponderance of evidence exists, some of it even supported scientifically, that death is not the end of life, but rather the simple shedding of this physical body and moving onward and upward to better things, to a higher level of consciousness. We have seen that experiencers, though clinically dead for at least a known one hour, with extensive damage to the brain having occurred, were returned to life in a normal condition. Surely that is scientific evidence that there is a spiritual force at work in the process of death and life after death.

Many strange things have been documented about dying people, especially those who die a lingering death as from terminal cancer. Quite often, just minutes or sometimes hours or even days before death, the patients find themselves without pain or discomfort. A sense of well-being prevails, and when death finally comes, their facial expressions reflect joy and serenity. I have personally witnessed that phenomenon in my work as a hospice volunteer.

Modern medicine knows a great deal about pain; what causes it, its symptoms and how it can be controlled, usually by substance application. It is all scientific fact. Patients, in cases like those above, find that the pain is gone without the use of medication. That is a proven fact, yet doctors don't know scientifically why it is gone. It has to be obvious that there is some other force that has brought it about.

Numerous cases have been documented of people who announce that they are going to die, that their time has come, even giving the day it is going to happen. They contact friends and relatives to say good-bye. It is not done in panic or anger, but with total acceptance and contentment. Their last days are spent in peace without pain or discomfort. We see this sort of thing time and time again, yet we ignore the obvious implication that death is not to be feared and that in some manner God has communicated this message to them.

Many terminally ill patients have pre-death visions in which they see and talk to others, usually relatives or friends who have died before. It is almost always attributed to hallucination, yet physical manifestations of those pre-death visions have been documented. Others have seen the person the dying patient was talking to. Others have seen physical objects in the room of the patient move, although they couldn't see the force that moved them.

Some true psychics can communicate with people who have "died" and graduated to the next life. They are often treated with disbelief, skepticism, even contempt, often by the theologians, although their remarkable talent has been proven beyond doubt.

A book called *We Don't Die* tells the story of one such psychic, George Anderson. It was written by Joel Martin and Patricia Romanowski. Martin was a TV and radio producer and talk-show host, who, being a hard-nosed skeptic himself, set out to "expose" Anderson. He used controlled tests, even attempts to "set him up." The results never varied; Anderson's communication with the "deceased" was always accurate. He revealed information to survivors that could only have come from their loved ones who had died. Information was exchanged about matters that occurred after their "death." Messages were received that they were alive and well, messages of love and hope, messages of forgiveness to those who were accidentally responsible for their death and even forgiveness for murderers.

Joel Martin turned from a doubter to a believer, saying, "Understanding that death is not a termination but a transition, that as human beings we have capacities and abilities far beyond our imagination. We don't die. That making this discovery--and seeing its proof--has changed our lives eternally, goes without saying."[2]

The London Society for Psychical Research has, for over a hundred years, been gathering volumes of material on psychic phenomenon that provide reasonable evidence that "death" is not the end, but simply a passage from here to there; that a supernatural force exists; that there is life hereafter; that death is not an unpleasant experience, but rather an incredibly joyous event and that our loved ones and friends who have gone before us are alive and well and will be there to greet us, even help us to make the transition from this life to the next.

But because we can't examine that phenomena under a microscope or even understand it completely, we refute or ignore it. We should not. As poet George Santayana said, "It is wisdom to believe the heart." Our "heart" tells us that there is more to our existence than this mortal life, and when it ends, our loving God and creator will take good care of us. Death is a spiritual matter that truly transcends religion. But it is a spiritual matter that we give little attention to. We shy away from it because we have, unfortunately, been conditioned all of our life to look forward to it with dread.

If we sought all the knowledge that is available about death, we would lose our fear of it and find ourselves more content and life less stressful. Perceiving that death is not something to be feared but welcomed and looked forward to with great anticipation also would greatly alter our outlook on, and behavior in, secular matters. For one thing we would cease the extraordinarily expensive and futile folly of transplanting organs so as to prolong this often less-than-wonderful life. Who would want to extend his mortal life knowing that an experience of awesome wonder and utter glory awaits us in the next life.

We would do away with the useless practice of preservative cryogenics, ostentatious funerals and the current way of grieving. Hospital procedures would change drastically; there would be no more "code blues" or human beings hooked up to elaborate life-sustaining devices. Materialism as a goal in life would fall to the wayside, as it has with the experiencers who understand the priorities involved in life and death. Spiritualism, with the goal of finding the right relationship with God and with one another, would come to the fore in our lives.

What if we looked at death as something good and as the ultimate goal to be achieved, rather than a bad experience and the end of life? What if we perceived death as one experiencer did: "As I reached the source of light I could see in. I cannot begin to describe in human terms the feeling I had at what I saw. It was a giant infinite world of calm, and love, and energy and beauty. It was as though human life was unimportant compared to this. And yet it urged the importance of life at the same time it solicited death as a means to a better, different life."[3]

When we deal with those who are known to be dying, we are more concerned with consoling them about having to leave this often less-than-pleasant life rather than giving them all the knowledge about death; that it is by far the best and most important event that will occur to them in this lifetime. We are often more concerned about the survivors and their loss rather than the gain of the one who is dying. Everything that we have been taught about death is wrong, even the grieving and mourning. To attend funerals and entertain thoughts of our loved one going to the grave and leaving us forever is simply a delusion, for the loved one is not there, but alive and well. How often have we read about or heard of a parent continuing to express great grief and anguish over a beautiful child who lies dead in the grave, gone before his or her time; not being able to enjoy life? The child is not there, but alive and well in the wondrous presence of its Creator. God takes loving care of all his creation at the time of "death."

As scripture tells us in speaking of our soul, our immortal self, we are "not slain when this its mortal frame is destroyed"....We are "eternal, universal, permanent, and unalterable; therefore, knowing it to be thus, thou shouldst not grieve!"[4]

Of course there should be sorrow and tears over the parting, but no more so than over any other temporary parting. And it should be softened and offset by the wondrous and glorious event that is taking place. It is not unlike a loved one graduating from college who then leaves the family to take up residence in some far place to go to work, perhaps get married, raise his own family, or generally pursue his own life. We celebrate their graduation, have a farewell party, and cry and hug them when we see them off at the airport, or send them on their way in their fully-packed automobile. We talk about when we will see them again.

So should it be with death. This life is a learning experience. When we die, it is simply a transition or graduation to another type of life. Some may graduate with honors, and some may have more learning to do. The "far-off place" we go to is beautiful, bright and wonderful. Total love that is unconditional and perfect understanding are found there. It is a place anyone would be reluctant to leave, even showing anger at having to leave, as some experiencers have related. We meet our friends and loved ones there. It is literally a reunion in paradise, where everyone is happy to see the other regardless of how the parting had been. We are completely whole in every respect.

Certainly there are differences from the college graduation simile. We can't write or call them on the telephone, although some have been known to communicate. We can't plan an airplane flight for the next meeting. And, of course, it isn't the same when a young child dies, having been taken from us so early in life. However, knowing that those who die, even the young children, are going to such a beautiful and glorious place where there is peace, joy and all-encompassing love, and that one day there will be a wonderful reunion, should be cause for celebration and tears of joy as well as sorrow at the parting.

We should change our way of doing things at funerals and in memory of those who have "died." Instead of expensive funerals and mausoleums, there should be a simple burial, or none at all in favor of cremation. To spend exorbitant amounts of money to inter a useless shell of a body, especially as the inhabitant is no longer there but safe elsewhere, is to be less than good and wise stewards of our resources. A much more appropriate use of those funds would be for the needy living. So also should it be with things such as eternal flames and life-long floral care of a grave.

Instead of a somber, tearful funeral service, a joyful wake would be much more fitting. A modest celebration with food, drink and music, suitable to the likes and beliefs of the family and the departed would be appropriate, along with tears and laughter. After all, it's an observance of joy and life, not death and despair. Part of my Will are instructions to my family to have that joyful wake. Food is to be catered so no one has to toil over preparation. Beer and wine is to be available. Music is to be big band oldies like Mantovani and Glenn Miller. I know they will have a good time with lots of laughter telling stories about me. And, of course, shed a few happy tears.

Death and eternal life are greatly misunderstood. We never die; we live forever. We have, in the form of our soul, existed forever as part of the vast immeasurable energy of God. As one experiencer put it, "I was peace, I was love. I was brightness, it (the Being of Light) was part of me...You just know. You're all knowing--and everything is a part of you--it's--it's just so beautiful. It was eternity. It's like I was always there and I will always be there, and that my existence on earth was just a brief instance."5

Another said, "I became aware that it (the Being of Light) was part of all living things and that at the same time all living things were part of it. I knew it was omnipotent, that it represented infinite divine love. It was as if my heart wanted to leap out of my body towards it. It was almost as though I had met my Maker."5

God is indeed our maker and when the body dies, we return to his presence in the spiritual world, retaining our individual identity but with a new spiritual body. Of course, we've always understood that our physical body dies. The scripture is clear about that when it says, "From dust you have come and to dust you shall return."6 We know that the body does turn to dust in the grave, or is burned to ashes during cremation, or is consumed perhaps by other animals or the fish of the sea, should the ocean be our grave.

The Church falsely teaches that on Judgment Day the "graves will open and the dead come forth." They base it on St. Paul's statement, "All the Christians who have died will suddenly become alive, with new bodies that will never die and then we who are still alive shall suddenly have new bodies too. When this happens, then at last this scripture will come true--Death is swallowed up in victory."7

The Christian theologians also base this belief on Christ's words in John 5, where he says, "And I solemnly declare that the time is coming, in fact, it is here, when the dead shall hear my voice--the voice of the Son of God--and those who listen shall live......Don't be surprised! Indeed the time is coming when all the dead in their graves shall hear the voice of God's Son, and shall rise again--those who have done good to eternal life; and those who have continued in evil, to judgment."8

Do you see how conflicting that information is? How can the dead in the grave listen to the voice of Christ? How can all Christians in the grave come alive again when nothing of them is there? The bodies of those in the grave have turned to dust. How about Christians who have died at sea and been consumed by sea creatures? The cells of their body have been absorbed into the cells of the fish as food. An omnipotent God could surely reassemble the bodies of the dead if he chose to. But it doesn't seem likely, especially as we are told by the experiencers, and even Paul, that we will have new bodies. Neither are their souls there in the grave, having departed elsewhere at the time of their "death." Just as Christ told the thief on the cross next to him that he would be in paradise with him that very day, and as Christ said of Abraham, Isaac and Jacob, they were alive and well in heaven, although they had been "dead" for hundreds of years, he also said, when we die, we rise and become as the angels in heaven. And, of course, the near-death experience provides reasonable evidence that this is so.

Surely what Christ was saying in John 5 is that those who are dead in their sins, who are spiritually dead, separated from God, will rise again, be resurrected from that spiritual decay, be renewed and be eligible for eternal life in God's presence when they listen to him and do what is right and good. Remember, he said, "the time is here" when the dead would hear his voice and live. Right then and there it would happen. Obviously it couldn't have been the dead in their graves, for they would have come forth then. It could only have meant that those who were not saved but destined for spiritual death would achieve salvation and eternal life by listening to his message and obeying it.

"Victory over death" is not achieved when we become Christian, and when "sin no longer has power over us" as St. Paul taught. It is not when the graves open and the Christians come forth. Victory over death comes when we understand and accept the messages of Christ and the other prophets about what God expects of us, which is to show love, mercy and forgiveness to one another.

Surely God would not send anyone to supposedly suffer in hell for eternity, or even temporarily, because they didn't know about Christ.

How do you justify such punishment, from a perfect-in-justice God, for simple disobedience or because they haven't been taught about Christ? How is it possible to reconcile it with Christ's statement that, "Those who don't realize they are doing wrong will be punished little?"9 Certainly hellish suffering isn't a small punishment! What of Christ's desire that "none shall be lost but all might be saved?" If only those who believe in Christ are saved, then literally billions will be lost and undergo some type of hell-like anguish.. How do we square such terrible punishment with God's compassionate and forgiving love for us?

The obvious answer is that God does not, indeed cannot, mete out such punishment. And if, either through our own stubbornness, ignorance, or negligence, or perhaps for reasons not of our own doing, we haven't learned what God expects from us in this lifetime, and therefore do not qualify for acceptance in his presence eternally, surely a merciful God would make available some course other than committing us to some type of hellish suffering--an alternative such as reincarnation.

According to a Gallup poll, 38 million Americans believe in reincarnation. A tremendous amount of material that presents reasonable evidence in support of reincarnation can be found in the scriptures of the world. The New Testament of the Bible is supportive of rebirth when Christ speaks of John the Baptist as the reincarnation of Elijah.10

The early Christians believed in reincarnation for about five centuries until that belief was suppressed, and writings concerning it were destroyed, by the Church fathers because it was not compatible with Christian doctrine which requires acceptance of Christ as savior and redeemer so as to gain eternal life. Or, if we do not believe in Christ or have no knowledge of him, we are damned by God for our "innate" sin, and after death, our soul goes to hell to suffer eternally. Christianity makes no allowance for a second chance by means of reincarnation.

Editors Joseph Head and Sylvia Cranston in their book *Reincar-*

nation: The Phoenix Fire Mystery have done an incredible amount of research in bringing to the public knowledge about rebirth. The Rev. John Andrew Storey says about their work, "Such is the wealth of material contained in this book that the reader may well conclude that all the great thinkers of mankind have been reincarnationists, and indeed such a judgment would not be far from the truth."[11] Anyone who desires to know the truth about reincarnation would do well to read this work.

To deny reincarnation assails our sense of justice, which tells us that God would give a second chance to one who has never been taught the message of salvation. Reincarnation is an expression of God's mercy to those who have not learned in one lifetime the requisites necessary to be one with him forever. Eternal life means there is no more death and rebirth. It is as Christ says in John 20, "They which shall be accounted worthy to obtain that world (heaven), and the resurrection from the dead (spiritual death), neither marry, nor are given in marriage; neither can they die anymore; for they are equal unto the angels; and are the children of God, being the children of the resurrection." Surely God desires that all of humankind should experience heaven.

HEAVEN, HELL AND THE DEVIL

Heaven is thought of as the place to which we eventually ascend to if we are good or meet certain requisites, often as set forth by a religion. When we make that journey to heaven is also subject to various beliefs. Hell is usually thought of as the fiery pit or caverns we descend into after we die, because we have been bad or haven't accepted a religion's theological beliefs. These are narrow and erroneous concepts of heaven and hell.

It is also likely that the idea of the devil or Satan as a person or a being is errant. Satan is simply the temptation that we generate through the wrongful thoughts and desires of the mind. Satan is defined as the great adversary or enemy of man. Wrong thought certainly fits that description. Thoughts of worry, paranoia, greed, fear, hate, anger, superstition, covetousness and negativity, to name a few, are indeed man's enemies, often creating a veritable hell for him.

Scripture also supports this concept of Satan. When Christ told his disciples that he was going to suffer at the hands of the elders and chief priests and die, Peter rebuked him, in effect telling Christ that it wasn't necessary to do that. Then Christ in turn scolded Peter, saying, "Get thee behind me, Satan."12 Surely, Christ didn't think Peter was Satan, but only that Peter's suggestion that Christ didn't have to go through with his suffering and dying represented temptation. Christ was putting that tempting thought from his mind. According to scripture, Christ agonized over what he had to do.

Christ's temptation in the wilderness13 is also supportive of that idea. Because the scripture records a conversation between Christ and the "devil" or "tempter," one might draw the conclusion that the devil was a person. But it is more likely that the entire story of Christ's temptation is simply an allegory, a form of communication frequently used in scripture to make a point. An allegory is defined as representation of an abstract or spiritual meaning through concrete or material forms; figurative treatment of one subject under the guise of another.

When we examine the story, one can easily see its abstract meaning through the use of material forms. The wilderness simply represented this materialistic world in which temptation often confronts us. Turning stones into bread represented materialism. That would seem quite clear from Christ's reply that, "we don't live by bread alone, but by the word of God."14 The high-mountain scenario and the "devil's" offer to give Christ all the kingdoms of the world would be representative of power. And, of course, the devil (the tempter) represented temptation itself.

Even Christ's final words in the matter, "Get thee hence, Satan: for it is written, thou shall worship the Lord thy God, and him only shall you obey,"15 could clearly have an abstract meaning. We are to put away the tempting thoughts of the mind that lead to wrongdoing and obey God and his instructions for right and just living.

To accept the story as reality is not very credible. It is not likely that Christ could turn stones into bread. That would violate God's natural laws. How was it possible for the devil to set Christ on the pinnacle, the pointed spire, of the temple? How did he transport Christ to the high mountain? No "exceedingly high mountains" can be found near Jerusalem, or, for that matter, anywhere in the world, from which Christ could see "all the kingdoms of the world, and the glory of them!"

Further, the teaching that Satan is an angel gone bad, fallen from God's grace, banned from his presence and who is continually battling with God for men's souls is illogical, if not absurd. My feeling is that no person or angel who has ever been in the presence of God and the total love and joy that exist there could ever do wrong or wish to leave that bliss. And certainly, "Satan" would be no match for the omnipotent God in a battle of any kind! The concept of the battle for man's soul is only within man himself. It is waged within the mind by the thoughts of right or wrong. No, it is not likely that there is such a person as the devil who makes his abode in a place called hell. More about hell later, but first let's examine the concept of heaven.

The New Testament tells us, "Heaven can be entered only through the narrow gate! The highway to hell is broad, and its gate is wide enough for all the multitudes who choose its easy way. But the gateway to life is small, and the road is narrow, and only a very few ever find it."16

Almost two billion Christians are living today who believe they are traveling that narrow road and are going to go through the narrow gate and get into heaven. That is certainly not a very few, even reckoned as a percentage of the population. And that's only those living today. What about all those who have died and all those yet to be born? How is it going to be possible for that great multitude to get through the narrow gate, especially as Christ said there will be only a very few.

If that passage is true, then a lot of Christians had better start worrying about who that handful, those very few, are going to be. They should also wonder about what's wrong with Christianity such that so very few are going to make it to heaven! The above scripture either has to be suspect, or has a hidden meaning, or a misunderstanding exists about the definition of heaven. It is probably a combination of all three. It surely could not be true literally, for then there would be little hope, but rather great despair for mankind.

To accept as apparent truth the idea that very few are going to enter the "gateway to life" does not correlate with other scripture, which tells us how easy it is to get to heaven. We need only to love our neighbor as ourselves, and we shall live in heaven forever. That's not hard to do. Christ says those who listen to his voice shall never die. We can do that, too. We need only to feed the hungry, "clothe the naked" and generally take care of others in need and then we shall inherit the kingdom of heaven. A great many do all of these things and will surely enter the gateway to life in heaven. The concept of few getting to heaven does not relate to Christ's statement and wish that all shall be saved. It doesn't even relate to the teaching of the Christian Church that we have only to believe in Christ as the sacrificial lamb in order to get to heaven. Billions have held this belief over the centuries. Surely then, that statement must have another meaning.

The scripture speaks of heaven both as a place and a condition or state of being. Genesis says God created the heaven and the earth and he called the firmament Heaven. Both the Old and New Testament tell of a new heaven and a new earth. And, of course, we are all aware of the reference to God the Father in Heaven. Similar references to heaven as a place can be found throughout the Bible.

But Christ speaks of it also as a state or condition. "The kingdom of heaven is like to a grain of mustard seed, which a man took, and sowed in his field: which is indeed the least of all seeds; but when it is grown, it is the greatest among the herbs, and becometh a tree, so that the birds of the air come and lodge in the branches thereof."17

Further, Christ says, "The kingdom of heaven is like unto leaven, which a woman took, and hid in three measures of meal, till the whole was leavened."[18] Christ uses the kingdom of heaven and the kingdom of God interchangeably. He says we are to seek the kingdom of God first, and then the necessary material needs will accrue to us.[19] He tells us that we can't see the kingdom of God; it is neither here nor there, but is within us.[20] That would certainly imply that it is a condition rather than a place.

It would seem that the kingdom of God or the kingdom of heaven is something we can attain here on earth, a state of being that is highly prized and should be sought after. As it is like leaven that leavens the whole loaf, it would be a way of life that serves as an example such that when others see it, and the rewards thereof, they too choose that way of living.

Surely the kingdom of heaven is the way that God wishes us to live and what he has always intended for us. After all, he placed us in paradise. Who can deny the beauty and wonder of this world where man has not destroyed it? But because we have used our free will to make the wrong choices, we have made this earth something less than a paradise and in some respects, a veritable hell.

But it doesn't have to remain that way. We can change things. We can reverse the damage we have done, and with the help of God in his constant renewal of nature, find that paradise, that "kingdom prepared for us from the beginning."[21] To do so we have to listen to what God has been telling us from the beginning, which is to show love to our fellow human beings and live in peace and harmony, not only with one another but with all of creation. When we do that, then will we find and experience bliss, the joy of heaven, supreme happiness and the "peace that passeth all understanding." We are meant to enjoy life fully. Surely that is the heaven that Christ is speaking of when he says that the gate to it, the gateway to that life, is narrow. Indeed, few find it. At least, so far!

Scripture tells us that it is God's pleasure to give us the kingdom of heaven: that blissful life of happiness, joy and contentment. But we foolishly choose not to accept it, rather making the choice to travel the wide path that leads to "hell;" the path of hate, anger, violence, worry, condemnation, cruelty, vengeance, covetousness, promiscuity, greed, irresponsibility and indifference to the needs of our fellow human beings.

Although almost no one believes it anymore, Christian dogma places hell in the nether regions of the earth. The Church teaches that Christ, after his death on the cross, descended there and stayed for three days as part of the punishment he received for our sins. Christ did not descend into hell after he died. He said to the thief on the cross next to him, "Today, you shall be with me in paradise."[22] That fits beautifully with those who undergo the near-death experience, finding themselves in some paradise-like place immediately after the body dies. The Church completely ignores these words of Christ, arguing whether just his soul or both his body and soul made the descent into hell for those three days. Christ never said he was going to hell to be punished for the sins of all mankind.

Given that God has perfect love and mercy, it is not likely that he created such a place as hell, where he sends some people to suffer eternally. From a historical standpoint, hell was an old, Aramaic, idiomatic word used to describe mental torment signified by burning fires in the city dumps. Later the idea of torment by fire changed to "Gehenna of Fire," a place of extreme torment, and then in further biblical translations to "Hell," which biblical writers then undoubtedly associated with punishment and the devil.[23] Hell is assuredly none of those, but a condition or state of being, one that we bring upon ourselves or inflict on others. It is a state that we can experience either here in this lifetime or in the next.

We experience it when we fail to love and respect ourselves, abusing our bodies by irresponsibly ingesting substances that we know cause disease, suffering and death. Anyone who has watched a loved one or friend suffer and die from an overdose of drugs, or from lung cancer as a result of smoking for forty years, can testify to the hell that person went through. Anyone who has witnessed or perhaps even experienced the withdrawal from the abuse of alcohol knows well the hellish suffering that occurs.

We can create a mental hell for ourselves in our thoughts. By excessive, even unwarranted worry we can suffer great pangs of anxiety, causing harm to our mental well-being, sometimes resulting in physical debilitation as well. By our conditioned thoughts of anger, hatred, racism and discrimination we create discord, often leading to violence, suffering and death.

We create a hell for ourselves and others when we do not love and respect nature, which is a manifestation of God, and by polluting and destroying the environment thereby causing disasters such as floods, dust bowls, starvation and death.

Just look at the hell mankind has produced by turning plowshares into swords, manufacturing massive amounts of weapons of destruction, hanging humanity, especially the children, on a "cross of iron," as Dwight Eisenhower once so aptly described the clouds of war. Do you think Hiroshima and Nagasaki, and their aftermath, weren't the epitome of hell, especially to those who lived there and survived? Think of all those babies and young children of Somalia, slowly and hellishly starving to death. Think of the hell that young girl in Somalia went through, aware that she was being buried alive. These things happened in Somalia because the "civilized" nations of the world provided the warring factions there with weapons enabling them to perpetrate that horror! What of those babies in Haiti, dying of disease and starvation because the "good guys" used their military power to blockade Haiti economically in the name of democracy?

All that hell we create for ourselves and others here on earth is due to one thing: disobedience to God and the instructions he has given us, which, if observed, would preclude all that suffering. Just observing his one command to love our neighbor as our self would do it. We have the complete ability to do it, if we were taught so, and that it is what God requires of us in order to attain the glorious bliss of heaven. But, instead, we are conditioned to believe that we cannot, that we are poor sinful beings whose nature it is to create all of this hell!

As to the hell in the afterlife, it, too, is a state of being and of our own doing. A loving and forgiving God could not sentence us to everlasting punishment in the pits of hell because we have been disobedient and judged unfit to be in his presence. The hell, the "weeping and gnashing of teeth," that the scriptures refer to is simply the anguish and remorse that we will feel and endure when we become fully aware of the harm and sorrow we have caused others, in this lifetime, either deliberately or through our indifference to their needs.

As experiencers have said, "You are shown your life...and you do the judging. Had you done what you should? It's the little things... maybe a hurt child that you helped or just stopped to say hello to a shut-in. These are the things that are important...You are judging yourself."24 One experiencer said, after witnessing her life review and all the things she had done to others, that the suffering and distress she felt was as close to hell as she could imagine.

The Being of Light, undoubtedly a manifestation of God, asks the questions, "What have you done to advance the human race?" "How have you loved others?" And you have to answer. If you can't answer satisfactorily, there may literally be hell to pay. You may have to pay with a state of mental agony. Some experiencers have encountered hellish conditions during their NDE. Some near-death experience researchers have speculated that what the experiencers see during their brief journey to that other world is based on the perceptions of the afterlife that they were taught and believed in during this lifetime. Or, in other words, the "visions experienced were projections from the mind of the participant; that mental images held in this lifetime determine what is met after death."25

It is more likely that all the visions experienced are a reality of the afterlife. In the hell-like conditions, the experiencer was witnessing the mental agony that some suffer when they understand and feel the distress and torment they have inflicted on others. Visions of gray zombie-like beings moaning and crying in great distress fits with the scriptural description that there will be "weeping and gnashing of teeth."

This condition could last a long time if one's deeds have been exceedingly wicked without showing remorse or repentance. Although the scriptures speak of some that will remain in that state forever, knowing that God is forgiving, it is not likely. Christ does speak of those who refuse to obey God, "And shall go away into eternal punishment."26 If it is so, it will be those who are extremely cruel and evil, and knowing God's will, still refuse to believe and obey him.

Christ said, in speaking of blasphemy, that those who spoke against him can be forgiven, but those who blaspheme the Holy Spirit (God) will not be forgiven and are in danger of eternal damnation.27 Do you see the contradiction here? They can't be forgiven; however, they are only in danger of damnation, not necessarily damned for certain. If they aren't forgiven or damned either, there would have to be an alternative, such as reincarnation. Or it could be an inaccurate reporting of what Christ actually said. Many experiencers feel that we will all be "home free" eventually, and that, as Christ implies elsewhere in the scripture, God wants everyone to be saved so that "not one is lost!"

There is a simple and easy way to escape judgment and any kind of hellish suffering. Love, mercy and forgiveness are the way. God has told us that if we have been merciful to others, his mercy will win out over any judgment. He has told us that if we have loved much, we will be forgiven much. We have been told that if we forgive others, God will forgive us. Obedience to and living by those words of God is the perfect formula for avoiding "hell" and achieving heaven, both in this life and the one to come.

Many people have a complete misconception as to what living by God's word means. They envision a life of strict piety or total commitment to religious obligations, perhaps joining a monastery, taking the cloth or becoming a missionary in some far-off land. It is often associated with a very restricted lifestyle which precludes the joys of living and requires a great deal of time on one's knees in church with hands folded. Nothing is further from the truth. Living by God's word results in the true joy of living.

These misconceived ideas can be a part of doing God's work, but they do not ensure that one will be living according to God's word. It is much more and, at the same time, more simple than that. God's work is doing good to others. We live by God's word when we show compassion and forgiveness to our fellow human beings. It is doing "random acts of kindness." It is the little things we do for others: a smile, a cheery good morning, a friendly wave, a kind word or a compliment. As one experiencer said, it is the little things that count. Living by God's word is living in harmony with all of creation. It is using the environment wisely, not ravaging and destroying the earth out of greed and for profit. When we give of ourselves and do what is right and good, we will be living by God's word and will find that we are enjoying life to the fullest.

Heaven is a state of being that we can achieve and enjoy here in this lifetime, but it is also the place where we will all eventually find ourselves; a place where we will forever delight in the indescribable yet glorious presence of God. Hell is only a condition that we ourselves are responsible for, either here on earth or in the life to come. Although those who have not met the necessary requisites to escape judgment should be concerned about the mental anguish they may have to suffer, they should not fear death. That anguish will not endure forever. Or God, in his loving mercy, may offer a choice, such as further learning or service to others which may take place in the afterlife or by way of reincarnation. We need to trust in the absolute love of God.

An obvious question arises that needs to be asked and answered here. If there is nothing to fear from death and it is so joyous, why would we not all seek death, such as in suicide or reckless and dangerous living? Why would anyone who is ill or suffering from a disease, especially one that is terminal, wish to get well?

The scriptures tell us that we are not to kill, not to take life, which obviously would include our own. Experiencers, who have found themselves in that near-death encounter as the result of suicide, are told that they were wrong to do it. Yet God is kind and compassionate and will give those who take their life another chance in some manner. Nor is it likely that there will be any condemnation or judgment of those who have ended their life to prevent undue suffering. If they have lived a good life, the taking of their own life, out of despair, will be overlooked by God.

Life is a gift from God. It is not our prerogative to take it, either our own or another's. The experiencers understand that life is precious, that it is to be highly valued and protected. Our own common sense, as well as the wisdom of the "heart," tell us that this is so. We are given life to enjoy and learn. We should make the most of every moment of it. Although we should look forward to "death" with anticipation, we need to await that magnificent experience with contentment, understanding that our purpose in life is to enjoy it, do good and let our light shine, making the world better.

All who have concerns about the death that is to come for themselves or a loved one, or are still in anguish and despair over a family member, especially a child, who has died, should search for knowledge about what happens at the time of "death." Put aside your preconceived beliefs about it. Read the literature on the near-death experience. There is a great deal of it, but it isn't necessary to read it all. Just a few of the books will give you sufficient insight that will change your views forever. Search the scriptures as well.

When you do so with an open mind and heart, then you will no longer fear death for yourself or a loved one. Your perspective about death for any human being, even the victims of murders and massacres that are happening around the world, will change. Instead of anger and despair at the loss of their lives, you will feel sorrow at any suffering they may have incurred, but also relief knowing that they are being taken good care of by God. As to the perpetrators, your malice and hatred toward them will turn to pity and sorrow, and perhaps, even forgiveness. Even should someone have killed your loved one, you may find that your animosity, desire for vengeance, and inability to forgive has been assuaged. You will never think the same about death again.

If you have led a less than good life, you are likely to find that your new knowledge of death will change your lifestyle. Experiencers who have been drug users, alcoholics and criminals undergo a complete turnaround in their lives. Just reading about their experiences and gaining knowledge of life, death, and what God expects of you can alter your own life as well. Your new understanding will spark a desire for even greater knowledge that will lead you to a better life. It can lead you to a healthier life, even the healing of any infirmities you might have.

—— *Chapter Twenty* ——

HEALTH, HEALING AND MEDICINE

This is the story of Jean, the daughter of longtime friends. It is a story of love, courage, faith and healing. Jean was in her twenties and nearing graduation from university when she was very seriously injured in an automobile accident. She had been hit broadside by a drunken driver and sustained extensive damage to her head and brain. She was in a coma for almost two months. One evening while her father was with her at the local hospital, the pastor came to visit and give support. Prior to leaving, he held Jean's hand and commenced to say the Lord's Prayer. Part way through the prayer, Jean began to move her lips, saying the prayer along with the pastor and her father. Jean then opened her eyes bringing tears of joy to her father and the pastor.

But the real miracle hadn't occurred--at least not yet. Considerable damage had occurred to Jean's brain on the side where the memory function takes place. She could remember very little. Her vocal cords were paralyzed. She could hardly speak. Her entire left side was also paralyzed. She could not use her left arm, nor could she walk.

The best brain surgeon in the West was consulted. His prognosis was not good. She was told she would never walk again. She would be confined to her wheelchair for the rest of her life. She could never finish college; she simply didn't have the necessary faculties for learning and remembering anymore.

But Jean and her family would not accept that prognosis. She started a hydrotherapy program. Daily, her father took her to a nearby pool for exercise. She began work with a psychiatrist who also was a hypnotherapist. He encouraged her in her goal to overcome her handicaps and taught her the techniques of self-hypnosis. She began to see progress, with improvement in her speech and motion of her left extremities. It was slow, hard work, but she never gave up, nor did she entertain thoughts of failure. She believed and was convinced that she would regain her full faculties. And she did indeed overcome every one of her handicaps.

She has long since discarded her wheelchair. Today, Jean speaks normally and walks just like anyone else. She has regained the feeling in, and use of, the left side of her body. Through self-hypnosis, she has learned to transfer her memory function to another area of the brain. On occasion, she has small memory lapses, but they are rare. Jean finished college, and went on to work with handicapped children, teach sign language at the college level, and to conduct her own hypnotherapy practice.

She is a dynamic, warm, loving and caring person. She loves to help other people and takes great satisfaction in showing them how to overcome their problems through self-hypnosis. Hers is a marvelous story of success in overcoming adversity in healing of the body when the normal medical practices are helpless. She attributes her recovery to absolute belief that she would get well, the loving support of her parents and family, the power of the mind and the use of self-hypnosis in harnessing that power.

We all have power within ourselves that can heal, but few realize it or would accept such a philosophy. Most people would accept such disabilities as Jean's as irreversible, continuing to live out their lives in a handicapped state. It is much the same with terminal illness. When such a prognosis is offered, it is usually received with denial, or thoughts of death, and perhaps resignation to the fate that has been decreed. Little thought is given to recovery from the illness. Some do and fight it, often in every way known to medical science, but in the end they succumb. Some simply accept their circumstances, refusing to go through the often difficult trials of treatment such as chemotherapy, and in the end concede defeat in the battle for life. A very, very few beat the odds and recover, somehow having come up with the answer to miraculous healing.

Usually they chalk it up to their faith in the power of God to heal them, and call it a miracle. But they can't explain how God accomplished the healing, or why he chose to heal them and not others who also believe in God and his power to heal. In a sense, it is God who does the healing, but it is more accurate to say that the primary effort is by man.

The human body that consists of our physical self, the mind and the soul is, indeed, a self-healing organism. In the chapter on the Nature of Man, we touched on the healing processes of the body: how the intelligence in the body mobilizes its resources to effect, for example, the healing of a wound. The body can even mend a broken bone, if not too severe a fracture, without the help of medical procedures, or even without any effort of the mind. Even compound fractures, with assistance from doctors, are mended by the intelligence within. Medical practitioners acknowledge that they are not responsible for the healing; they only facilitate it.

But obviously, the ability of the body to heal itself has limits, succumbing to injuries such as massive wounds that destroy major organs. Almost always it yields to deadly diseases such as AIDS and amyotrophic lateral sclerosis, commonly known as Lou Gehrig's disease. More often than not it surrenders to cancer. But what of those instances of cancer and even AIDS where people have beaten the odds and continue to live long and healthy lives? What of the many miracle cures that have been documented? Why do certain people recover and others do not when the circumstances of the illness are basically the same? There is a very simple answer. Let's look at a few cases of "miraculous" recoveries, as well as some who didn't recover. Then we will analyze them all and find that answer.

Jackie Pflug was a passenger on Egypt Air Flight 648 when it was hijacked in 1985 and forced to land at Malta. She was chosen for execution by the hijackers, along with two other American passengers and two Israelis. As the gun that was pressed against her head exploded, she felt herself falling from the front aircraft exit to the tarmac where she lay for five hours in and out of consciousness, yet still aware that she needed to remain still and act dead. When the hijackers allowed a morgue detail to retrieve the five bodies, she knew she was going to survive.

The bullet had shattered the whole right side of her skull and the bone fragments damaged a large part of her brain. The doctors told her that, although her survival was a miracle, she would never be normal. They told her she would never be able to drive or work and would never be able to read above the third-grade level. She had lost most of her vision and severe epilepsy had destroyed her short-term memory. She could not tell time nor count money.

But, like Jean, she proved the doctors wrong. She literally willed herself to be healed. Prior to being shot, and after worrying for an hour about her possible fate, she said, "I just stopped struggling. I just closed my eyes and went into a place that was very safe. A place of non-worry, knowing that everything would be all right, no matter what happened. I started to pray and I asked God for my life, and I felt like it would be OK after that, whether I lived or whether I died, even though I'm not a religious person. We are not our bodies. We are spirits, and spirits move on."[1]

Later she said that her ability to will herself healed was connected to the "place of non-worry" into which she escaped before she was shot. She said that, through that experience, she felt that she was "taking God out of heaven and putting God inside me. Every morning, I get up and get myself quiet and get in touch with that power. I believe we can have heaven on earth by touching that power."[1]

Jack Colern, hospitalized and dying of AIDS, almost in an unconscious state, heard the doctors and nurses saying it was unlikely he would last through the night. But he didn't feel that way. "I had the unusual sense that I was going to make it; I was at peace." Not only did he make it, but today he lectures and shares his new spiritual and emotional strength with others. He says, "I am no longer afraid. Today, I don't just survive. My life is full of wonderful things. My sense of spirituality today is real simple, let go and let God. Once

I let go I'm shown the way." He says the world is besieged with misery and destruction, but it doesn't have to be that way, even if you have a debilitating illness. "I don't want to be part of that, I want to be part of the solution."2 He is indeed!

Bert, at age 70, was dying from severe coronary artery disease and diabetes. He was given, at the most, three months to live. A year and a half later, he was still alive. The doctors told his wife they didn't understand what was keeping him alive. But she knew and I, the hospice volunteer that worked with them, knew. Bert and his wife soon would celebrate their 50th wedding anniversary. It was about a year and a half away from the time he received the news about his terminal illness. All during his illness they made big plans and talked a great deal about the coming event. All the children, grandchildren and many friends were coming. Although not able to express himself very well due to his illness, it was obvious that Bert enjoyed the big celebration. In a matter of days after their anniversary he died. It was clear to his wife and me that Bert had literally willed himself to live so that he could celebrate his 50th anniversary.

John battled cancer for twelve years. In the early years it was in his lymph nodes in the neck area. He underwent both radiation treatment and chemotherapy, losing a lot of weight and all of his hair. He would wear a baseball cap most of the time. He was a devout Christian and had great faith in God. His attitude was amazingly positive; he was sure he would beat it. And he did. And got his hair back, too.

Jerry also had cancer. He was riddled with it, in the lungs, stomach and liver. Although it was widespread, it was not so severe that his activities were curtailed. However, he was considered terminal and given about a year to live. He was a very negative person, took to his bed and simply resigned himself to his coming fate. He had little use for God or spirituality. In three months he was gone.

There are a few more cases that are appropriate to discuss which shed light on the answer of why some die and some recover from the same illness. They are from Deepak Chopra's book, *Quantum Healing*.3

Chitra came to Dr. Chopra after removal of a breast due to a malignant tumor, which also had spread to the lungs. She had about a 10 percent chance of surviving for five years. She was concerned about dying, not for herself, but for her family, particularly her husband. Conventional therapy had done all it could for her, and she hoped that Dr. Chopra could help.

He started her on a new course of treatments involving Ayurvedic techniques. They consisted of a change in diet with special meals, use of medicinal herbs, oil massages, simple yoga exercises and meditation. It is a technique designed to bring the day-to-day existence into a deep state of rest and relaxation, the foundation for healing. She was very faithful in continuing the program and trusted that Dr. Chopra would make her well. After a year, x-rays showed no cancer cells at all, and there was mutual jubilation.

But that isn't the end of the story. Doubt began to creep in. Chitra began to entertain thoughts that the cancer would return. She was disturbed that her "miracle cure" was only a temporary stay of execution. She became extremely anxious, fearful and depressed. You can probably guess the rest. Cancer showed up again, this time in the brain, and in her extremely agitated and depressed state, she died rather quickly.

A man complaining of a painful chest cough was found to have a very large tumor between his lungs which, after biopsy, was diagnosed as oat-cell carcinoma, an extremely deadly and very fast-growing malignancy. The doctor told him he must have immediate surgery to remove the tumor and enter into radiation and chemotherapy treatment. But he refused treatment and left the office. The doctor lost track of him. Eight years later a man came to see him with an enlarged lymph node is his neck. Biopsy showed it also to be oat-cell carcinoma. The doctor soon realized it was the same man. When he asked the patient what he had done for the earlier chest tumor, he said he had done nothing--he had just decided he was not going to let himself die of cancer.

Laxman Govindass was a patient in a hospital in New Delhi.

He was a peasant farmer whose drinking had gotten out of hand--an alcoholic with cirrhosis of the liver. His family had abandoned him, and he was deteriorating very rapidly, extremely emaciated and down to less than eighty pounds in weight. Doctor Chopra, taking his medical training at the hospital, had struck a rapport with him, visiting him frequently, just sitting with him to ease his loneliness and apprehension.

When it came time for Dr. Chopra to rotate to a village dispensary sixty miles away, he went in to say good-bye to Mr. Govindass and told him he would be back in about thirty days to visit him. The man said to him, "Now that you are leaving, I have nothing more to live for--I will die." Doctor Chopra replied, "Don't be silly, you can't die until I come back to see you again." He left thinking that he really wouldn't see him again because no one expected him to live more than a week.

A month later when he returned to the hospital he was greatly surprised to find the patient still alive, albeit little but skin and bones. When Dr. Chopra gently touched him, he opened his eyes and said, "You have come back. You said I could not die without seeing you again--now I see you." Then he closed his eyes and died!

A Boston fireman entered the emergency room of a suburban hospital complaining of sudden, sharp pains in the chest. The resident examined him and could find no evidence or irregularity in his heart function. He returned another time with the same complaint, and Dr. Chopra, as the senior physician, gave him a thorough examination, with the same results. He returned repeatedly, certain that he had a heart condition, but no test, including sophisticated cardiograms and angiograms, detected the slightest defect.

In the face of his extreme anxiety and its adverse effect on his work, he was recommended for disability retirement, but the fire department's medical examining board refused to approve it on the basis that there was no evidence of a heart condition. Two months later he showed up in the emergency room, on a stretcher, the victim of a massive heart attack. Within ten minutes of his coronary, which destroyed 90 percent of his heart muscle, he died.

Let's review one more case, and then we will analyze them. A woman of fifty came to Dr. Chopra complaining of severe abdominal pains and jaundice. Believing it to be gallstones, she was scheduled for surgery. But when the surgeons opened her up, they found a large malignant tumor that had spread to her liver and abdominal cavity. Judging the case inoperable, they closed the incision without further action.

After her daughter had pleaded with Dr. Chopra not to tell her mother the truth, he informed the older woman that the gallstones had been successfully removed, rationalizing that her family would break the news in time, and that in all likelihood she had only a few months to live. Eight months later he was astonished to see the same woman back in his office for a routine checkup. The examination showed no signs of jaundice, no pain and no cancer. Later she told Dr. Chopra, "When I was so sure I had cancer and it turned out to be just gallstones, I told myself I would never be sick another day in my life." Her cancer never returned, and Dr. Chopra writes, "The woman used no technique; she got well, it appears, through her deep-seated resolve, and that was good enough."

Perhaps you already see the common denominator in these cases of miraculous healing. There was a decision made by the mind to be healed: "She had absolute belief that she would get well." "She willed herself to be healed." "I had the unusual sense that I was going to make it." "He was completely convinced he would get well." "He had absolute unwavering belief he would get better." "He just decided he was not going to get cancer." "I told myself I would never get sick another day in my life." "Through her deep-seated resolve, she got well."

It is the same with the two cases in which Bert and Mr. Govindass lived well beyond the medical prognosis given for their condition. Bert literally willed himself to live until his 50th wedding anniversary. Mister Govindass told himself and believed that he could not die until he had seen Dr. Chopra again. But they also believed that when those specified times had passed, they would die, and so they did.

It also works in reverse. Through decisions and thoughts of the mind, we can literally bring on disease and cause death. The Boston fireman was certain he had a heart condition. Jerry resigned himself to his fate; he was a very negative person. For Chitra, doubt began to creep in; she became anxious, fearful and depressed.

These are not isolated cases, they happen all the time. A man who had inoperable cancer was given a new drug that was reported to be effective in curing his type of cancer. His cancer disappeared. But later when he read a medical report that the new drug was not reliable in effecting cancer cures, doubt set in, his cancer returned and he soon died. The thoughts of our mind are very critical to the state of our health.

We have proof of that in the placebo effect. In scientific experiments, test groups may be given a placebo, a substance that has no medicinal value whatsoever. They are told that it has certain medical properties that will help or cure their problem. Subjects quite frequently show improvement and sometimes are even cured of their ailment. It seems logical that the thought of the mind and belief that the pill would help brought about the healing.

It is very likely that it is the placebo effect, the thought and belief of the mind, that is responsible for the results often realized from alternative methods such as faith healing and laying on of hands. The person believes with his mind that he will be healed. The reason that others are not healed is because they don't really believe; there is doubt. It is most probable that the same holds true for voodoo. For example, the sticking of pins through the heart of a doll resembling the victim, or invoking a hex, cannot, in itself, possibly cause harm if the target has no knowledge that it is being done. It is only when the victim becomes aware, believes that harm is possible and thoughts of fear and death are implanted in the mind, that those results may occur. It is also likely that substances like ground apricot pits, pulverized rhinoceros horn, bear gallbladder and other "health aids" work for some people because they believe these substances will help.

We simply do not understand the power of the mind. It is the dominant force, not only in shaping our behavior but also in determining the state of our health. It is the freedom and power that God has given us in the form of free will. The intelligence within us, our soul, knows how to maintain perfect health and how to heal if we are injured or incur a disease, but it needs the cooperation of our mind.

Sometimes the only cooperation it needs is for us to get out of the way with our negative and anxiety-ridden thoughts. That is why meditation is so effective in healing. The state of peace, relaxation and serenity that accompanies meditation lays the foundation for healing. It is why we sleep--so the body can restore itself. When our mind is at rest in a state of meditation, self-hypnosis or sleep, free of worry, frustration, anger and all thoughts of negativity, then the soul is free of those dominating forces and can go about its function of healing and restoring the body.

That is what is often referred to as 'letting go and letting God.' That is the way Jack Colern, hospitalized and dying with AIDS, was healed. As he said, "My spirituality is simple, let go and let God. When I let go, I am shown the way." Yet it is not God who directly does the healing, but God within us in the form of our soul, our spiritual self, that sustains life in our body and makes every effort to return it to normal when things go awry from disease and injury.

But, even better than "getting out of the way" by putting aside the negativity of the mind, is the decision to cooperate fully with the soul, aiding in the healing by thinking good, happy, positive thoughts; by providing the body with proper nutrition and exercise; as well as making firm, confident decisions to recover from the disease or illness. Or, even more specifically, by use of the visualization technique; carrying in the mind the thought of being whole, healthy and cured.

Disease or illness is a disruption of the harmony between the mind, body and soul. The tendency of the soul is to maintain our body in perfect health. Our soul is that field of energy given to us by God. It has the intelligence to form and perfect our bodies from the moment of conception through birth and growth to adulthood. It is the force that sustains our life and knows how to heal. But it is still subordinate to the mind. Although it is unalterable and indestructible, its abilities can be overridden by the mind. With our minds we can literally think ourselves ill and even to death.

More individuals often do not respect the body, but abuse it both by the less-than-healthy thoughts we entertain, as well as the undecidedly unhealthy substances we take into our body, either intentionally or unknowingly. We cause harm to both our mental and physical self when we dwell on such thoughts as anger, hatred, frustration, impatience, worry, bitterness, paranoia, lust, covetousness and many others. We often ingest substances that are not the best for us, such as junk food, too much animal fat, excessive amounts of sugar, too much caffeine, tobacco smoke, immoderate quantities of alcohol, trans-fats, legal and illegal drugs, preservatives, pesticides, synthetic dyes and many pollutant-type chemicals that are spewed into the air that we breathe.

We have absolute proof that all those negative thoughts and harmful substances are generally detrimental to good health and often the cause of disease, yet we do little if anything to change our lifestyles to avoid them. And, of course, the food industry, the chemical manufacturers, the advertising media, the medical establishment and even government have not always acted responsibly nor been forthright in advising the public about the harmful effects.

The ulterior motive of profit often governs the production and promotion of the legal yet harmful products that are offered for consumption. A prime example is tobacco. Smoking is the greatest cause of preventable disease and death, increasing governmental health costs by about $22 billion annually in the United States alone. Over 420,000 Americans die each year from smoking-related illnesses. Tobacco is the cause of more death, debilitation and destruction than amphetamines, marijuana, opium, crack and cocaine combined.

What does that say about a government that makes narcotics production and use illegal while at the same time that same government subsidizes tobacco? It speaks loudly of politics. The tobacco industry is a multi-billion dollar business. It spends $4 billion annually just to promote its products while the government spends about $1 million in anti-smoking advertisements. The politicians in Washington have been cowed by the powerful tobacco lobby and the political leaders from the tobacco-producing states, often giving in to their opposition to anti-smoking measures in exchange for their support in other areas.

Certainly, tobacco farmers are not evil or anything of the sort. Growing tobacco is a long-standing and honorable tradition. But now that we have become aware of the harm that it causes, its production should be discontinued. Common sense would dictate that if we do not have the right to use marijuana, opium and cocaine because they are harmful to individuals in particular, and to society in general, then neither should we have the right to use tobacco, which is much more injurious and costly to both the individual and to society.

Land that is now used for the output of tobacco should be converted to the production of healthy products such as vegetables, fruits, grains and herbs. Their use is on the rise and will increase dramatically as we come to learn more about their nutritional value in maintaining good health and combating disease. With recent disclosures about the tobacco industry and the increased opposition to cigarette smoking, the handwriting is on the wall. The wise tobacco farmer will make the switch to other products.

The United States has spent $23 billion in the last few decades to find the cause of and a cure for cancer, but there has been very little progress. Meanwhile the incidence of cancer has increased. The problem is that medical research is looking in the wrong place and for difficult solutions when the answer is probably quite simple. The cause of cancer likely lies in environmental and food chain contamination, diet and the state of the mind.

We know that eighty percent of cancers are caused by identifiable factors that can be controlled such as smoking, other dietary factors, toxins and stress. Granted, control of all those causes can often be difficult, but we do have the complete ability to do so!

Studies show that if a parent or grandparent died of heart disease or ovarian cancer, for example, the offspring have a higher risk of dying from the same thing. In addition to the genetic or hereditary connection, more attention should be given to the possibility of a learned lifestyle correlation. One may be predisposed toward a disease that the parent died from because one often follows in the parent's footsteps when it comes to lifestyle and the types of food and drink one consumes. An inclination toward similar temperamental factors such as anger and worry is also a factor.

But even the genetic link can be altered by the power of the mind in cooperation with the ability of the soul to perfect the human body. Jordan Houghton was born with a defective gene that causes severe enzyme deficiency, most often resulting in death at an early age. It had already killed his brother, Beau, at 18 months of age. But scientists reported that "Jordan managed to heal himself, returning a flawed gene to normal. Somehow, at some unknown time, Jordan's body rewrote his genetic legacy and stopped his disease."[5] Jordan's beliefs, his positive attitude and love of music surely contributed to the healing. About a dozen examples of such natural gene fixes have been reported. Every one of us has the capability to heal our self and maintain perfect health by deciding with our dominant mind, to cooperate fully with the life-sustaining and life-perfecting intelligence within us called the soul.

In the United States, there are over 20 million surgeries performed every year. Annually, about one million people die from heart disease, 150,000 die from strokes and 600,000 from cancer. About 75 million people are suffering from allergies at any given time. Arthritis affects, to some degree, about 75% of the elderly population. It has been estimated that 60 million baby boomers will have arthritis by the year 2020. Depression, diabetes, high blood pressure, vision problems, obesity, indigestion and many other ills plague our society, causing tens of millions of people considerable discomfort and a restricted, less-than-enjoyable lifestyle. And it's all so unnecessary! Most disease can be eliminated! The elimination of disease is to be found in prevention. Prevention is to be found in responsibility. When we are irresponsible and disease overtakes us, then cure can be found in returning to responsibility and belief in the healing intelligence within us.

The medical establishment is starting to lose the battle for the health of mankind. Disease is winning! Illnesses such as heart disease, cancer, arthritis and AIDS are epidemic and ever-increasing in their rate of occurrence. We are spending billions upon billions of dollars on research in order to find a cure, but are little closer than we were at the start.

Heart bypass surgery has been touted as one of medicine's greatest achievements in fighting heart disease. But just how effective and safe is it? It is estimated that 50 percent of all bypass grafts clog up again after five years and 80 percent within seven years. There is risk of heart attack, stroke and death. Bypass surgery and angioplasty are only temporary restorative measures unless one changes his or her lifestyle by improving the diet and state of mind, for example.

Synthetic drugs and the scalpel are the standard "cure" for heart disease. Why should we use drugs and surgery as a cure when known, gentler and safer methods are available? Who would want to go through the expense and risk of heart bypass surgery, angioplasty and dangerous prescription drugs for cardiovascular disease when a non-surgical, safe, painless, inexpensive and even enjoyable procedure is available?

Rare is the doctor who would recommend the non-surgical way. And those with the disease can't ask for it because few know about it. Or, if they do ask their doctor, it would likely not be approved despite the fact that the procedure is generally known to the medical profession. Nor would the AMA or the American Heart Association approve of it because they consider it untested, which isn't true. It has been tested both in Europe and this country.

We have seen that Doctor Dean Ornish has scientifically proven that heart disease can be reversed without surgery. In his book, *Program For Reversing Heart Disease*,6 he reveals research and studies that show that diet and lifestyle not only prevent heart attacks, but actually have reversed the clogging of the arteries. His program involves healing of the heart emotionally and spiritually as well as physically. *The Washington Post* says, "There is emerging evidence that Ornish, with his non-invasive techniques, is accomplishing the same ends as are his scalpel-wielding colleagues."6 The National Institute of Health says, "Dr. Ornish's program can lead to a better life as well as a longer one. It is the only program, scientifically validated, to begin reversing even severe coronary disease without using cholesterol-lowering drugs or surgery."6

Forty million people in this country have heart disease and that's only those who have been diagnosed. Sixty million have high blood pressure and 80 million have cholesterol levels that are too high. Over 1.5 million people suffer heart attacks in this country each year. Still, the primary treatment for all this misery continues to be surgery and drugs.

Infection is becoming a serious problem with super strains of drug-resistant bacteria emerging as a result of overuse of antibiotics. Until that problem is resolved, you can do your part by using natural products that have antibiotic capabilities. Usnea, Petasites Officinalis and Nasturtiums are plentiful, just to name a few. A combination of Echinacea and Goldenseal is quite effective. I've used it for sinus infection and it works. Natural antibiotics can also be found in garden cress, watercress, and horseradish. You can protect yourself and your children from disease by using vegetables and herbs with antibiotic capabilities in your everyday diet. Garlic, especially fresh garlic, is very effective. It not only adds a wonderful flavor to the food but is a potent deterrent of infection. You don't need anyone's approval to use these products, and therein lies the basis for disease prevention and good health.

Just as we are individually responsible for our behavior and salvation, so are we personally responsible for the state of our health.

Unfortunately, there has been a great deal of irresponsibility when it comes to the care and condition of our bodies. What we eat, drink and breathe in, as well as the state of our mind, is very important. Of the utmost importance is how we perceive the nature of our being. The latter can overcome deficiencies in the former. If we believe that we are self-healing organisms and that the soul has the ability to perfect and maintain our bodies in good health, with the cooperation of our mind, then a deficiency in the kind and amount of the food we eat, for example, need not cause us health problems.

For instance, look at the diet of some of the cultures around the world. Some of the Peruvian Indians who live at high altitudes live almost entirely on a corn diet. They eat fresh corn, corn mush, corn bread and even drink corn beer. They eat very little in the way of green vegetables or meat. Still, they are magnificent specimens, with large lung capacities to compensate for the thinner air at higher altitudes. They have great endurance and are capable of running long distances with little effort.

By our nutritional standards, these people should be riddled with diseases such as scurvy, rickets, arthritis and osteoporosis due to diet malnutrition; yet they are not. It seems the only possible answer is that they *believe*, simply accept, that what they eat is all they need to eat. They believe they have the ability to exist and enjoy good health on what they eat. The lack of chemical pollutants in their daily environment is another positive factor. The soul, without their awareness to the contrary, does the rest.

So you see there is still that need for the cooperation of the dominant mind and the life-sustaining intelligence within us that is our soul. But we are often uncooperative, making bad decisions with our mind that tend to overwhelm the soul. We ingest harmful products that are not good for our body and do not have the understanding to call upon the intelligence within us that can offset their harmful effects. Or we eat, drink and breathe in harmful substances knowing, with our mind, that they are detrimental to our health, and so they become.

The best of all worlds is to consume and enjoy the things we know are good for us, avoiding what we know is harmful, and maintaining a state of mind that is free from stress. At the same time, we should hold the belief that we are truly, wonderfully made with the totality of our being able to sustain perfect health despite attack by antibiotic-resistance strains of bacteria or any other disease-causing organism.

This is the formula for enduring good health, healing, and even the cure for such diseases as cancer and AIDS. We prevent as well as cure disease by being responsible in what we ingest, in maintaining a positive mental attitude and believing in the ability of our life-perfecting soul and the power of the mind to assist.

In recovering from disease, a good and balanced nutritional program must also insure that a cleansing takes place at the start in order to eliminate all the toxic substances that have accumulated in the body. We have seen how our bodies are literally assaulted with toxins, including certain prescription drugs. They are a major factor in poor health. Research scientists say we don't have enough hard evidence to make such a judgment. Nonsense! We need to use our common sense and open our eyes to the empirical evidence. It is most certainly there. We saw that a University of Toronto study showed how bad reactions to prescription drugs were the U.S.'s fourth leading killer in 1994.7

The Food and Drug Administration approves drugs and other substances after lengthy testing to determine if they are safe. But insufficient attention is given to the cumulative effect, which can become toxic, or the combination effect of taking a variety of drugs at the same time which can be deadly. If a specific substance shows no harmful effects, the FDA pronounces it as safe. It probably is when taken individually. But when we ingest multiple substances, along with the chemicals we breathe in and harmful foods that we eat, the cumulative effect, especially over time, can be lethal. Many of us know of people, especially the elderly, who are taking a half-dozen, and in some extreme cases as many as twenty, drugs at the same time.

Many of these people just get sicker and sicker.

Older people are given prescriptions for drugs that they should almost never take; drugs that can produce amnesia and confusion, and others that cause serious side effects like heart problems or respiratory failure. Investigators said there is no need to prescribe these drugs to older people, either because safer alternatives are available or because the drugs are simply not needed."8 Most of those people would be better off throwing their medications down the toilet, starting over with a medical doctor who also practices nutritional and holistic medicine and making sure that their system is cleansed of these synthetic, often toxic, drugs.

The cleansing can be done on a fresh-fruit, fresh-vegetable and pure-water diet. The fruits and chlorophyll-rich vegetables are very powerful detoxifying agents. This regimen should be accompanied by the use of special cleansing herbs for the blood, liver, kidneys and colon. But you need to be informed. You also must beware of remedies that do not do what their purveyors claim. A lifetime of accumulated toxins in the body cannot be eliminated overnight, or even in a few weeks, as some claim. It takes time and patience. An herbalist can be helpful. Do not fast; this only weakens the body.

When you are generally in good health, your body can tolerate a certain amount of toxic substances. But if you are ill and fighting diseases such as cancer or AIDS, your body and the healing intelligence within you can better accomplish the task of restoration to health without having to contend with all of those harmful substances.

If you feel uncomfortable trying to do this alone, then look for a medical doctor who also practices nutritional and holistic medicine. It is ideal to find a doctor who will work with you. Your input and desires need to be considered. Avoid any doctor who is not willing to listen to and try your suggestions, especially one who tells you that he knows best.

Then you need to make sure that your nutrition program excludes the many harmful products that are offered for consumption. Get most of your protein from plants such as nuts, beans and mushrooms. Eliminate refined sugar and white flour. Don't use products that contain artificial sweeteners. Keep the chlorine out of your body by using pure water, both to drink and shower with. In a steamy shower, you both inhale and absorb chlorine from the tap water. Filters are available that will eliminate the chlorine, as well as other impurities. Air filtering units are available that can eliminate most harmful particles and gases.

Much of supermarket-packaged food is processed, pasteurized or preserved, taking out nutritive value or adding substances that are not good for you. Avoid these foods whenever possible, choosing to use fresh foods when they are available. Look for certified organically grown products. Farmers' markets offering these products are coming back and can be found in most cities. Even supermarkets are beginning to carry some organically grown produce.

Everyone should educate him or herself on the benefits of proper nutrition. A lot of material is available in the library that will help. Subscribe to publications such as a good vegetarian magazine and perhaps a reliable health newsletter. Many good books have been published on the subject. A new paradigm in health care is appearing with emphasis on proper nutrition and exercise as the way to prevent, as well as cure, illness. Albeit reluctantly, the government is beginning to recognize the importance of diet and lifestyle in fighting disease. The Surgeon General's office estimates that 66 percent of all deaths in this country are diet related.

In general, the medical establishment does not acknowledge the importance of a properly balanced diet in preventing as well as curing disease. Certainly, many in the medical profession do so, but the vast and primary emphasis is on extensive and expensive testing, surgery, radiation and prescription drugs. That is not to say, of course, that most doctors are not sincere and dedicated. They are simply locked into the long-standing medical practices that are taught in the medical schools. Nutritional medicine is seldom a part of their training.

This is very unfortunate, for nutritional, holistic medicine is the better way. It's the way of the future. The medical establishment and the pharmaceutical industry would do well to recognize this and speed up the transformation that is already taking place. Certainly there have been some great triumphs in the field of medicine, such as conquering polio and small pox. Medical technology and pharmaceutics have done wonders in relieving human suffering due to illness. Still, we shouldn't have to wait until we get sick to start the doctoring, when we know how to prevent most illnesses. We do it through good nutrition, a healthy environment and a proper mental attitude.

We have to change our perceptions in this matter of our health, understanding that we are in charge of and responsible for the state of our health. We need to make the decisions as to how we are going to prevent disease and treat our illnesses and not leave it up to the medical establishment, the pharmaceutical industry or the government. You say we don't have the knowledge and expertise to do so? We do! We may not have the knowledge at our fingertips, but it's readily available and easily understood. And we certainly have the know-how to both make the decisions and carry out the treatment.

Maintaining good health is so simple; it's a shame we have ignored it for so long, choosing to suffer so much. The evidence is overwhelming that improper diets--not enough fruits, vegetables and whole grains; using intemperate amounts of refined sugar, fried foods, fats, excessive alcohol, too much starchy food and too much animal fat--are hazardous to our health. It is common knowledge, yet we choose to stuff ourselves with cookies, candy, ice cream, donuts, French fries and hamburgers. Of course, we are egged on by the food industry and advertising media. Neither have the government nor medical establishment, who are fully aware of that evidence, fulfilled their responsibility in this matter.

We are especially remiss in the matter of health when it comes to our children. For example, the overuse of antibiotics for children is dangerous. Earaches, ear infections and fluid in the middle ear are very common among children and the incidence is rising. It is very likely that the basic problem is diet related, as children start their junk food diets at an early age influenced by television and in turn influencing their parents. The standard treatment for those problems is antibiotics and surgery. Continued use of synthetic antibiotics results in building resistance to them to the point that they may no longer be effective, putting the children more and more at risk.

About 650,000 surgical procedures are done annually to relieve ear conditions, the most common being to pierce the ear drum and insert small tubes to drain middle-ear fluid. Recent studies show that most of these surgeries were not necessary; that if left alone the condition would have cleared by itself without negative repercussions.

"Cleared by itself," of course, meaning that the healing intelligence within the child handles the problem. Children usually don't get in the way of that healing with negativity of their minds. They are, for the most part, happy and content, not having yet learned about stress, although, in this day and age, stress is becoming more of a factor in the lives of our children. But they do hinder the healing by their less-than-proper diets.

Many parents are failing their children, not only by neglecting to teach and show them proper values and good behavior, but in the way that they feed them. Shamefully absent from their meals are fruits and vegetables. Notoriously present are all the wrong kinds of foods: sugar-laden cereals, whole milk, too many proteins and fats and too much starchy food, such as are found in baloney and cheese sandwiches, hamburgers and hot dogs, chips and pastries. Their liquid diet consists of a great deal of artificially colored and flavored water called soda pop when they should be given juices and nonfat milk as well as pure water. They are fed too many foods that contain pesticides, preservatives and synthetic substances.

Most diseases and illnesses can be treated naturally. God knew what he was doing when he made the blueprint for this body and our environment. "Nature" contains everything we need, both to stay healthy and cure disease. Within nature can be found the source of disease prevention. When we are irresponsible, bringing illness upon ourselves, or even if it should overtake us through no fault of our own, then nature also provides the natural medicine and remedies to assist the mind and soul in healing and restoring the body to perfect health.

We have already seen the importance of nutrition in reversing heart disease. The associated problem of high blood pressure, currently afflicting 60 million Americans, has a very simple, natural and effective solution: Reduce the fat in your diet, and eat lots of fruits, vegetables. Bananas, almonds and unpolished brown rice work well. White rice has much of the nutritive value removed, thus losing its effectiveness in restoring elasticity to the blood vessels. Recent studies show that a dominant diet of fruits, vegetables and whole grains can significantly reduce blood pressure in as little as two to three weeks.

Standard treatment consists of drugs that lower blood pressure but do nothing to resolve the basic cause. Those drugs can have very unpleasant side-effects such as impotence, fatigue, depression and an irregular heartbeat. Why would anyone opt for such treatment when a better way is available naturally without any side-effects whatsoever?

Malignant melanoma, the most dangerous form of skin cancer, is on the rise, despite the fact that sunscreens are touted as a good preventative and used by many people. All this leads scientists to wonder how effective sunscreens really are and whether they may inadvertently increase the risk of cancer and other disease by providing people with a false sense of security, as well as depriving them of the vitamin D benefits of the sun.

New research at the University of Texas in Houston suggests that "sunscreens can protect against sunburn, but not against melanoma," says the study's co-author, Margaret Kripke. "In addition, experts now speculate that the sun's ultraviolet A rays may be more harmful than once thought, rendering the many sunscreens that protect only against the burning ultraviolet B rays less effective than believed. Another factor may be the decrease in ozone concentration, the earth's 'sunscreen.' As a result, we're getting more radiation now than people did in the past."[9]

It is quite probable that another factor is involved in skin cancer, but it has been given little, if any, consideration. Why is it that some people who spend a great deal of time in the sun, over their entire lifetime, never develop skin cancer? The answer would seem to be that people are diverse; their chemical makeup is different, or some have stronger "immune systems." But what determines the chemical makeup of the body? It is the nutrients that we take into the body or the lack thereof that does so. Or body chemistry is altered by toxic substances that we ingest. Even though body chemistry can be genetic in nature, it can be altered by a change of diet. Although the sun and, perhaps, a reduction in the strength of the ozone layer may be contributing factors to skin cancer, it is more likely that faulty nutrition and ingestion of toxic chemicals are the primary cause. That melanoma is frequently showing up on parts of the body that are not exposed to the sun would lend support to this premise.

There is a basic rule of health: When we abuse the body there are consequences often showing up in the way of disease. These bodies that we possess are indeed wonderfully and respectfully made, but they are not invincible. We need to respect and take proper care of them. Then, should we incur illness or disease not of our making, we need to use remedies that are naturally provided for us rather than synthetic drugs and treatments that are often harmful. God, in his role of "mother nature," has provided us with a natural pharmacy without equal. But we need to educate ourselves in their use, as well as insisting that the medical profession and the pharmaceutical industry take advantage of that pharmacy.

To be fair, we can't put all the blame on the food industry, advertising, the medical field and the government when it comes to our health. Most of us know what's good and bad for us, but we're often weak-willed, lazy and irresponsible. We don't respect or appreciate our bodies. We welcome the fast food convenience and don't want to take the time to properly prepare the right foods.

Or we attempt to make sure we get proper nutrition by adding vitamins and nutritive supplements to our regular, often poor, diets. If you make sure you get a balanced diet, you don't need these supplements; although there are exceptions. For example, if you are suffering from a condition that requires more of a chemical or nutrient to correct than you would normally get from your regular diet, you should take a supplement until your condition has been alleviated.

Of course, we are conditioned to think that food needs fat, salt and sugar to taste good, and we are, therefore, often willing to take the risk. Or we live by the philosophy that it "won't happen to me." Except for the basic taste sensations of sweet and sour, bitter and salty, our tastes are cultivated and conditioned by the mind. We remember how we hated spinach and eggplant when we were young, yet somehow, when we got older, we began to like them. Baked eggplant Parmigiana is wonderful. Those who have gone on a low-salt diet out of medical necessity, and remained on it for some time, will tell you how unpleasant salted foods have become for them. Although now, the experts are telling us that salt is not the villain that they once thought it to be, and use of salt is not a factor in high blood pressure for most people. If, over a period of time, you gradually reduce your use of milk from whole milk to 2 percent, to 1 percent and then to nonfat, you will find that the nonfat milk tastes just as good, and that whole milk no longer tastes just right on your natural cereal or with your veggie sandwich.

Many believe that use of less meat and a vegetable-dominant diet deprives one of the joys of eating. Nothing is farther from the truth. Numerous and varied dishes can be prepared from nuts, grains, fruits and vegetables and they are absolutely delicious.

A veggie sandwich? Sure, they taste great. Use whole-grain breads without preservatives. Warm the slices very lightly in the microwave, but not too much, for they will turn to "cement." Toasted is great, too. Use low-fat mayo, mustard or lite butter. For the filling try any combination of romaine lettuce (it has the better nutritive value), a slice of vine-ripened tomato, sweet Oso or Vidalia onions, fresh avocado slices (avocado has gotten a bad rap; it's good for you, even helping to lower your cholesterol), fresh sliced mushrooms, red bell pepper (it has more nutritive value than the green, but green is okay if you prefer), mild green chili peppers, or anything else that your heart desires. Experiment and you will find some wonderful combinations. Then top it off with a low-fat cheese of your choosing. After you add the cheese, pop it in the toaster oven and call it a veggie melt. Some of the low-fat cheeses don't have much taste, so regular cheese is okay and won't hurt you as long as you don't use it habitually. Try soy cheese--some have great taste. Use different herbs and dressings as seasoning for your sandwiches until you find one, or a combination, that you really enjoy.

A variety of pasta dishes abounds. Pasta primavera (with broccoli, carrots and zucchini) topped with a marinara sauce and lightly sprinkled with Parmesan or Romano cheese is wonderful. The list of vegetarian foods seems endless: dozens of potato dishes, soups, salads, breads, pizzas, rice, nuts, stir fries, all kinds of beans and more. But be cautious of the starchy foods. There are varied dressings for your salads that are low or even non-fat with zero cholesterol. Some are made with all-natural ingredients. Vinegar and oil are okay if you use a good oil like extra-virgin olive oil. We need oil in our diets, but the beneficial kind. Have you noticed that the Italians have such good complexions? They use olive oil and garlic liberally in their cooking, both of which are good for the skin.

You don't even have to give up your hamburgers and hot dogs. There are different burger and Frankfurter products on the market made from soy and other vegetable produce. They look like hamburger patties and frankfurters, with texture and taste being very similar. When you add the onion, lettuce, ketchup, mustard, pickle and chili, there is even less difference in the taste. Yes, chili! The burger-substitute product makes wonderful chili, as well as Sloppy Joes. Nor do you have to give up sweets. Use natural sweeteners like honey, molasses and real maple syrup. But keep your use of refined sugar to a minimum. A piece of cake, pie or candy once in a while isn't going to harm you.

Nor do you have to give up Fettuccini Alfredo, chili Relleno, eggplant Parmigiana or Chinese food. The grams of fat in a small helping of those foods constitute approximately one's maximum suggested fat allowance for one day. Just don't eat any other fat for that day. Your body size and daily calorie intake may dictate no other fat for two days. When you fix such recipes at home you can lower the fat content to half or less, without losing significant taste, by using reduced-fat ingredients, a lesser amount of them and appropriate herbs to enhance the taste. Many restaurants are beginning to prepare such dishes with reduced-fat calories. Those kinds of dishes occasionally will not be detrimental to your health as long as your regular diet consists of plenty of fruits, vegetables and grains, and you keep a positive mental attitude about it.

Why would anyone not want to go on a nutritional program, knowing that you are not denying yourself the pleasures of eating and that you are going to be healthier, happier, more able to fend off disease and cure the illnesses that you already have? The beauty of such a program is that you will never have to be concerned about your weight; it will automatically take care of itself. Throw away your bathroom scales and calorie counter. Your grocery bill will be smaller. You will have fewer headaches, colds and backaches. Indigestion and constipation will disappear. Your over-the-counter medicine bill will be much smaller and likely nonexistent. Your breath will be fresher, and your need for deodorant will decrease. You will have more energy. How we think with our mind is very important.

THE MIND CONNECTION

Equally important is the mental aspect of the healing program. We can generally live with a certain amount of stress in our lives, but if you are battling cancer or AIDS, it is imperative that you eliminate the stress in your life which comes from anger, hatred, worry and any other source. Granted, it isn't always easy, especially when you have to deal with people who are a source of anxiety. Certainly it's difficult not to worry if you believe that you are going to suffer and die, particularly if you entertain thoughts about the concepts of death that are prevalent in our society today. You should never be afraid of or concerned about dying; it is the suffering that you want to avoid. But it can be done; you can achieve peace of mind in any circumstance.

You can always remove yourself from a situation or location that causes stress; for example, a job. But this kind of drastic action normally isn't necessary. You can learn to eliminate the stress, whatever its source, by the power of your mind. It can be done through hypnosis or meditation and changing your perceptions.

We should really call it self-hypnosis, for it is actually accomplished by the individual and not another person. One uses learned techniques or follows instructions imparted by another. The concept of hypnotism is greatly misunderstood. It is often thought of as a trance-like condition in which you are unaware of what is happening to you. Self-hypnosis is simply a state of total relaxation of the body and mind. Your body is as thoroughly relaxed as in the sleep state. The mind is clear and at rest but completely aware, as in the fully-conscious state. Hypnosis is an altered state of consciousness in which your mind is free from outside distractions and highly receptive to thoughts and suggestions.

Another common misconception, even among most hypnotherapists themselves, is that during a hypnotic state the subconscious mind can be programmed. It cannot! As we have already discussed, in the chapter on the Nature of Man, the subconscious or soul is constant, unalterable and immovable. It is the conscious mind that is being programmed. We know that thoughts, happenings and ideas that are implanted in the memory of the mind, particularly with repetition or great emphasis, are very powerful in influencing our behavior. For example, we remember that certain actions bring unpleasant consequences and so we avoid them. On the other hand we recall with the mind that certain behavior results in pleasure and so our conduct is influenced accordingly. Just like Pavlov's dogs, we respond to a program with which we have been conditioned and remember. It is the conscious mind that has been programmed, not the "subconscious." Clearly we respond with a decision of the mind. It is the values and beliefs that we have thought about with our mind, stored in the memory and held with deep conviction that control our behavior.

Hypnosis should be used as a means to relax and program the mind with beneficial thoughts while in that state of repose. A great number of books are available on hypnosis, including do-it-yourself manuals. You can use self-hypnosis to learn relaxation techniques, remembering that any thoughts you are entertaining while in that state constitute a programming of the conscious mind and memory, not the "subconscious."

Meditation is very much like hypnosis. To meditate is to engage in thought or contemplation, usually on a given subject, often in order to gain understanding or peace of mind. Or, meditation can take other forms, such as listening to music that you enjoy, walking on the beach, looking at the stars or lying in a meadow, smelling the fragrance of the flowers and feeling the soft breeze upon your face. Still, the purpose is to promote peace of mind, good health and mental well-being.

Another type of meditation does not involve thinking about a given subject, but rather is the absence of thought. It is called transcendental meditation. The idea is to transcend thought, sitting silently without thinking about anything whatsoever. The goal of transcendental meditation is to get in touch with your inner self, freeing your mind of all conscious thought and letting that inner self influence or "speak" to you. It is not easy to do, at least initially. Except when in the state of sleep, thoughts of some kind are always running through the mind. When you close your eyes and first try to empty the mind of all thought, within a matter of seconds, some thought will pop into your mind. Emptying the mind takes practice. Books that are helpful are available, as well as people who can teach you meditation.

Different postures can be assumed during meditation. A traditional one is sitting with legs folded and hands in the lap in the lotus position. But if one is not experienced with that posture, cramping will soon overtake the muscles, making meditation difficult if not impossible. Some believe that sitting erect and/or slightly swaying forward and backward is important. The ideal situation is to assume a position that is completely relaxing, such as sitting in an easy chair, so that no muscles are being used.

A mantra, some word that is continually repeated during meditation, is frequently used. Its continued use eliminates other thoughts. All these things work, but still require activity of the mind. One has to send thoughts to the muscles to remain in an erect posture or sway, as well as speak the mantra. Other techniques involve narrowing thought to the inhalation and exhalation of the breath or picturing blackness. As you see, they all require thought, so you need to decide which works best for you. When you become more experienced in the practice of meditation, those techniques become pretty much automatic so that the mind is relatively free from thought.

To free the mind completely from conscious thought is very helpful in achieving peace of mind. But the greater benefit is to get in closer touch with the soul. When we get out of the way of the busy and often negative thoughts of the mind, then the inner or higher self, the soul, can go about its work of perfecting us both physically and spiritually. Meditation is an excellent way to achieve this.

Both self-hypnosis and meditation can be very instrumental in removing all forms of stress from the body and mind. Even when thrust back into a situation that is the cause of the stress, frequent use of hypnosis and meditation can help reduce its impact. Regular exercise is also very important in reducing and controlling stress. There is a last step that will literally eliminate stress from your life: CHANGE YOUR PERCEPTIONS! You need to change how you think about the stressful situation or the cause of the stress. "Get yourself new minds and hearts," as God has told us; as well, we need to remember that "as we think, so are we!"

For example, danger and challenge are stressful to most people, still there are those who thrive on them. It's all a matter of how they think about such activities. Whitewater rafting can be both challenging and dangerous, and to those who think of it that way, it is stressful. The veteran rafter finds it enjoyable, exhilarating and even relaxing because he thinks of it as such.

Driving an automobile in traffic can be a great source of trepidation and even downright hazardous to one's life and limb. Speeders, slowpokes, lane weavers, traffic tie-ups, confusing signs, honkers, drunken drivers, finger-givers, fist-shakers, rain, snow, sleet, heat and many other factors contribute to the tremendous stress that can be experienced. Although most of us consider ourselves good drivers who don't do these things, or aren't unduly influenced by them, we still often respond in kind. We honk, we curse and swear, fret, stew, shake the fist, shout, call other drivers names, won't let other drivers in and often drive too fast for road conditions, all of which drive our blood pressure sky high and are detrimental to both our physical and mental well-being.

None of these reactions on our part need occur if we just change our perceptions. It is possible to be calm, cool, relaxed and even enjoy driving under these conditions. The first thing we need to think about, understand and accept is that these kinds of reactions to bad drivers do not adversely affect them or change them. The harm and change that occurs is to ourselves. We become stressed, our blood pressure goes up, we get angry, feel unhappy, and our health and peace of mind suffer. Why would we do this to ourselves when it isn't necessary?

Through thought and power of the mind, we can simply tell ourselves that we are not going to jeopardize our well-being by allowing unsettling reactions to others. We refuse to react in that manner. Rather we can choose to stay calm, let the other driver in, ignore and avoid the reckless driver, and adjust our driving to the conditions. If traffic is backed up and we're going to be late, we simply tell ourselves that we can do nothing to change it, so there's no gain in getting upset. Relax, tune in to your favorite music, and enjoy it. Think about pleasant things, smile, laugh, sing and be courteous. Every one of us can do it, but it takes time. Behavior that we have been conditioned to for so long is often difficult to change.

These basics of changing our perception and, thus, our behavior apply not only to driving, but to all of our relations with others; at home, in the office or wherever we are. Life can be wonderful! Why unnecessarily make it otherwise? Take charge; be in control! Show love, kindness and patience to others, perceiving that this is what God tells us is essential for achieving heaven on earth, as well as in the hereafter.

Can we truly eliminate all stress from our lives? What about drastic situations, such as losing one's job, bankruptcy, losing our home or divorce? Or perchance being face to face with violent death? How could anyone's anxiety level not be drastically elevated with a gun held to the head? The answer is "yes," we can eliminate stress and remain calm and unaffected in every one of those situations!

Again, the solution is to change our perception! No matter what confronts us, we have to believe that everything will be okay. For it will be! As one experiencer said, "I remember that I knew that everything, everywhere in the universe was OK, that the plan was perfect...I was just an infinite being in perfection. And love and safety and security and knowing that nothing could happen to you..."10 God's plan is perfect, but because man chooses to do wrong, suffering often results. That is not okay. Still, in the end, everything will be! As the scriptures say, "Who can be against us if God is for us?"11 And he is indeed! Nothing can separate us from the love of God, no tribulation whatsoever! When we think like that, we can face anything that confronts us with serenity and composure.

Yes, even the gun to the head! Do you remember Jackie Pflug, who was aboard a hijacked airliner, scheduled for execution and shot in the head? Prior to being shot, and after worrying for an hour about her possible fate, she said, "I just stopped struggling. I just closed my eyes and went into a place that was very safe. A place of non-worry, knowing that everything would be all right no matter what happened....whether I lived or whether I died."

We all can live in that belief, that everything will be all right, no matter what happens. Every one of us can find that place of non-worry. Jackie found it through prayer in her dire need. We, too, can find it when trouble confronts us. But we can have it right now by changing our perception of our own nature and the nature of God. We claim it by accepting that we are divine and immortal, as well as human and mortal and by believing that "we are spirits, and spirits move on," as Jackie Pflug says. It is ours by understanding that God is for us, and nothing can stand between us and his unconditional love; by understanding that all of us, without exception, will eventually be reunited with God.

We now have three of the four ingredients for good health and healing. One is to cleanse our bodies of the toxins that we have consumed with our food and the air that we breathe. Then make sure that we avoid, as much as possible, any further consumption of them. Two is to change our diet, eliminating or at least minimizing, the foods that we know are not the best for us, making sure that we eat primarily natural foods, without preservatives and preferably organically grown. Three is to get control of the stress in our lives, working toward the goal of complete serenity.

The medical establishment, researchers, the government and most of the rest of us are already aware of the above information; however, for varied reasons, choose not to avail ourselves of such a program or teach its benefits. That is so unfortunate, for we could eliminate so much suffering of the human race if we would do so. Yet, the handwriting is on the wall; the spiritual, nutritional and health revolution has already begun. Why not join in, get aboard and enjoy life?

Few are aware of the fourth factor. Or, society in general has failed to realize its significance, although its presence is known and its benefits proven. It is a factor that is very beneficial in preventing disease and sustaining good health, an element that is absolutely essential in avoiding the suffering from diseases. That factor is the power of the mind. It has been emphasized throughout this text. We know how the thoughts of our mind can affect our behavior. We even know that we can make ourselves ill or well by the thoughts that we hold in our mind. But those in the field of medicine haven't made the connection as to why this is so. They have failed to find the link because of false perceptions.

They have not perceived the human body as a true and efficient self-healing organism. Although it is acknowledged that healing ability is possessed by the body, it is widely believed that modern medicine, in the form of drugs, high-tech equipment and surgery, is absolutely essential in solving the health problems of mankind.

The greatest misconception concerns the total nature of man. Although most doctors and medical researchers probably believe in the soul, they aren't aware of its function in sustaining life and its ability to heal and perfect the body. Most unfortunate is the unawareness of the relationship between the mind and that healing intelligence within us called the soul. Even those few who promote mind/body and spiritual healing have not made the final connection--that the mind is dominant; that it is the free will that God has given us and that, when the mind is programmed with negative thoughts and ideas, negative results occur.

Thus, when a doctor makes a terminal prognosis and so informs a patient, he is pronouncing the death sentence. For when that thought is planted in the patient's mind and, usually after a short period of denial, he accepts the prognosis and believes he is going to die, he will die, just as surely as God made little green apples. The only time the "death sentence" can be commuted is when the patient changes the perception that he is terminal.

We have a great deal of evidence that all of that is so. Some of it has been presented at the beginning of this chapter in the cases of those who have recovered from terminal illnesses, as well as those who have not. It is only when the patient rejects the prognosis and believes he is going to get better, that terminal illnesses such as encountered with some cancers and AIDS, for example, can be overcome.

It is that decision by the mind that makes the difference. I want to reemphasize that the proof is in the results: "She had absolute belief that she would get well." "She willed herself to be healed." "I had the unusual sense that I was going to make it." "He was completely convinced he would get well." "He was sure he would beat it." "He had absolute unwavering belief he would get better." "He just decided he was not going to get cancer." "I told myself I would never get sick another day in my life." "Through her deep-seated resolve, she got well." And they all did!

In all of those cases, the individuals themselves, through the power of the mind, commuted their "death sentence." All of us in the totality of our being, our body, mind and soul, have the ability to heal ourselves of disease. God has given this power and authority to us. After all, we are made in his likeness which would include the capability to heal. It is an endowment that we all possess. Of course, we must have possession of our mental faculties. When we do not, such as with certain mental diseases, then others must help, using modern medicines, nutritional medicine, prayer and belief.

The medical establishment should eliminate the prognosis of "terminal." Rather, patients should be advised that they have a life-threatening illness, but that it need not be terminal. If you have been diagnosed and pronounced terminal, you must totally reject it! You must get yourself a "new mind and new heart." A new mind that perceives your illness as only temporary and which can be overcome, a mind that understands that you are wonderfully and respectfully made, a self-healing organism, with the total capacity to heal itself. You must get a heart that believes, with deep conviction, that those abilities do constitute your true nature and that recovery from the disease is possible.

When you get all four of those healing and disease-preventing factors working for you, then you will be on the road to perfect health and recovery from any disease you may have incurred.

In Chapter Three, we discussed the need for a new paradigm concerning health, healing and medicine if we are to win the battle with disease that is rapidly overtaking and threatening mankind. We need to take primary responsibility for our own health. We must improve the quality of our food supply, eliminating, or greatly reducing, synthetic chemicals that are used to grow and preserve it. We need to be aware that convenience is proving harmful to us, and we need to get back to preparation and use of natural foods. It is important that we get on with cleaning up our water and air supply. Progress has been pitifully slow. The World Water Council has estimated that at least "five million people die each year due to filthy drinking water, caused by massive amounts of pollutants, including sewage, industrial wastes and hazardous fertilizers being dumped into the world's lakes and rivers."12

The medical establishment must speed up the transition from drugs and surgery to natural and nutritional medicine, for it is the wave of the future; the true, natural and God-given solution to our health problems. All of us need to be aware of the importance that good nutrition and lifestyle play when it comes to the state of our health, and make changes as necessary.

Of the utmost importance is the need to change the perception of our own nature concerning disease prevention and the ability to heal. When we understand and accept the presence of an intelligence within us that is capable of sustaining and perfecting life, with the cooperation and assistance of the mind, then we can conquer disease, and illness will be a thing of the past. Then will we "die" only of old age. We could live to the age of 120, or perhaps even 969, as did Methuselah, and enjoy every minute of it. There is no need for mankind to suffer as we do from disease and illness. It is time to set aside all the false beliefs and ulterior motives that are present in our health care system and enjoy good health!

──── *Chapter Twenty One* ────
CONCLUSION

There are a great multitude of people waiting for the world to be destroyed in some Armageddon-like cataclysm. They believe it is coming, especially as they witness conditions waxing worse and worse, and they perceive mankind as descending into completely uncivilized behavior and depravity. Many believe it is relatively imminent. It isn't going to happen! This world is going to continue until humanity learns to live in peace and harmony. Only then will some form of a new heaven and earth come into being. Scriptures tell us that all of God's laws must be fulfilled,[1] that his will is to be done on earth as in heaven,[2] that God's ways will reign supreme[3] and when (not "if") the world is full of the knowledge of the Lord, then there will be no more harm in all the earth.[4]

So let's not continue to suffer and let the deterioration of the world proceed. Let's get on with searching for knowledge of God and fulfilling his laws in order to return this world to the heavenly paradise that it was intended to be. We have the complete ability to do so. It's time to take charge of our lives and accept responsibility for our actions and the things that happen in this world. By false perceptions, especially of our own nature, we have let circumstances and the thoughts of our minds shape our lives and environment, to our detriment and sorrow.

James Allen, author of *As A Man Thinketh*, says it well: "Man is buffeted by circumstances so long as he believes himself to be the creature of outside conditions, but when he realizes that he is a creative power and that he may command the hidden soil and seeds of his being out of which circumstances grow, he then becomes the rightful master of himself.... Man, as the lord and master of thought, is the maker of himself, the shaper and author of his environment.... Man has but to right himself to find that the universe is right."[5]

Let us summarize how we have adversely shaped ourselves, our surroundings and what we must do to right them and, thusly, the world. Primarily through religious beliefs we have made the human being a poor, inadequate, mortal creature, with few redeeming qualities, whose destiny is to struggle through life, continually doing that which is wrong, and who can do little if anything of his own accord to change all that. We have been conditioned by others and our own thoughts to think in these terms and so it is what we have become. As we think, so are we! It is an image of mankind that must be totally rejected. We are better and much more than that.

We must accept what God tells us about ourselves: that we are made in his likeness, that we are wonderfully and respectfully made, that we are the salt of the earth and the light of the world, that we can bring forth good things from the goodness of our hearts, that we can turn from our wrongdoing and do what is right and good..

We must perceive ourselves as magnificent, sentient beings who are masters of our own destiny who can control circumstances along the road that leads to it. We need to understand that we are responsible for our lives, our own good health, the condition of this world that God has given us to live in and our salvation. He has provided us everything that we need to make our habitat a paradise, live in bliss, and achieve heaven. He provided us with a soul that gives and sustains life. In accordance with God's blueprint and the free will he has given us, we create for ourselves a powerful, dominant, conscious mind with which we can control all aspects of this life as well as our destiny. In what we call Nature, God has supplied us with our food, shelter and everything else essential to our well-being. All he asks of us is that we show one another love.

But, in order to do that, we must change the perception of our nature from that of an error-prone, poor, sinful being to one who is fully capable of goodness and fully capable of letting our love show forth so as to make the world a better place as God has instructed us to do. We must learn to love our neighbor as our self. But first we need to discover how to love ourselves. How can we possibly do that if we continue to perceive ourselves as that sinful being whose nature it is to do wrong? How can we achieve self-love when we are bombarded with such concepts as being rotten, depraved beings with nothing but evil in our hearts? We must reject all such teachings by men and believe only God.

We must also believe him when he tells us that we are responsible for, and will be held to account for, our actions in this lifetime. So, let's start thinking of life that way, rather than blaming other people and events for our problems and the condition of the world. When we change our ways, taking responsibility and doing that which is right and good, then our lives and the world will change for the better.

Molli Nickell, author and publisher of *Spirit Speaks* magazine, said it beautifully: "The moment you begin to take conscious responsibility for your life, it will change dramatically. Owning your thoughts and deeds moves you into the status of being in charge of your own life as you create it and recreate it moment by moment. You'll discover self-empowerment which will lead to increased feelings of freedom. You'll become a happy creator, taking responsibility, making conscious choices, and being the awesome, powerful and joyful being you were always meant to be. Go for it!"[6]

But we have often been very irresponsible in our lives. Perhaps the greatest bane is the belief that materialism equates to happiness and success, and thus we strive to accumulate treasure and power. In doing so, all kinds of bad things happen to mankind and the world. Greed, political corruption, selfishness and indifference raise their ugly heads. By-products are poverty, debt, crime, violence and war. Certainly this isn't true of all people. Gaining wealth, as long as it is used properly, is not wrong. Many use their material gains wisely, not storing up great wealth, providing jobs for others and helping those in need. But the predominant philosophy in the world is to "look out for number one; you can never be too rich; let the other guy fend for himself and do unto others before they can do unto you."

God has told us that the first priority is to seek his kingdom and his righteousness. God's kingdom is an earth that exists in peace and harmony. We think of war as inevitable. It is not! World peace is achievable. We simply have to change our perception, believing that it is attainable. Then we must take responsibility for what we have done in arming the world to the teeth, acknowledging that it was wrong and take steps to right that wrong.

We must change the perceptions that "might makes right" and provides security; that there will always be evil in the world and therefore we must be prepared to battle it with guns and explosives. Military might eventually results in insecurity. Love is a much better and more effective "weapon" against evil. We must listen to God, who has told us not to kill, rather than to governments and leaders who tell us that it's okay. If we believe God, then there is no need for weapons.

Nor do we need them to defend ourselves when we accept God's instructions that we are to turn the other cheek, love our enemies, and do good to those who persecute us. It's a hard philosophy to accept and live by, but God's wisdom is flawless. Using weapons to kill animals for food or to thin the herds and flocks is okay. Killing them simply for the sport of it, is not. Sport is defined as activity requiring skill or physical prowess, of a competitive nature, as in racing, ball games and hunting. Sportsmanship is defined as fair and courteous conduct while engaged in a sport. Is it competitive and fair to blast innocent and helpless doves out of the sky with a shotgun? Is it sporting to blow away a defenseless deer with a high-powered rifle and a pinpoint-accurate telescope? We must adopt the mindset that commands that we change swords into plowshares; that realizes that only love can conquer hate.

In the interim, until we realize the abolition of armies and armament, the world's military establishment can use its resources for humanitarian relief. A very great need exists for such action. Funds currently being spent for the production of weapons of war, as well as space exploration, can be redirected into the manufacture of equipment and the use of manpower to ease the problems that confront mankind.

For example, water is plentiful in the world. It's just not accessible for various reasons. It's too salty, too much rainwater runs back into the ocean, or it needs to be transported great distances. We can build catchment systems, water pipelines and waterways. Desalinization technology is here. It's expensive, but only a portion of the money that is spent on space exploration, "defense" and weapons of war would provide all the fresh water we need to turn much of the desert and drought-stricken area of the world into farmland and veritable green pastures, eliminating hunger as well as easing political turmoil. A major point of contention in the Middle East is the control of the limited water supply there. The Israelis have done a remarkable job of turning the desert into fertile and productive land. The same can be done for much of the other arid land in the Middle East, with the result that dispute, violence and war over territory there will greatly diminish, if not cease.

There are many other forms of "plowshares" that the military industrial complex can transition to for the benefit of mankind, without disrupting profits and employment. World peace is elusive, but not impossible. We only need to change our perceptions and actions will follow. And, after all, scripture tells us that, "Nation will not lift up sword against nation, neither will they learn war anymore."7 Knowing that the peaceable kingdom is coming, why wait? Let's get on with it now!

We will never achieve harmony on earth until we change our perception of one another. Racism and discrimination are alive and well in the world. When we look at one another we see and think such thoughts as white, black, fat, thin, tall, short, beautiful, ugly, rich, poor, American, Jew, Arab, and on and on. We think that way because we are conditioned all of our lives to do so by parents, educators, literature, religion, governments and media, and thus prejudice, intolerance and disunity come into being and thrive. Surely we have to be realistic, but when we classify people like that for the purpose of judging or criticizing them, which is commonly done, then it is wrong.

We need to deliberately change the way we think. When we

look at a person we should see a being made in God's image, one who possesses the qualities of love, goodness and compassion even though they may be suppressed, one who is wonderfully and respectfully made and one who is to be respected and held in high regard, as God has told us to do. We should see all people as our neighbors to whom we are required by God to show love, kindness, caring, mercy and forgiveness. When we do so, then bigotry and injustice will have disappeared, and we will have found God's righteousness; we are right and acceptable to him.

We also have been incredibly irresponsible when it comes to our children. We have failed to bring them up in the nurture and admonition of the Lord; failed to teach them love and respect for others. It is not enough to tell them about love, respect, courtesy, kindness and all the values that are essential to a civilized and harmonious society. We must set the example. The model that children predominantly see today is one of disrespect, rudeness, impatience, anger, hatred and violence.

They are bombarded with that example from all sides: parents, peers, governments, literature, movies and especially television. No matter how much we preach values to them, it is the example from which they learn and which they then imitate. How can we expect children to be respectful and courteous when they see a parent who is rude to other drivers, shouting, cursing and using unfriendly gestures? How can they learn patience when they are treated with impatience? How can they learn to be kind when parents are unkind to them and each other? How can they learn love when they see so much hatred in the world?

The violence and sexual innuendo in books, magazines, movies and television are appalling. It is present even in children's books and videos. Those who produce that material are grossly irresponsible. The First Amendment gives us freedom of speech and expression, but does not give us license to teach such detrimental material to our children, which is surely what we are doing. That material is also bad for adults, for they too, are adversely influenced by it.

We rationalize by saying that parents can control what their children read and view. Or that adults don't have to buy the material and they know where the "Off" switch is. Producers of that material say they are providing only what the audiences want and demand. Many contend that it is not harmful, citing their experience with such material when they were children and that they turned out all right.

All of those premises are faulty. We are assailed by so much material that parents can't always control their children's access to it. Or the parents are not always in the position of being at home to regulate television viewing. They shouldn't have to put a lock box or "V" chip on the TV. Much of the material is insidious. The producers are not responding to what the audience wants, but what they have been conditioned to want by the tremendous volume and incessant flow of that kind of material, as well as the lack of good, decent non-violent viewing matter. Radio is not innocent, either.

Also the programs and material of today are more violent, explicit and frequent than those of past generations. There can be little doubt that such material affects the behavior of the viewer. Children can become so negatively conditioned that they think it is normal behavior. Clearly they imitate what they see and read. There are many cases of crime and violence in which the perpetrator remarked that they had learned about it on television.

We don't seem to have grasped the concept that the continual programming and conditioning of the mind with the violence, sexual behavior, hatred and anger that is so prevalent on television can manifest those things in our actions. Is it any wonder that crime and violence among and by children is skyrocketing? It's time to take responsibility and clean up television and other forms of irresponsible media that are so adversely affecting us and our children. If they won't do it themselves, then we must do it for them through regulatory agencies and/or on an individual basis by other means, such as boycott.

We need to "empower" the children with good values, teaching them love, kindness, patience, politeness, caring and forgiveness *by example.* That is our responsibility. God holds us accountable. He has declared woe unto those who lead the little ones astray. Not woe that God is going to inflict, but that which is even now being experienced by society. We need to right ourselves, change our ways, and begin to raise our children properly.

We have been much less than responsible in sexual matters, such as indulgence and pregnancy at too early an age, as well as promiscuity among adults. They all have caused harm, both to the individual and society at large.

Sexual intercourse constitutes a very intimate and emotional experience. To enter into such a relationship when one is young and immature can be detrimental to one's well-being. Young people find it difficult enough to cope with the demands of life in getting an education, perhaps having to work, and dealing with peer and family relationships, without having to contend with a sexual relationship and concern about pregnancy and disease. Of course that can hold true for adults as well, especially those who are promiscuous in their sexual relationships. Promiscuity for both the young and adult is not only hazardous to one's health, but shows disrespect for one another, a deficiency in discipline and a lack of the caring kind of love that God expects of us.

Fortunately, some young people have good minds and are learning those things. Many are rejecting the advice of those adults and "experts" who say we are sexual beings whose nature it is to engage in sexual activity as soon as we are able; that children are going to do it anyway, so don't preach abstinence, but rather safe sex. A growing abstinence movement among teenagers reflects their wisdom.

To become pregnant either as a teenager or adult, when it is not desired, is most certainly careless and irresponsible behavior, regardless of the passion of the moment. To abort pregnancies further compounds the irresponsibility. If a society cannot agree on whether or not abortion is acceptable, surely most can agree that unwanted pregnancies are not and that steps should be taken, both collectively and personally, to prevent them, knowing that to abort them can be harmful both physiologically and psychologically.

To bring children into the world when they cannot be supported and provided for physically, economically and emotionally also shows a lack of responsibility. To oppose conception by means of birth control, on the basis of God's instructions to go forth and multiply, is illogical and irresponsible. Surely, we can do both, controlling conception, unwanted pregnancy and the number of offspring, at the same time that we propagate the species. What of celibacy? Would that not be disobedience to God's command to go forth and multiply?

How about homosexuality? Is it an abomination, or could it possibly be acceptable? Surely, it has been a major factor in the spread of AIDS. It would seem that it is not natural. By both biological and biblical standards, it is man and woman who constitute the basic relationship involving family and reproduction. Homosexual relationships cannot bring forth offspring.

What of the sexual act itself between members of the same sex? Although sex is an important and enjoyable part of living, it is not the most important thing in life. Why do we put so much importance on it when it comes to the relationships between those of the same gender? If we do not condemn oral and anal sex among heterosexuals, why should we between homosexuals? The answer, of course, is that we should condemn no one! Unconditional love will eventually sort it out. You can be sure that when anyone in such a relationship shows the kind of love that is kind and forgiving to their companion as well as to others, they are acceptable to God.

What of "living together" and having children out of wedlock? Although those lifestyles are becoming more common, such relationships are still frowned upon and even considered "sinful" by many, including most religious authorities. Is that really a sound and accurate assessment of those actions? What about Adam and Eve? Surely, God didn't hold a wedding ceremony for them and issue them a marriage certificate! Nor were their descendants, for many years, involved in such ceremonial procedures. The marriage ceremony and certificate are institutions of man. There is nothing wrong with that, but other aspects of marriage are more important.

There is much ado about the number of teenagers having children "out of wedlock." Wedlock should have little to do with it. If there was a marriage certificate, would that make it okay? Of course not! It is having children without the emotional and economic ability to care for them that is the problem. In our legalistic society, the marriage certificate does have importance when it comes to financial benefits, Social Security and inheritance, for example.

But the ceremony and certificate don't seem to have much, if any, value when it comes to marriage relationships, the children and staying together. If two can't get along or they aren't completely satisfied with the marriage, a common procedure is to forget about the children, get a divorce and try someone else. You can be sure that God is not pleased with marriage as it is perceived, instituted and practiced today. Of far greater importance to him is caring, courtesy, commitment and respect on the part of the participants. That is where the emphasis should be, rather than on ceremony and certificate.

All of this talk of irresponsibility is not to say that there aren't a great many people who do live good, decent and responsible lives. It is only to show the trend of irresponsibility and the misconceptions about responsible behavior that plague us.

Humanity has displayed a lack of good judgment and accountability in other areas. Much of the world has lived beyond its means, incurring excessive debt that threatens financial Armageddon. Politicians around the world have caused a high level of cynicism among the people, which has bred distrust and pessimism. Politics is a major polarization factor. It is the prime cause of the financial dilemma that confronts much of the world. Politics is frequently the root of discord and violence, often preventing reasonable solutions to world problems. It is imperative that we reform the party system.

Governments have fostered materialism through misguided priorities in spending and frequent indifference to the needs of the people of the world. The medical establishment has taken a wrong turn in the road that leads to good health and the prevention of disease, failing to recognize that God has naturally provided all that we need to achieve those goals. Although religion has provided comfort and guidance to a great many people, it has inadvertently divided mankind because leaders who have formulated religious doctrine have listened to other men rather than to God. All of those things must change and will change. We may as well get started.

We can resolve all the problems of the world if we wish to. World leaders, both secular and religious, must stand up and tell the people the truth, fulfilling their responsibility as leaders, regardless of political consequences. We need more secular leaders with vision like Vaclav Havel, the former Czech President. In his address in Philadelphia on the 218th anniversary of our Declaration of Independence he declared that, "Only a new spiritual vision, cosmic in its dimension and global scope, can rescue civilization." Further he cites the notion that "Human beings are mysteriously connected to the universe" and that "The Earth is a mega-organism on which all of us depend."[8] Those concepts are not so mysterious, Vaclav; their reality is unfolding before us.

All of us as individuals must do our part, generally sacrificing self-interest for the good of the whole. We must search for knowledge, always listening to the wisdom of the "heart," for it is the better part of knowledge. We need to understand and accept the truth that "Man has but to right himself to find that the universe is right;"[9] that we have the complete ability, through the power of our minds to do so. Of the utmost importance is that we perceive love as the true panacea; love that is caring, kind, compassionate and forgiving! The kind of love that is the way to heaven--both in this lifetime and the one to come!

"The command, as you have heard from the
beginning, is that you must all live in love."[10]

REFERENCE INDEX

Most biblical references are from the Living Bible

Chapter Eleven
RELIGION: THE GREAT BARRIER

1. The Great Religions, Ross & Hills, Crest Books
2. The Great Religions, Ross & Hills, Crest Books
3. Luke 10:25-27
4. San Diego Union 8/28/93
5. Luke 14:26
6. Mark 10:21
7. I Corinthians 7:7,8
8. I Corinthians 11:6
9. I Corinthians 11:14
10. I Corinthians 7:15
11. I Corinthians 14:34
12. I Corinthians 14:37,38
13. Romans 13:1,2
14. Romans 13:4
15. I Corinthians 6:2
16. John 12:47
17. I Corinthians 7:29-31, 10:11
18. Romans 13:8-10
19. I Corinthians 7:25
20. The Christian Conspiracy, Moore, Pendulum Press
21. Matthew 24:35

Chapter Twelve
THE NATURE OF OUR WORLD

1. Quantum Healing, Chopra, Bantam New Age
2. Romans 5:3
3. Isaiah 11:6-9

4. We Are The Earthquake Generation, Jeffrey Goodman
5. Jonah 3:10
6. San Diego Union 5/25/94
7. San Diego Union 6/1/94
8. Luke 21:10-11
9. Luke 21:23
10. Matthew 5:45
11. Mark 11:24
12. As A Man Thinketh, Allen, Running Press
13. Reversing Heart Disease, Ornish, Ballantine Books

Chapter Thirteen
DOES GOD REALLY EXIST?

1. Newsweek
2. Matthew 7:12
3. Closer To The Light, Morse, Villard Books, 1990
4. Reflections on Life After Life, Moody, Bantam Books
5. Understanding The Present, Appleyard, Doubleday, 1992

Chapter Fourteen
THE NATURE OF GOD

1. Ezekiel 18:20
2. John 14:9
3. II Corinthians 4:4
4. Here I Stand, Bainton, Abingdon Press
5. Genesis 1:26
6. Genesis 1:28
7. John 4:24
8. John 6:63
9. John 4:24
10. John 6:63
11. Quantum Healing, Chopra, Bantam New Age
12. Quantum Healing, Chopra, Bantam New Age

13. John 4:24

14. Matthew 25:40

15. Acts 10:34

Chapter Fifteen
THE NATURE OF MAN

1. Luke 23:43

2. Koran Surah 2:154

3. Koran Surah 6:61

4. Bhagavad-Gita Chapter 2:25-27

5. Reincarnation: The Phoenix Fire Mystery, Head and Cranston (The Tao Te K'ing)

6. Genesis 6

7. Genesis 4:4

8. Great Religions of the World, Ross & Hills, Crest Books

9. Psalm 51:5-13

10. Matthew 5:8

11. Romans 5:18-19

12. Matthew 9:13

Chapter Sixteen
AS WE THINK SO ARE WE

1. Proverbs 23:7

2. 60 Minutes Television Magazine

3. Matthew 12:35

4. Ezekiel 18:31

5. San Diego Union 8/27/93

Chapter Seventeen
MATERIALISM AND SPIRITUALISM

1. Matthew 6:33

2. Philippians 3:19

3. Matthew 6:19,20
4. Luke 14:13,14
5. Ephesians 6:4

Chapter Eighteen
THE EXPERIENCERS

1. Heading Toward Omega, Ring, Quill-Morrow 1984
2. Other World Journeys, Zaleski, Doubleday, 1992
3. Closer To The Light, Morse, Villard Books, 1990
4. Coming Back To Life, Atwater, Ballantine Books 1988
5. Heading Toward Omega, Ring, Quill-Morrow, 1984
6. Closer To The Light, Morse, Villard Books, 1990
7. Recollections of Death, Sabom
8. The Light Beyond, Moody, Bantam Books, 1988
9. Closer To The Light, Morse, Villard Books, 1990
10. Heading Toward Omega, Ring, Quill-Morrow 1984
11. The Light Beyond, Moody, Bantam Books, 1988
12. Heading Toward Omega, Ring, Quill-Morrow, 1984
13. The Light Beyond, Moody, Bantam Books 1988
14. Heading Toward Omega, Ring, Quill-Morrow, 1984
15. I Corinthians 13:13
16. Romans 13:8
17. Matthew 22:36-40
18. Isaiah 11:6-9
19. Matthew 6:33
20. Matthew 7:1
21. Heading Toward Omega, Ring, Quill-Morrow, 1984
22. Closer To The Light, Morse, Villard Books, 1990
23. Matthew 7:1-5
24. Matthew 7:15-20
25. Mark 12:26,27
26. Matthew 22:30
27. I Corinthians 15:50-52

28. The Koran

29. Matthew 8:12

Chapter Nineteen
THE JOY OF DEATH

1. Heading Toward Omega, Ring, Quill-Morrow, 1984

2. We Don't Die, Martin

3. Heading Toward Omega, Ring, Quill-Morrow, 1984

4. The Bhagavad Gita

5. Heading Toward Omega, Ring, Quill-Morrow, 1984

6. Genesis 3:19

7. I Corinthians 15:52-54

8. John 5:25-29

9. Luke 12:48

10. Matthew 17:11-13

11. Reincarnation: the Phoenix Fire Mystery,
Head & Cranston, Point Loma Pub., Review

12. Mark 8:33

13. Matthew 4:1-10

14. Matthew 4:4

15. Matthew 4:10

16. Matthew 7:13,14

17. Mark 4:31,32

18. Matthew 13:33

19. Matthew 6:33

20. Luke 17:21

21. Matthew 25:34

22. Luke 23:43

23. Journal of Near-Death Studies, IANDS, Vol 10,
PMH Atwater, 1992

24. Heading Toward Omega, Ring, Quill, Chap 3

25. Journal of Near-Death Studies, IANDS, Vol 10,
Atwater, 1992

26. Matthew 25:46
27. Mark 3:29

Chapter Twenty
HEALTH, HEALING AND MEDICINE

1. Seattle Times, 11/1/92 - (Rochester Democratic and Chronicle Times)
2. San Diego Union, 3/25/94
3. Quantum Healing, Chopra, Bantam New Age
4. Good Medicine, PCRM, Spring 1994
5. The San Diego Union, 7/2/96
6. Reversing Heart Disease, Ornish, Ballantine Books, Reviews
7. Newsweek, April 27, 1998
8. PCRM News Release, 6/29/94
9. Family Circle, 6/28/94
10. Heading Toward Omega, Ring, Quill
11. Romans 8:31
12. The San Diego Union, March 20, 1998

Chapter Twenty One
CONCLUSION

1. Matthew 5:17,18
2. Matthew 6:10
3. Koran Surah 8:36-40
4. Isaiah 11:9
5. As A Man Thinketh, Allen, Running Press
6. Body Mind Spirit Magazine, June 1994
7. Isaiah 2:4
8. Newsweek, 7/18/94
9. II John 1:5,6

CPSIA information can be obtained
at www.ICGtesting.com
Printed in the USA
FFHW012209050919
54765960-60443FF